The Employment Relationship

A psychological perspective

Peter Herriot

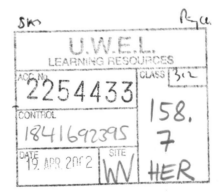

ROUTLEDGE
ROUTLEDGE
Taylor & Francis Group

First published 2001 by Routledge
27 Church Road, Hove,
East Sussex, BN3 2FA

Simultaneously published in the USA and Canada
by Taylor & Francis Inc
325 Chestnut Street, Suite 800, Philadelphia, PA 19106

Routledge is an imprint of the Taylor & Francis Group

Typeset in Goudy by RefineCatch Limited, Bungay, Suffolk
Printed and bound in Great Britain by
TJ International, Padstow, Cornwall

British Library Cataloguing in Publication Data
A catalogue record for this book is available from the British Library

Library of Congress Cataloging in Publication Data
Herriot, Peter.
   The employment relationship : a psychological perspective / Peter
Herriot.
      p.   cm.
   Includes bibliographical references and index.
   ISBN 1–84169–239–5
   1. Psychology, Industrial.   2. Work—Psychological aspects.
   3. Organizational behavour.   4. Industrial sociology.   5. Industrial
relations. I. Title.

HF5548.8.H398 2001
158.7—dc21   00–059234

ISBN 1–84169–239–5 (Hbk)
ISBN 1–84169–240–9 (Pbk)

The Emplo

The Employment Relationship presents a controversial perspective on an area hitherto dominated by industrial relations experts and radical sociological theorists.

Exploring some of the metaphors commonly used to describe the employment relationship, Peter Herriot argues that it is often their dark rather than their bright side that best expresses how employees really feel. Human resources sometimes feel like human discards! The main culprits in this situation, he suggests, are the top managers who fail to treat employment as a relationship and employees as individuals. He concludes that management rhetoric must be replaced by real dialogue, and points to three issues where this is most crucial: employee compliance, contractual inequalities, and the need for organisational change.

The Employment Relationship will make essential reading for all managers and occupational psychologists. It will also be of interest to students of work psychology, human resource management or organisational behaviour.

Peter Herriot is a well-known commentator on organisations and employment. After a career as an academic psychologist, he has more recently been engaged in consultancy and research and was, until 2000, Editor of *The European Journal of Work and Organisational Psychology*. His previous publications include *New Deals* (1995, with Carole Pemberton) and *Trust and Transition* (1998, with Wendy Hirsh and Peter Reilly).

Contents

Illustrations

Figure

Tables

Acknowledgements

I would like to thank John Arnold, John Coopey, Wendy Hirsh, Paul Sparrow, Shaun Tyson, and Allan Williams for their helpful and penetrating comments on the draft manuscript.

Introduction

The change imperative

It is a truism to say that organisational change has become a constant feature of business life.[1] In our efforts to keep pace with business, technological, and social change, we put our organisations through all sorts of contortions. We expand or contract, devolve or centralise, plan for the long term or seize immediate opportunities.[2] Realising that these adjustments are not effective on their own in keeping us up with the pace, we initiate transformational change. We try to restructure the organisation to face its markets more effectively; we seek to redesign its business processes from scratch; we go for quality so as to attract and retain our customers; or we aim at no less than a radical change in organisational culture. And finally there are the bolts from the blue: the takeover bids, the new regulatory regimes, the collapse of regional economies, all of which force us to change. These changes are summarised in Table 1.

On the receiving end of all this change are employees. Commentators have not surprisingly noted a degree of change weariness in workforces.[3] Their initial anger at the breaking of the old deal of security for loyalty has given way to a recognition that their psychological contract has changed. If constant organisational change is the new order of the day, constant personal change is the inevitable corollary. Yet constant personal change can be difficult as well as exciting. The types of transition that employees are continually being asked to make are numerous. They are also often simultaneous. They do not only require the acquisition of new skills and knowledge;[4] they may also involve fundamental changes in identities.

Table 1 Some organisational changes

Ebbs and flows	Restructures	Management initiatives
Expand or contract	Downsize	Total Quality
Devolve or recentralise	Internationalise	Business Process Re-engineering
Opportunistic or strategic	Mergers and acquisitions	Culture change programmes

For example, one of the major aims of many businesses is to increase the functional flexibility of all their employees.[5] Operatives with a specific craft are expected to become multi-skilled. Research chemists have to acquire project management skills. Production engineers find themselves in the HR function. Yet a key characteristic of these people may well be their occupational or professional identity, which they are now being asked to surrender, or at least dilute.

So not only do employees have to prepare for, encounter, and adapt to changes in their work roles; they also have to come to terms with the changes in their identity that these role changes imply. Add the practical difficulties of transferring to shift working in our 24 hours a day, 7 days a week service culture, or of learning to make do with a part-time instead of a full-time wage, and it is clear that change may pose profound personal difficulties.

We are certain, however, that the pace of change is likely to increase. The pressure becomes overwhelming. As a manager in a world-class pharmaceutical company put it to me: 'The demands are stupendous, and there is no light at the end of the tunnel, no breathing space to look forward to.' The big issue forces itself upon us with a stark clarity: how are employees going to get through yet more change? How are we going to maintain motivation, morale, and commitment? How can we retain what goodwill they have left?

The answer I propose is not some new motivational lever to pull, or button to press. Nor is it another management fad, a reinvention of the wheel dressed up in new verbiage. Rather, I suggest that we take a long hard look at the nature of the employment relationship in our organisations. For it is the quality of that relationship which is the motor for change. If it is sound and trusted, then employees are more likely to agree the need for change, if it is required, and to implement it with enthusiasm.

Metaphors with a flip side

Yet we may not often consciously think and talk about the employment relationship. We may sometimes take it for granted, or we may delegate it to employee relations professionals. This could be a mistake. The enhancement of the quality of the employment relationship is central to strategic attempts to gain competitive advantage. Moreover, success is not dependent upon esoteric professional knowledge. Rather, we have the theory inside our own heads already. My purpose in this book is to extract it and make it more explicit, so that its implications for practice become clear. This task of extraction is not a difficult one, since our theory of the employment relationship can be discerned from the language we use about it. In particular, it can be drawn from the metaphors with which we pepper our conversations.[6]

Our typical way of trying to make sense of something is to compare it with something else with which we are more familiar.[7] So, when trying to make sense of organisations themselves, we speak about them as though they were machines or people. We talk of 'pulling the appropriate levers', or 'business process re-engineering': organisation as machine. Organisations, we say, have a 'life-cycle', or they 'learn', or they become 'leaner and fitter': organisation as person. After a while, the metaphors lose their metaphorical quality and become part of our ordinary descriptive language. So we forget that a word such as 'motivation' is really originally a metaphor: getting people moving.

We have had a lot of problems thinking up other appropriate metaphors for organisations. Authors have had to resort to comparisons which seem a little far fetched: organisations as brains or as psychic prisons, for example.[8] But there is no such difficulty in the case of the employment relationship; we have a wide range of other relationships with which we habitually compare it. There are eight such comparisons which I will take up in this book, but there are many more which we could find useful. The eight metaphors which I have selected are Family, Crusade, Contract, Club, Resource, Democracy, Partnership and Customer. They are all metaphors which people already use more or less frequently when talking about employment relationships. We may not hear these actual words very often, but we do frequently hear related and derived words that are bound up with the metaphor in question. Whatever the words we use, our purpose is clear: to point to one or two key features of something which we don't understand too well by comparing it with something else which we do.

So Families are primarily known for their care; Crusades for their vision; Contracts for mutual obligations; Clubs for their membership; Resources for their value; Democratic citizenship for rights and responsibilities; Partnerships for mutual interests; and Customers for service and support. When we use these metaphors for the employment relationship, we are saying that these are its key features.

Now the one thing about relationships that we are all convinced of is that there is always a potential flip side. Families can break up and conduct appalling feuds. Crusades can turn into mere shams, where everyone merely plays at being soldiers. The mutual obligations embodied in the notion of Contract can rapidly degenerate into the law of the jungle if trust and enforcement fail. Clubs, usually so convivial and collegiate, can become exclusive *laagers*, making even some of the members feel they are outsiders. Resources, we are only too aware, can be wasted, exploited, used up, and discarded, as well as used, nurtured, and developed. As for Democracy, the lessons of history indicate that the price of freedom is eternal vigilance, in the absence of which we fall into slavery. Partnerships can easily degenerate into disagreement and mutual isolation. And finally, the Customer relationship is sometimes a sham; it degenerates into a rip-off, a clever way of getting more money out of people.[9]

So the metaphors which I have chosen not only point to some features of the employment relationship which are central to its functioning; they also demonstrate how those features can be destroyed as the relationship degenerates into its flip side. Our metaphors can thus not only help us to understand the relationship when it is working well; they can also explain why it so often fails. They can, in other words, chime in with our own experience of the good, the bad, and the ugly.[10]

The basic theme of the first half of this book, then, is this: *There are many good employment relationships, but they all have the potential to turn on to their darker flip sides.* If we can understand how this happens, we may be able to take steps to keep the shiny side uppermost. Each of the first eight chapters of this book will deal with one of the metaphors. First, the metaphor itself will be analysed for its key features. Then the potential seeds of decay will be described, followed by the worst scenario, the full-blown flip side.

So the book is not a cool analysis in terms of Human Resource Management (HRM), assuming a rational disposal of human assets. Rather, it is an attempt to explore in more depth employees' existing highly charged experiences, which are encapsulated in the metaphors which they use about them. We may not recognise our own employment relationships in some of the eight metaphors, but this is because different types of organisation typically give rise to different sets of metaphors.

Family, for example, is not surprisingly used often of family firms, small and medium sized enterprises, and locally based firms. Voluntary sector organisations often seem like Crusades, as do those public sector organisations which refuse to agree that their main purpose is to provide the cheapest service possible. Included amongst Crusades are often those private sector organisations which insist that service excellence, not profit, is their prime concern; get the first right, they argue, and the profits will follow. Contracts are typical of short-term transactional deals, such as those between merchant banks and their currency dealers, although of course many forms of contract exist. Organisations of professionals resemble Clubs, while many large private sector organisations use Resource language, with employees construed as assets to be utilised to leverage competitive advantage. Meanwhile in the public sector, ideas of Democracy and citizenship still survive, whilst notions of stakeholder rights are much talked of in private sector managerial discourse too. The idea of Partnership is used in professional organisations, and also in industrial firms which have opted for a collaborative rather than an adversarial relationship with unions. And finally, where else would we find the Customer metaphor more explicit than in the retail sector, and especially in (super)markets?

This is not to say that each metaphor is aligned with a particular type of organisation in any hard and fast way. Rather, it is quite likely that if, for example, we run a voluntary organisation, the Crusade metaphor among others will ring bells. So we need not expect all of the metaphors to be personally relevant. On the other hand, we do not need to assume that only one of them applies to our own experience with our current employer. That experience is varied, and we may feel as though we are in a congenial Club one day but being sold to as a Customer the next. Moreover, we all recognise that different relationships obtain for different employees: for some the Club analogy may be appropriate most of the time; for others within the same organisation, Dictatorship is more often the preferred metaphor.

But we do need to retain our confidence that we are using the right methods of enquiry. For these metaphors would not have an existing place in our language and thinking if they did not contain essential elements of our experience. Table 2 provides a summary.

The psychological approach

After the eight metaphors in the first part of the book, I go on to ask in the second what causes the metaphors to flip. Why should Family degenerate so often into Feud, or Crusade into Play? The answer is to be found in the nature of people's relationships and their concepts of their selves. These are recognised in the metaphors' top sides, but have subsequently been down-played or ignored. The consequence is the turn over to the flip side.

The employment relationship is ultimately a relationship between human beings, and as such is subject to the same fundamental psychological con-straints and influences as are other human relationships. Thus whilst other writers have explored the employment relationship by concentrating upon the economic, political, social, and philosophical nature of employment, I will emphasise its psychological commonalities with other relationships. Chapters 9 through to 12 explore the psychology of the employment rela-tionship in the light of what we know about human relationships in general. Throughout these chapters, however, and indeed throughout the whole of the book, a very difficult question lurks unanswered: who are the parties to the employment relationship? The answer that comes immediately to mind is that they are the organisation and the individual. But if relationships are

Table 2 Employment relationship metaphors

Metaphor	Flip side	Core elements	Typical location
Family	Feud	Care, dependence, security	SMEs, family and local firms
Crusade	Play	Vision, values	Voluntary, public, 'excellence'
Contract	Jungle	Obligations, transactions	Short-term organisations
Club	Outsider	Belonging, fitting in	Professional organisations
Resource	Discard	Assets, utilisation	Large private sector organisations
Democracy	Dictatorship	Rights and responsibilities	Public sector
Partnership	Conflict	Shared interests	Unionised workplaces
Customer	Rip-off	Consumer, customer, service	Retail sector

between people, who is or are 'the organisation' and, come to that, who is 'the individual'? Is there any form of relationship at the individual level?

First, it is important to understand that a relationship is an ongoing process between parties, in which the actions of each party are responded to reciprocally by the other. Responses are not merely a function of what the other party has done, however. They also result from the self-concept of the respondent. What is more, that self-concept may itself be changed as a result of the other's or one's own actions. Thus the 'individual' and the 'organisation', as the parties to the employment relationship, have to be defined in terms of that relationship.

Self-concepts are of course unique to individuals. However, there are major cultural differences which affect the likely order of prominence of elements of people's selves. For example, those who live and work in more individualistic cultures are more likely to give priority to elements that differentiate them from others: their achievements, perhaps, or their occupation. Those from more collectivistic cultures, on the other hand, are more likely to define themselves in terms of their social relationships: their family, locality, or religion, for example. Employment relationships which fail to take account of such cultural differences in selves are unlikely to succeed.

Clearly, the essence of relationships is that they are between people. Yet the abstractions that we use when thinking about the employment relationship obscure this truism. We talk of 'the individual' and 'the organisation', when what we mean are people. In particular, 'the organisation' is normally in this context an abstraction for the top managers of the organisation. The question then arises, how each of the two parties exercise their influence over the relationship. I argue that whilst top managers usually hold most of the aces, employees have many ways of influencing the *course* of the relationship. However, even when the relationship is one merely of compliance of employees with the demands of top managers, the exercise of unilateral power is likely to prove unproductive.

Instead, the parties need to engage in dialogue. Dialogue involves listening to the other's account of the relationship, past, present and future, and providing one's own. However, it is not merely an intellectual exchange, but is rather conducted primarily through emotions and feelings. Dialogue involves the search for understanding of the other party. Rhetoric, on the other hand, seeks simply to persuade them.

Four dialogues for the future

Finally, Chapters 13 through to 16 indicate the areas with which these dialogues should be concerned. I argue that, contrary to current management orthodoxy, organisational cultures are moving towards greater managerial control of most of their employees through rules and the setting of targets.

Hence a major problem arises in dealing with employees who are less and less inclined to conform.

A second area for dialogue is that of difference. Organisations are becoming markedly segmented, with different employment relationships being enjoyed by different categories of staff. Management will have to temper its demands for flexibility by enquiring about employees' preferred flexibilities.

The third dialogue concerns the all-pervasive need for change. Again, I argue against current managerial orthodoxy, which stresses the need for top managers to lead a constant programme of change. Rather, there are immense dangers to the organisation in radical top-down change, and in the managerial rhetoric used to justify it.

Finally, dialogue is required regarding the nature of the employment relationship itself: a dialogue about dialogues. Unless top managers take active steps to initiate dialogue and to reflect upon its course, the competitive advantage they so eagerly seek will go to those who have better integrated their people into the business. I argue that the conditions needed for emotionally charged mutual disclosure are seldom to be found in today's organisations. However, the answer lies in the political process: that is, dialogue between those of differing interests.

So *the overall argument of the book* runs like this. Employees appear to experience the flip side of the employment relationship just as often as its top side. The unremitting optimism of the typical management guru is unjustified. But why? The answer is to be found in the psychological nature of relationships. Relationships depend upon ongoing dialogue between the parties which seeks at an emotional level to understand the other and takes account of the other's self. Not many top managements engage in such dialogue with employees at present. Yet if they do not rapidly initiate dialogues about compliance, difference, change and the employment relationship itself, they will fail to engage their employees in the ever more difficult task of organisational survival.

References

1 Hamel, G. and Prahalad, C. K. (1994) *Competing for the Future*. Boston MA: Harvard Business School Press.
2 Herriot, P., Hirsh, W. and Reilly, P. (1998) *Trust and Transition: Managing Today's Employment Relationship*. Chichester: Wiley.
3 Noon, M. and Blyton, P. (1997) *The Realities of Work*. London: Macmillan.
4 Drucker, P. F. (1993) *Post-Capitalist Society*. Oxford: Butterworth-Heinemann.
5 Emmott, M. and Hutchinson, S. (1998) Employment flexibility: Threat or promise? In P. Sparrow and M. Marchington (eds) *Human Resource Management: The New Agenda*. London: Financial Times and Pitman.
6 Morgan, G. (1980) Paradigms, metaphors, and puzzle solving in organisation theory. *Administrative Science Quarterly*, 25, 4, 605–622.
7 Grant, D. and Oswick, C. (1996) Getting the measure of metaphors. In D. Grant and C. Oswick (eds) *Metaphor and Organisations*. London: Sage.

8   Morgan, G. (1997) *Images of Organisation* (2nd edn). Thousand Oaks CA: Sage.
9   du Gay, P. (1996) *Consumption and Identity at Work*. London: Sage.
10 Guest, D. E. and Hoque, K. (1994) The good, the bad, and the ugly: Employment relations in new non-union workplaces. *Human Resource Management Journal*, 5, 1, 1–14.

Part I

Mixed metaphors

Chapter 1

Family and Feud

Care in the family

On 23 August 1998, the London *Observer* columnist, Melanie Phillips, wrote a valedictory piece. She explained how she had gradually come to realise that the liberal consensus represented by that great newspaper was actually, in her view, deeply authoritarian and contrary to the interests of those whose well-being she most desired: the poor and the vulnerable. Clearly feeling that this represented a radical move which established her own independence, she concluded her column as follows: 'The *Guardian* and the *Observer* have been to me like my extended family. After 21 years, though, it's finally time to leave home.'[1]

We use the Family metaphor to enrich our understanding of so many areas of our lives that it is hardly surprising that we apply it to the employment relationship. Those twin areas of maximum emotive potential, politics and religion, are replete with family members. Politics, for example, provides us with numerous dictators calling themselves the father of their nation; the mother country, that fantasy beloved of expatriates; brothers and sisters in the unions struggling for workers' rights; the sisterhood of feminists or the Daughters of the American Revolution; and so on. And as for religion, we have God the Father and God the Son, mother church or mother earth, the brotherhood of saints or the brotherhood of man.

So Family is a well-practised metaphor in all sorts of arenas. But it also has a great historical resonance in the history of business. This history is replete in the USA and the UK with family owners who believed that they should consider their companies as extensions of their own families. Indeed, some of the founding families have gracefully retired from the scene and from the parental role altogether. In China and Italy, on the other hand, family dynasties survive and flourish and are the mainstay of the economy.

The central belief of many of these founding families was that it was their duty to care for the wellbeing of their employees. They did not do so because it was good for their business, but because it was simply the right thing to do. And surely care is the central feature of Family: the fundamental purpose of that threatened institution is to care for children so that they can develop in infancy and childhood in as secure an environment as possible; and then negotiate adolescence to become independent and adult people. They will as a result develop a degree of trust in their parents, and believe that they have their wellbeing at heart. Parents will enhance this trust by demonstrating reciprocal trust in their growing children to act sensibly, honestly, etc.

If and when we use the Family analogy to describe the employment relationship, then we are surely referring primarily to this fundamental duty of continued care by the employer, leading to trust and confidence that employees will be supported and enjoy a consequent feeling of security. We may merely refer to 'a family atmosphere' or 'feeling like one of the family', but ultimately we are talking about care and support.

Care at a premium

Now all this sounds very old-fashioned indeed, at least in Western post-industrial societies. Victorian philanthropists are from another era (although we do not seem to have jettisoned quite so easily the equally Victorian Samuel Smiles and his distinction between the deserving and the undeserving poor). It may be a long time since we ourselves thought or spoke in such terms. But the Family metaphor for the employment relationship is still alive and well and in everyday usage. Here are two heartwarming contemporary examples:

> My field service manager has been unstinting in his help to me personally. He has been like a father in many ways. My own dad died while I was still at school. My problem is that I am very shy, lack confidence, and at one time would have thought it impossible to do my job of going into factories, hospitals, offices, etc. to repair their vending machines. I just could not have faced going into strange environments, dealing with people I had not met before, even talking to you like this would have been an embarrassment. F***** said he understood the problem and would help me with it. He came out with me in the early days, we went into jobs together and I saw how he coped with receptionists, secretaries, porters, etc. . . . Without that help I would have been a good mechanic stuck in the workshops. I would never have had the use of a company car or gone to such interesting places. I have substantially conquered my shyness and blushing. Two years ago I would have said it was impossible for me to do what I am able to do today. The organisation in the person of F***** has made this possible.[2]

> The organisation I work for is ********, the major leisure group that is probably the largest hotel operator in the UK. I would say that the one thing it does that is above general employment conditions in any organ-

isation (let alone the catering industry) is the way it recognises long and loyal service. Our first recognition comes at five years, when the employee is given a small cocktail party in their honour, a certificate, and a small presentation. After 10 years, etc. . . . At 15 years, etc. . . . At 20 years it is two weeks at any hotel, and a weekend away every year thereafter. It really makes you feel important and appreciated. The wives become totally committed to the organisation. My wife wouldn't let me leave even supposing I wanted to! The group has a nil turnover of management grade staff. It becomes like a large extended family.[3]

These are definitely exceptions, we may tell ourselves, and may not match our own organisations. There may be mutual care and support amongst our immediate colleagues, but most of us would hesitate to construe the management role as that of parent, or employees as family. Yet, as we ponder the recent past and the uncertain future, managers might reasonably be asked for some parental-style care and support.

That organisational change is a constant, rather than a passage between periods of stability, is now commonly stated. But what is often ignored are the transitions which these changes at the organisational level force upon individuals' working lives.[4] They may be thrust into a much more responsible job after a merger, but be unsure whether they have the experience and the confidence to carry it off. In the interests of flexibility they may be expected to work part-time or on shifts; or they may be asked to broaden their range of skills, with the result that they can no longer keep up to date in their real expertise. Or they may simply be told that they are surplus to requirements and made redundant.

Such transitions are profoundly important to employees. In the case of redundancy, their very livelihood may be at stake. In all of them, fundamental elements of their identity are involved: their self-esteem in the promotion, their professional identity in the job enlargement, their role as wage earner supporting any dependants in the case of redundancy. They need support and care from their employer, when they are preparing for such transitions, when they encounter them, and when they are adapting to them.[5]

Enhanced trust

Support and care through their children's transitions are a parental duty. All parents will recall the perils of negotiating together the first tentative steps into adolescence. As far as employers are concerned, support and care are also good business, for the following reasons. First, if transitions are becoming more and more frequent, then a decrease in the time taken to get up to speed in the new role will become a major source of competitive advantage. More important, however, care and support, consistently and reliably given result in employee trust in the employer and in feelings of security, just as they do in the child–parent relationship.

These latter consequences are worth exploring further. Trust is the fundamental glue cementing any relationship; employees need to have a degree of confidence that management will reciprocate before they are willing to act on their behalf. Trust based on regular support from the employer has been termed *knowledge-based* trust.[6] It is based on the belief that if they have supported us regularly in the past through our transitions, they are likely to do so this time round. As a consequence, employees may be willing to embrace organisational changes of which previously they would have been deeply suspicious and afraid.

Indeed, once we feel we can trust the other party on the basis of our experience of their reliability, a deeper form of trust may develop. We may come to understand more fully what the other's wants and needs are, so that we can effectively act on their behalf and identify with them. We know what really matters to them, and as a consequence it really matters to us too. The Family metaphor is irresistible here, as many of us recall the pride with which we returned home to find that the children had dealt with an emergency in just the same way as we would have done. If this level of *identification-based* trust exists in our organisation, then employees are willing to believe that top management has their wellbeing as one of their concerns when they are planning the next change. Moreover, employees may embrace the change because they want the same outcomes as top management.[7]

Yet the sequence is important. Only when employees have come to be confident in management's support and care will they develop a knowledge-based trust; they know they can rely on them for support when they need it. The further development of identification-based trust is likely to depend upon the prior establishment of such reliance. This level of identification with an employer therefore has to be earned over a long prior period of reliable care and support. The easy assumption that employees will identify with the company and recognise and act upon the supposed imperative for change is thus facile and dangerous if care and support have not been the norm. Trust is not the next snake-oil to follow Business Process Reengineering. It is the cement which makes any relationship viable; and it takes time to solidify.

Other benefits of caring

However, the immediate benefits of care and support are considerable, as well as those of the trust and security which regular care and support finally engender. Research indicates that if members of six different occupations perceived that they were valued and cared about, they were more likely to be conscientious in their duties, involved in the organisation, and willing to innovate without reward. In a second study in a manufacturing organisation, employees who perceived they were supported showed a greater affective commitment to the organisation, believed that good performance would be rewarded, and were more willing to make constructive suggestions for improving the manufacturing process.[8] Prior experiences of development and promotion were amongst the antecedents of the perception of support discovered by another research project, while its consequences included organisational citizenship behaviour, affective commitment to the organisation, and intention to stay.[9]

To put some flesh on to these dry bones of research, here is the beneficial outcome of the support for the shy and blushing mechanic whom we met earlier:

> I really try to give the company a good day's work, and to be a good ambassador for them when dealing with the clients. I keep the car immaculate, and always try and look smart and efficient. Where I do a lot more than many other mechanics is that I accept calls right up to normal business closing time. This means that I can sometimes have long drives home in my private time. Others insist that their last call is near home, otherwise it must be delayed to the next day. I must be more productive than some of the others.[10]

An increased feeling of security, the other outcome of regular care and support, also has its benefits. Organisations which have given assurances that there will be no compulsory redundancies, and have stuck to their word, have reaped the benefits in continuously improving motivation and morale. But there is a more specific benefit of security, which is especially important at the present juncture. It is the benefit of increased innovation. Only when employees feel secure enough about their jobs and about their value to the organisation are they likely to take the risks that are necessary if innovation is to occur. For then they are confident that they will be supported through any mistakes which they may make.[11]

So the outcomes of the most fundamental feature of the family relationship, parental care and support, seem to be beneficial to both parties to the employment relationship. As the psychoanalysts have argued, parents can provide a 'holding relationship' within which children can both feel secure but also become independent. But what happens when the family starts to feel the stresses and strains? What happens when the flip side becomes a possibility? Just as real families can over- or under-react to external pressures, so the employment relationship can threaten to flip to its savage reverse side: revenge and feud.

After all, the trends and pressures are all too real. Today's parental relationships have often become serial monogamy: a succession of exclusive relationships between adults. The children often have no say in the matter.

They have to get used to new 'parents' who are not their natural ones. It takes time, effort, and goodwill to develop such new relationships, as is attested by the age-old myth of the cruel stepmother. This development in the current state of the family carries over to the employment relationship. For there too, relationships are now seldom for life. Employees have a series of organisations as parents, and often have little say in who their new parents are (as in the case of mergers and acquisitions). The difficulty of forming new relationships whilst the old ones are part of our histories is immense.

Families that care too little or too much

The traditional family is under grave stress in most Western societies. All sorts of reasons have been adduced for its apparent decline, amongst them the so-called liberal consensus with which this chapter started. Whatever the causes, the reactions to external threat by the family itself have tended to follow two patterns. In the first of these, the family builds a stockade to protect itself against the nasty dangerous world outside; children are kept under tight control so that they come to no harm, either from outsiders or from their own folly. Or else, secondly, parents are so busy out there fighting for their share that they have no time to care for their children, excusing their neglect by such weasel phrases as 'quality time'.

It is the former response that has dominated our thinking about the family. We have been seduced into this emphasis by the impact of psychoanalytic ideas upon our post-nineteenth-century thinking. We forget that this whole intellectual edifice was constructed on the basis of Sigmund Freud's experience of middle-class middle-European families. We fail to see that, overall, the more frequent response is probably lack of care rather than too much of it. So we spend our time talking about paternal dominance and family dependence, each reinforcing the other in a vicious circle. Instead of children developing into independent adults, we emphasise the dangers of their internalising the stern demands of their father and being emotionally imprisoned as a consequence.

So we may neglect the opposite danger: too little care. Whether by ignorance, choice, or necessity many families simply fail to provide the degree of care required to enable their children to grow securely into adulthood. Whether we are rich or poor, we can neglect to care for our children. Readers of this book may care to reflect on the number of hours they spend working in relation to the number of hours they spend with their children. And we may also reflect on the long-hours culture of many organisations which results in those working less than excessive hours being branded as lacking commitment.[12]

We are not overburdening the Family metaphor if we take it this step further. If we use the Family metaphor for the employment relationship, it is because care and support are the central features of Family which we believe should also be embodied in employment. Both Family and the employment relationship are therefore at risk if care and support are in doubt.

Organisational family rhetoric

Many organisations use metaphors as rhetoric, in efforts to persuade employees to perceive the employment relationship in the way they want them to. This is particularly true in the case of the Family metaphor. Organisational rhetoric, too, points to the fact that, as in the family, there are two possible risks: too much care by management, and too little. Historically we have seen many examples of the one big happy Family rhetoric.[13] In spite of regular redundancies, some organisations continue to put out the idea of the employer as the good parent who really cares despite having to do unpleasant things periodically ('it had to be done in the interests of the family as a whole'). Such rhetoric also seeks to persuade 'family' members of their duties and obligations if they are to merit such care.

More recently we have seen the opposite rhetoric, which seeks to persuade employees that the employer has been caring too much. In the bad old days of dependency, runs this rhetoric, the company treated employees as though they were little children. All that has gone, and gone for ever. Nowadays we empower you; we give you your head, as adolescents on the verge of adulthood, to take your own decisions. Our ultimate intention is to deal with our people as adult to adult, since we all have to become grown-ups who recognise the realities of today's business world.

Organisations which care too much

If organisational spin-doctors have got to work on it, then we can be sure that there lies a real issue lurking somewhere in the background. So how can we discover if the parent employer 'cares too much'? As Freud and many subsequent thinkers about the family have pointed out, early dependence on the parent is likely to lead to internalisation of what their children believe the parent's wishes to be. Children take on board for themselves the duties and obligations which they believe their parents want from them, and have a bad conscience when they fail to fulfil them. They internalise the demanding parent.

Psychoanalytic writers on organisations argue that it is this actual childhood transference and projection which is at work in the employment relationship.[14] But there is no need to assume this causal relationship; we need not necessarily be playing out our childhood struggles in our working lives. Rather, we can simply recognise the same sort of process at work: if employees become too dependent on their employer, if their employer 'cares too much', they may become internally driven. They may, in fact, become willing, or at least obedient, slaves to sales targets, budget targets, time deadlines, and all the other ways in which organisational control is exercised.

The next step on this particular downward slope towards Family Feud is increased parental dominance. People who are internally driven may become competitively masculine.[15] The caring parent becomes the overtly demanding and bullying father. The Managing Directors of the different businesses of the corporation compete to achieve the highest targets, and smaller fathers all the way down the organisation compete in the same way, bullying their subordinate children to achieve. Even the mentoring Director, who supposedly looks after his protégés and inspires admiration and intimacy, secretly protects his back in case he loses his power to them before he formally hands over the baton.[16] No wonder that, under these pressured conditions, employees suffer increased stress and its consequences for their wellbeing and ultimately for their physical and mental health.[17]

Organisations which care too little

But what of the other danger: too little care? Again, there are many explanations in the psychological literature to explain real parents' failure to care for their children. Most of them have in common the idea that some parents are too immature and self-centred to bring up their children. They are so concerned with caring for their own needs that they fail to care for their children's. Or else parents may simply be ignorant of the sheer helplessness and dependence of infants and young children, and so fail to realise what their parental duties are. And even if they do realise, they may not have the necessary skills and patience to carry them out.

Again, the parallels with the employment relationship are not fanciful. How often have employees attributed top management's salary rises and share options to greed and to their lack of concern for employees' situation? They are like greedy little children who are always wanting more, employees may feel, rather than acting as responsible leaders of the organisational Family. They are in it for themselves; they don't care about the rest of us.

Alternatively, employees may believe that top management are simply so blinkered and so bullied themselves by the shareholders that they look only to the bottom line, ignoring entirely the people factor. How can accountants who by definition only think in terms of balance sheets possibly understand that profitability depends on people?[18] Ignorance rather than selfishness is management's problem in this case, employees believe.

Here is an example from the public sector of a lack of care through a mixture of ignorance and the desire to cut costs:

> [An example is] the provision of decent working conditions after a member of staff was murdered in one of our offices. It was premeditated murder by a psychiatric patient from the hospital. Following this incident it was promised that we would be moved away from the dead-end offices that are up a dark back staircase of the building. That was six

months ago now, so I guess it is clear that nothing is going to be done. The late girl's fiance also works in the department, and has been off sick since the tragedy. They are now cutting off his sick pay, and speak in a throw away manner about getting rid of him so that his post can be advertised for a replacement. The dead girl's job has been frozen as a cost saving measure. We were all emotionally hurt by this experience, and the organisation is failing to give us appropriate concessions and help and support.[19]

Whatever cause employees attribute to top management's failings, however, the consequences for the employment relationship construed as Family are clear. Employees in some organisations have lost trust in management's *motives* as parents: they care for themselves more than they care for us, they feel. Or else they have no confidence in management's *competence* as parents: they don't seem to know what it is they are supposed to do or how to do it. And out of the window with trust goes any feeling of security and confidence in the relationship itself. It is now that the Family really starts to fall apart.

Break-up, revenge, and feud

These however are only preliminaries to when exploitation and abuse start in earnest. When employees have identified with a parent, they can tolerate the occasional failure to care.[20] But when they are betrayed and treated without respect, they are devastated.

Redundancies, for example, can and should be conducted in a caring way.[21] Explanations can be offered, choice of those to be made redundant can be transparent and fair, terms can be tailored to meet individuals' needs, and regrets and gratitude can be expressed. In sum, the employment relationship can be ended with respect and with fairness. If it is, then employees will be more likely to feel that there has been interactional and procedural fairness,[22, 23] and to attribute the redundancies to the organisation's unfortunate situation rather than to the malevolence or incompetence of top management.

However, many recent redundancies have been conducted with brutal inhumanity. This is hardly surprising, for several reasons. First, public utterances are put out for the stockmarket's benefit rather than for that of the redundant. It is from the market's perspective an achievement to reduce headcount and therefore costs, so many organisations parade redundancies as an achievement. Second, top management has to cope with being held responsible for the redundancies but surviving themselves. Many cope personally by becoming 'executioners'.[24] They may be well-adjusted, resilient and hardy, successfully rationalising what they are doing. They may reduce their anxiety by control, concentrating on the details and doing things properly. Some become abrasive and aggressive, devaluing those dismissed as 'deadwood'. Others dissociate themselves from the situation and act in an emotionless way, while others again escape into non-stop action to prevent themselves feeling any unpleasant guilt. None of these modes of coping is calculated to endear top management to redundant and surviving employees. On the contrary, all give off the message that top management does not really care.

Redundancy has been a key theme of the last decade. Yet perhaps a more pervasive demonstration of lack of care is *pressure*. Some managements put employees under extreme pressure to meet deadlines, make budgets, enhance quality, and cut costs, regardless of the contradictions implied, and regardless too of the consequences for individuals. Managers push themselves: a recent report from the UK Institute of Management[25] indicates that 54 per cent of UK managers often or always work in the evenings, and 34 per cent often or always work at weekends. So they expect employees to do the same.

The internalisation of 'father's' requirements is a subtle way of exerting pressure. But for those who fail to push themselves, a push from the boss is often given. Bullying and domineering management does not need or engage commitment: it rules through fear. A recent UK Trades Union Congress report[26] gives us this example:

> My former boss used to manage his staff by humiliation. He would make people who did not reach the impossible targets he set stand in a corner wearing a dunce's cap. The worst thing was he was convinced his behaviour made him a good boss, that it would increase productivity. But the staff were terrified. Some of them jumped every time he walked into the room.

Yet efforts to engineer a Family atmosphere may even now still be made. Top management lay on Christmas parties and other grisly rituals, little realising that the fault lines in the 'Family' are absolutely certain to gape open wide given such a golden opportunity.[27] Consider, for example, the case of the young man who gets drunk and insults the guest speaker: 'The next sweepstake will be on how long Eric Minton will stay on Branfield's payroll.'[28]

However, by this stage things have gone too far wrong to be patched over by rituals and pretence. Employees feel betrayed by people they mistrust as incompetent, greedy, or malevolent, who appear simply not to care a fig about them. Again, there are different ways to react. Some employees regress back to early childhood and become more dependent on authority figures on whom they cannot realistically depend. Others feel angry and stunned at the breaking of trust, ruminate alone or in a group about it, and try to take revenge upon their 'bad parent'.

There are all sorts of ways to take revenge.[29] Here is one where the lack of care and consideration by the boss stimulated immediate revenge:

I work for a chiselling conniving bastard. Anything the staff does against him is richly deserved, and is only restoring the balance, do you see what I mean? If we get the chance, we pocket some of the money from clients without putting it through the till. But that's not very often. Even though I am paid on commission only, the bastard will not give me a moment off work to attend to private needs. What I do is to book in phantom clients, and N**** the receptionist can spot them because I use the brand names of Scotch whisky, for example Linda Bell, Sylvia Haig, Mrs Whitehorse, Joyce Teachers, etc. If I want to leave at say 5.00pm latest next Thursday, then I book in a two-hour perm at 4.00pm. About 3.45pm I get my girl-friend to phone in and cancel, so that it will then be too late to fill the slot. By about 4.30pm latest, I can then pack my bag and leave because there is no work for me.[30]

Others are not so fortunate: they have to exact their revenge only in their fantasies, although they take a lot of pleasure in them. Or they avoid the perpetrator, or withhold their own support. They may try to humiliate him or her in public, or privately spread evil rumours about them. They may leave the 'Family' entirely. Or, horror of horrors, they may commit parricide and literally kill the father: murder at the workplace is the fastest growing form of homicide in the USA,[31] and 40 per cent of these homicides are followed by suicide.

So the slippery slope is from support and care in a family atmosphere, through an excess or a lack of care, to estrangement, abuse, breakdown, and revenge: from Family to Feud. This is not to discount the possibility of reconciliation. But since it is the loss of trust in management which has resulted in Feud, its re-establishment is a necessary condition for reconciliation. And the regaining of trust takes time, since motives have to be reattributed, and a reputation for care, competence, and trustworthiness re-established. The transition from Family trust to Family Feud is shown in Table 3.

Metaphor fix

So how do we know where we ourselves stand with regard to the Family metaphor? Whereabouts are we on the continuum: Family, Flip, or Feud? Is it

Table 3 From Family to Feud

Family	Flip	Feud
Employer: Care and support Employee: Security and trust	Care too much or too little Dominance, dependence, or mistrust and injustice	Abuse, bullying Regression, revenge

still a meaningful metaphor to talk about our organisation's employment relationship as a Family one? Is the organisation on the slippery slope? Or is it already full of feuding revenge seekers? Here are some signs to look for:

- Who uses the Family metaphor and the words associated with it? Mainly employees? Top management and employees alike? Or mainly top management?
- What causal explanations do employees come up with for redundancies? External events outside top management's control? A mistaken attempt to save/improve the business? Personally motivated as a result of greed, fear, etc.?
- What are the current organisational stories and myths about? Support and care bringing success? Over-demanding or unconcerned management? Or managerial bullying and employee revenge?
- Have there been any critical organisational events or turning points where employees' trust in top management's intention to support and care for them was suddenly lost? What were they?
- If there have been such events, has top management recognised that trust has been lost as a consequence? Has it given any indications that it believes that this loss is important for the business? Has it taken any steps to try to re-establish trust? Have they had any effect?
- Does the organisation have proper grievance procedures? Employee assistance programmes? Encouragement and opportunity for whistle-blowing? Health and safety provision over and above minimal legal requirements? Active mentoring and/or support groups? Career workshops?

References

1 The *Observer*, 23 August 1998.
2 Manning, W. E. G. (1993) Unpublished PhD thesis, Birkbeck College, University of London.
3 Manning (op. cit.).
4 Herriot, P., Hirsh, W. and Reilly, P. (1998) *Trust and Transition: Managing Today's Employment Relationship*. Chichester: Wiley.
5 Nicholson, N. and West, M. A. (1989) Transitions, work histories, and careers. In M. B. Arthur, D. T. Hall, and B. S. Lawrence (eds) *Handbook of Career Theory*. Cambridge: Cambridge University Press.
6 Mishra, A. K. (1996) Organisational responses to crisis: The centrality of trust. In R. M. Kramer and T. R. Tyler (eds) *Trust in Organisations: Frontiers of Theory and Research*. Thousand Oaks CA: Sage.
7 Lewicki, R. J. and Bunker, B. B. (1996) Developing and maintaining trust in work relationships. In R. M. Kramer and T. R. Tyler (eds) *Trust in Organisations: Frontiers of Theory and Research*. Thousand Oaks CA: Sage.
8 Eisenberger, R., Fasolo, P. and Davis-Lamastro, V. (1990) Perceived organisational support and employee diligence, commitment, and innovation. *Journal of Applied Psychology*, 75, 1, 51–59.

9 Wayne, S. J., Shore, L. M. and Liden, R. C. (1997) Perceived organisational support and leader–member exchange: a social exchange perspective. *Academy of Management Journal*, 40, 1, 82–111.

10 Manning (op. cit.).

11 Ghoshal, S. and Bartlett, C. A. (1998) *The Individualised Corporation*. London: Heinemann.

12 Collinson, M., Edwards, P. K. and Rees, C. (1997) *Involving Employees in Total Quality Management*. London: Department of Trade and Industry.

13 Casey, C. (1996) Corporate transformations: Designer culture, designer employees, and post-occupational solidarity. *Organisation* 3, 3, 317–339.

14 Hirschhorn, L. (1988) *The Workplace Within: Psychodynamics of Organisational Life*. Cambridge MA: M I T Press.

15 Kerfoot, D. and Knights, D. (1993) Management, masculinity, and manipulation: from paternalism to corporate strategy in financial services in Britain. *Journal of Management Studies*, 30, 4, 661–677.

16 Roper, M. (1994) *Masculinity and the British Organisation Man*. Oxford: Oxford University Press.

17 Cranwell-Ward, J. (1998) Stress. In M. Pool and M. Warner (eds) *Handbook of Human Resource Management*. London: International Thomson Business Press.

18 Rucci, A. J., Kirn, S. P. and Quinn, R. T. (1998) The employee–customer–profit chain at Sears. *Harvard Business Review*, 98, 1, 82–98.

19 Manning, (op. cit.).

20 Lewicki, R. J. and Bunker, B. B. (1996) Developing and maintaining trust in work relationships. In R. M. Kramer and T. R. Tyler (eds) *Trust in Organisations: Frontiers of Theory and Research*. Thousand Oaks CA: Sage.

21 Noer, D. M. (1993) *Healing the Wounds*. San Francisco: Jossey Bass.

22 Folger, R. and Cropanzano, R. (1998) *Organisational Justice and Human Resource Management*. Thousand Oaks CA: Sage.

23 Brockner, J., Konorsky, M., Cooper-Schneider, R., Folger, R., Martin, C. and Bies, R. J. (1994) Interactive effects of procedural justice and outcome negativity on victims and survivors of job loss. *Academy of Management Journal*, 37, 2, 397–409.

24 Kets de Vries, M. F. R. and Balazs, K. (1997) The downside of downsizing. *Human Relations*, 50, 1, 11–50.

25 Institute of Management (1998) *The Quality of Working Life*. London: IoM.

26 Trades Union Congress (1998) *Bullying at Work*. London: TUC.

27 Rosen, M. (1988) You asked for it: Christmas at the bosses' expense. *Journal of Management Studies*, 25, 5, 463–480.

28 Fineman, S. and Gabriel, Y. (1996) *Experiencing Organisations*. London: Sage, p. 24.

29 Bies, R. J. and Tripp, T. M. (1996) Beyond distrust: Getting even and the need for revenge. In R. M. Kramer and T. R. Tyler (eds) *Trust in Organisations: Frontiers of Theory and Research*. Thousand Oaks CA: Sage.

30 Manning (op. cit.).

31 Thornburg, H. L. (1992) Practical ways to cope with suicide. *HR Magazine*, 37, 5, 62–66.

Chapter 2

Crusade and Play

Chivalry and cynicism

In 1095 Pope Urban II sanctioned a holy war. Whoever undertook the pilgrimage to the Holy Land to recapture the Holy City, Jerusalem, from the infidel would be freed from all penances, he promised. The biblical vision of the Holy City of God, the New Jerusalem, added spiritual splendour to this temporal task: 'And I, John, saw the holy city, new Jerusalem, coming down from God out of heaven, prepared as a bride adorned for her husband' (Revelation 21: 2).

'Deus vult, God wills it,' responded the Crusaders, adopting the words as their battle cry in the campaigns ahead. Forgetting local quarrels, Crusaders from all over Europe joined up en route. By the time of the Third Crusade (1189–1191), the romantic ideal was fully fledged. Richard Coeur de Lion, the charismatic leader of the Crusaders, engaged in chivalrous and courteous encounter with the noble Saladin for the highest of all possible motives.

Yet the vision of the City of God was soon debased. From the Fourth Crusade on, war was made against fellow Christians for gain, rather than against infidels for glory. Latin and Greek Christians fought each other, as soon did Templars and Hospitallers. Pope Urban's vision of a united Christendom degenerated into papal autocracy, and Western and Orthodox Christians parted for ever.

The story is one of an inspiring (though totally misplaced) vision, resulting in a mission undertaken by comrades sharing the same chivalrous values and led by charismatic leaders who embodied those values. But it is also a story of the betrayal of those values by people motivated by pride and greed. The top side of Crusade, with its distinguishing features of vision and charismatic leadership, flipped over to mere Play acting. While the values were still espoused, the reality was venality.

History is full of charismatic leaders who embodied their followers' aspirations in their persons, their deeds, and their words. Sometimes the vision remained untarnished, the mission was accomplished, and the values lived on in subsequent generations. Sometimes the coin flipped, the dark side became uppermost, and the followers reacted accordingly. Either they deserted the cause, disgusted and disillusioned; or else they stayed on and partook of the same evil gains as their discredited leaders. However, this was at the cost of a cynical hypocrisy, by which they pretended still to be in search of the Holy Grail whilst in fact being motivated wholly by greed. Meanwhile all the hewers of wood and drawers of water who had been forced to come along by their lords and masters happily went back home to their normal lives, never having shared in the vision in the first place.

Crusade and corporate excellence

Over the last 25 years, Crusade has become a fashionable rhetorical metaphor for the employment relationship. Following on from *In Search of Excellence*,[1] it became accepted management dogma that charismatic leadership which provided *vision*, defined *mission*, and established *values* led to corporate excellence. So dominant is this assumption that one of the most common management initiatives of recent years has been the establishment of corporate vision, mission, and values statements, and their reaffirmation on every available free space on the wall.[2]

Clearly, such initiatives are rhetorical; that is, their purpose is to persuade employees that they should all accept the statements and sign up for a united and enthused journey together into the future.[3] However, it does not follow that, because much of the use of the Crusade metaphor is rhetorical, it is of no value in helping us to understand an important element of the employment relationship. Many do share vision, mission, and values. For example, many health employees have brought to their work a vision of free and effective health care for all according to clinical need. Many teachers would subscribe to the mission of enabling young people to develop as much as possible of their potential. Both groups self-selected for their occupations in the light of these visions. The fact that the rhetoric to which they are currently exposed stresses value for money and efficiency does not detract from the appropriateness of the Crusade metaphor in recognising their vocational values.

The other essential element of the Crusade metaphor is the role of the *charismatic* or *transformational leader*. Such individuals do not inculcate vision, mission, and values from scratch. Rather, they succeed in expressing the essence of what is already latent in others. By their symbolic behaviour, their symbol-laden speeches, the stories and myths which they tell and which grow up around them, they help others to make sense of their experience and to use that sense to drive themselves on.[4] Such leaders are often the embodiment in themselves of the essence of the vision. Winston Churchill was a previously failing politician who managed to look like a bulldog, talk like one, and periodically walk around with one, so making bulldoggery the symbolic essence of British resistance in the Second World War. What he succeeded in doing was to express the desire of the British people to win the war in such a way as to enhance their hopes of doing so. He articulated and communicated a vision, built trust in it, and helped others achieve it.[5] He was the right leader in Britain's wartime situation.

This last caveat draws attention to the danger of over-emphasising the capacity of transformational leaders to transform. They are in danger of themselves becoming a myth. They depend upon followers who already are minded to take their desired direction, and upon a situation that requires those capacities which they have to offer. As soon as that situation changes, they may become superfluous, irrelevant, or downright dangerous. And finally, their longer-term success may depend upon the extent to which they develop others to be leaders too (instead of carefully guarding their backs).[6]

Nevertheless, the management literature is replete with examples of visionary leaders who have enabled their organisations to survive and prosper in times of change. In one current volume, for example, we learn of at least six such heroes:[7] Poul Andreassen of ISS (International Service Systems); Percy Barnevik of ABB (Asea Brown Boveri); Livio DeSimone of 3M; Andrew Grove of Intel; Yoshiro Maruta of Kao Corporation; and Jack Welch at GE (General Electric). Ghoshal and Bartlett, the book's authors, suggest that what is common in most of these cases is that the efforts to transform the organisations

> followed a carefully phased approach that focussed on developing particular organisational capabilities in an appropriate sequence. And second, actual transformation occurred only when the structural configuration was reinforced by real and enduring change in the behaviours of individuals within the organisation.
>
> (p. 244)

A typical change process involves such leaders as those quoted above acting in the following sequence:

- rationalising structures and building discipline and support so as to enhance the performance of each business unit
- revitalising by building stretch and trust between units
- so that the entire organisation is regenerated as a result of highly integrated and highly performing units.

Such transformations require huge leadership qualities in our heroes. They seldom had a clear vision at the beginning of where they wanted to be at the end of the transformation process, but they developed one as they went along and they communicated it clearly at each stage. Jack Welch, for example, said at the first stage at GE: 'The new [psychological] contract is that jobs at GE are the best in the world for those willing to compete.' At the second stage, he had best internal practice teams touring the organisation encouraging learning. He also overcame his reputation as a savage cost cutter by meeting as many employees as possible and speaking with them in an atmosphere of plain-speaking, directness, and honesty. The third stage is still in progress, since the vision is 'to build a GE that renews itself constantly, exhilarates itself with speed, and freshens itself through constant learning' (p. 266).

According to Bartlett and Ghoshal, Welch and others like him have moved from the old notions of management as consisting of strategy, structure and systems to a framework of purpose, process, and people. They have to create a sense of purpose that will motivate and enthuse employees, since strategy, however clever, cannot do so. They have to create processes which provide the environment in which employees can take decisions for themselves. And they have to form relationships and communicate personally with a wide range of people. We should, however, remember that Bartlett and Ghoshal's book, and many others like it, exemplify the 'excellence' genre of management texts. Coming from the American business culture, authors have to discover heroes with whom their readers can identify. Rounded pictures, warts and all, are unlikely to result.

Vision and mission in the Inland Revenue

These are examples from international private sector corporations. They emphasise the transformational function of the charismatic leader. If they are to follow such leaders, employees need to be able to trust them in terms both of their motives and of their competence.[8] Here is an example from the UK public sector, where the leadership was exercised by several and the vision, mission, and values were generated by employees rather than being brought down from the mountain by Moses. The example derives from the British nation's favourite public servant, the Inland Revenue.

One of the most profound trends of the last 20 years has been the commercialisation of everything, including that of the public sector. This bottom line orientation has sat uneasily with the underlying vocation of many in the public sector, which is to serve the public and their country. That is often why they went into the public service in the first place. Their career anchors were service and security, rather than, say, entrepreneurship or pure challenge. Hence the importance attached to involving staff in the derivation of vision, mission, and values. Whilst the changed circumstances required the Inland Revenue to adapt, it was vital that the mission should reflect and build on the existing vision and motivation of the employees.

Wisely avoiding the use of such high-flown terms as 'mission', Inland Revenue expressed it in terms of what their job was:

> Our job (is) to provide an efficient effective and fair tax service to the country and Government by:

- helping people get their tax right first time and on time
- detecting and deterring people who do not voluntarily comply
- and approaching all our work in a manner that demonstrates best customer service and value for money.

The Inland Revenue also decided that whatever values it espoused should not be subject to change but should be enduring statements of how people should work with each other. The consultation process produced the statement:

The success of the Inland Revenue depends on all of us sharing common values:

- In our relations with others:

  - mutual respect
  - integrity
  - trusting people and earning their trust
  - being open and approachable
  - treating everyone fairly

- In working together:

  - fostering teamwork
  - encouraging initiative and innovation
  - taking a pride in our work
  - having determination to achieve our goals

- All managers providing leadership by together giving:

  - a clear direction
  - encouragement and recognition
  - visible support and training.

To prevent this becoming mere motherhood and apple pie, training was extensive, do-it-yourself toolkits were developed, and project managers appointed. To check that the programme was having the desired effects, attitude surveys were conducted, and complaints and absence records monitored.

Overall, this attempt at change management maximised its chances of longer-term success by involving staff from its inception and by building on their strengths. At the same time, the need to address issues of efficiency and customer service was not shirked.

Seeds of doubt

But the coin can start to flip; the Crusader may feel some seeds of doubt creeping into his mind. Does the Holy Grail really still exist? Is it really worth all this dirt, disease, and death in strange and savage lands? Am I really a chivalrous knight in shining armour?

One of the signals which we might pick up that all is not quite what it seems is that there appears to be an amazing similarity between visions and missions and values across organisations. It all seems like vision by numbers. If all the organisations whose vision is to be the best in the world were to race together, the result would be the biggest multiple tie for first place ever seen. And anyway, is the vision of, for example, selling more sweet fizzy water than anyone else in the world really worth Crusading for?

Other doubts may begin to surface. Employees may have been so swept along by the excitement of it all that they failed to reflect on how they started out on the Crusade in the first place. Was the initial presentation of the vision and the values by top management really aimed at transforming the organisation to enable it to adapt to the changed environment? Or was it simply a way of ensuring that what top management believed to be the right strategic issues were addressed?[9] Did employees have any say in what the vision and values were? Or were these simply handed down and employees were expected to comply ? Employees are unlikely to be truly committed if they merely complied.[10]

More seriously, is it really me, they ask? I may be well grounded enough in my own identity to know that whilst I may share some of the required values, there are different ones which are nearer the top of my own list which fail to appear on the official one. I may share a strong values base with my professional colleagues in my own division.[11] Or I may simply have a personal career anchor, for example security or service, which does not appear anywhere in the Crusader's creed.[12] To continue with the religious metaphor, employees cannot all sing from the same Crusader hymn sheet when some of them are confirmed agnostics or Buddhists.

After a while, employees may begin to doubt the motives of their leaders. They may reflect how they have come to view them. As parents who will nurture and guide them? As mystics, who know the path into the future? As heroes who can move mountains? As saints, driven only by their devotion to the cause?[13] Such idealised hero worship leads inevitably to disillusion. Can they really be such saints when they award themselves such huge salary rises?[14, 15] Are they more interested in themselves than in the cause?

Or perhaps dominance rather than greed is their real motive? Perhaps they enjoy the power over others which their charismatic gifts make possible. Charisma can lead to narcissism and worse, employees recognise. Leaders can become so grandiose that they start making unrealistic demands upon people, just like over-demanding parents. And employees dimly recognise that they have colluded in this process by blaming themselves for failing their leaders, but attributing all *their* mistakes to the rest of the world. Is this what has happened?[16]

Taken for granted

Various management actions may force employees to recognise that their leaders have come to take them for granted. Management initiatives introduced as ways of helping them to achieve the vision give them instead a strong hint that they are merely a means to an end. Total Quality Management (TQM), empowerment schemes, and culture change programmes in general all make assumptions about employees' willingness to continue the long trek to the promised land as the unsung footslogging backbone of the Crusading army:

- TQM urged them to get it right first time for internal and external customers, yet they themselves were not always supported in these efforts by top management.
- Empowerment was handed down as a big deal, but employees noticed some mixed messages;[17] how come we're ordered to be empowered, they asked. And why do we need champions to push it through: because we can't do it ourselves? And above all, why, if we are to be trusted with decisions, have they added to our accountabilities but decreased our resources?[18]
- Culture change programmes seek to homogenise us, employees feel, when we each have different things to offer and would like to be valued for that individuality or professional identity.[19]
- Why have they suddenly felt the need to spell out to us with a great fanfare a set of values which were the very reason we came into the public sector in the first place, ask long-suffering public sector staff.

Perhaps they have had a revealing experience like the following:[20]

A financial sector organisation adopted TQM, as have 51% of organisations in that sector since the late 1980s. The TQM vision was expounded in a booklet, which implied that everyone's skills and knowledge would be needed and used to ensure that all thrived and prospered with the business. Unity, teamwork, autonomy and empowerment were the key themes.

However, top management involved itself little in the programme. Contrary to the values of TQM, there were heavy corporate control systems in place to control the branches, and the branch managers in their turn adopted an authoritarian management style in response to the pressures upon them.

Training consisted of only four days for managers and two days for staff, but even so people were fired up at the end of it. Particularly powerful were the messages about seeing all one's work in the context of service to internal and external customers.

However, top management did not reinforce these messages and drift occurred. The Managing Director appeared not to recognise that some employees might need to be persuaded and would not automatically buy into the change. There was no infrastructure back at the branches to support and develop TQM practice.

Suddenly, as recession bit, unannounced and unexplained downsizing was the order of the day. Despite such downsizing being incompatible with TQM as expounded in the programme, some managers used TQM arguments to justify the redundancies!

Such experiences may start to make employees speculate further about their leaders. Why is it, they wonder, that they are so eager to embrace these Crusading fads? After all, such fads all appear to follow a sequence of initial enthusiasm, piecemeal implementation, disillusion, and decline. Are they so incompetent as to grasp at every straw, every new quick fix? Or do the consultants who sell them successfully appeal to their need to see themselves as bold brave risk-takers, saviours of the business?[21, 22] Consultants may play on top managers' fears for their futures, which will be in doubt if they fail to turn the business around: do it or perish. Or they may hold open the possibility of redemption, liberation and the new Jerusalem through the necessary suffering of revolution. Or they may offer a new identity as old-fashioned all-American hero, blasting through all the obstacles?[23] Whatever the sales pitch, employees suspect leaders who fall for it.

The leader from hell

Perhaps these seeds of doubt develop into full-blown cynicism. Knights in shining armour become mere toy soldiers; Crusade turns into Play-acting. What causes the coin, or indeed the Crusader, to finally flip?

One possibility is that the leader herself may flip as a result of all the burdens of charismatic leadership, causing the follower to come to her senses. Julie Maddrell[24] experienced a semi-religious conversion to the dream of 'Parfum Hypnotique'. She was promised no less than the casting off of the burdens of the past in a recreation of the good old-time religion. She would be rid of the everyday tedium of life, like the existing employees who gave their testimonies to their own salvation.

Apparently transforming herself in the same way, Julie hurled herself into the task of marketing and selling the dream. Her life was devoted to the dream, and revolved around the parfumerie and getting her manager's approval and friendship. She felt guilty if she stepped outside this micro-world for the briefest moment. However, her dependency on her manager was her Achilles heel (or rather, her toe-hold on reality). For her manager finally tired of playing her inspirational role perfectly, thereby demonstrating that for her at least the dream had faded. Julie realised that she too had been duped, and subsequently made sense to herself of her experience in terms similar to this paragraph.

Alternatively, charismatic leaders may become plain monsters.[25] They already possess those personal characteristics which predispose them to abuse power: they have a strong need for power, they are very self-confident, and they have very strong convictions. So, when employees collude with their narcissistic view of themselves as God's gift, when they present them with the admiration they crave, then they are dicing with danger. Employees and colleagues forgo the possibility of ever finding any blemish in their leader's perfection because if they try to point one out they are scapegoated; the loyal followers are let loose upon them. If employees accept responsibility for a major task, they can be sure the narcissistic leader will fail to give it full support in case they become identified with failure. And they had better not succeed too well or the leader will think they are trying to usurp his of her position. Indeed, it is better not to take any initiative oneself, since one's own initiative cannot by definition be totally under the leader's control. Much better to Play-act, to fawn and flatter, and to repeat the right mantras whilst keeping one's sanity by speaking one's true feelings about the leader in secret.

Playing at soldiers

For most people who play at soldiers, though, things are nothing like so dramatic. They do not have conversion experiences like Julie Maddrell's, nor tremble before tyrants as did the staff of Harold Geneen or Robert Maxwell. Rather, they collapse gently into a world-weary ironic cynicism. And this is hardly surprising. People are accustomed to being continuously bombarded by marketing rhetoric. They have learned to take it all with a very big pinch of salt, so much so that most of today's television advertisements contain a heavy dollop of irony. They are only too well aware that someone is trying to persuade them of a proposition which they do not currently believe strongly enough to go out and buy the product or service in question.

Employees are aware that top management's visions, missions, and values may also be rhetorical: that is, they are attempts to persuade them. This rhetorical action frequently has precisely the opposite effect from that intended. It draws employees' attention to the fact that management are trying to persuade them. What's in it for them? they ask themselves. Why are they exercising their persuasive skills like this? And employees may rapidly and cynically assume that as far as they are concerned, the message is just a marketing tool, a façade. What's their hidden agenda? they ask. More cost cutting? Getting more out of us for less? Trying to pretend that their interests and ours completely coincide?

Moreover, the contradictions in the rhetoric are only too obvious. How come, if we're such a valuable resource, that we're treated as a disposable commodity? ask employees. Why, if they value autonomy so highly, are they on our backs all the time? Ironically, those who do not need rhetoric to propel them, those with a true vocation, have often been sent the opposite message. Teachers, nurses, personnel professionals even, are a cost to be reduced, a drain on the rest of the organisation. And reduced they are, to the extent that science graduates shun teaching and there is currently a shortage of nurses. So those who work to live are dragooned into pretending to live to work, whilst those with self-generated vision and values feel taken for granted and undervalued.

So employees play at being soldiers. They say the words and go through the motions. Instead of rapturously merging their identity with the corporate cause, they treasure it as their own in all its quirky individuality. We'll be just as good at façades as they are, they tell themselves. We can keep hidden our commitments to our friends at work and at home, our families, what really matters to us. They can't touch us deep down.[26]

Emotional labour

Employees play their roles dutifully, though, since it is in their interests to comply. And nowhere is this more apparent than in what has come to be called 'emotional labour'.[27] This phrase refers to

> those (increasingly common) situations where service employees are required, as part of their job, to display specific sets of emotions (by verbal and/or non-verbal means) with the aim, in turn, of inducing particular feelings and responses among those for whom the service is being provided.[28]

So we are talking about bankers as well as waiters, supermarket staff as well as airline cabin crew, ticket clerks as well as receptionists; a whole range of employees over and above those who have traditionally been expected to 'put on a show'. Where competition has removed many of the price and quality differentials between companies, it is how the service is provided which has come to differentiate. The aim is to produce a more favourable psychological response in the customer than one's competitors succeed in producing. And this response can include feeling a better person through enhanced self-esteem and social status,[29] or even increased confidence in one's sexual attractiveness.[30]

Moreover, the level of customer satisfaction which is required today involves, paradoxically, being expected to go beyond what is normally expected. If customers are to be delighted at the service they receive, then they need to be surprised that the person providing the service has been so thoughtful and empathic. In other words, it is impossible to go the extra mile for the customer without getting involved, without genuine imagination and feeling. Putting on a show is just not enough to produce 'customer delight'. So the task of the employee who is unwilling for whatever reason to put their heart and soul into serving the customer is a hard one. They cannot hope to get away with merely greeting the customer using the right words ('Hello, my name is Tracy, how can I help yooooou'). They have to look them in the eye, smile winningly, and sound as though they really want to help and are actively searching for an opportunity to put themselves out on the customer's behalf. They either have to be authentic, or else they have simulate authenticity supremely well, since it is authenticity that is being required of them.

Just in case they are failing to perform authentically enough, they are checked up on constantly. Fake passengers travel on airlines, fake shoppers use supermarkets. Emotional labourers are put under covert surveillance. Customers are asked to rate the authenticity of their performance. The strategies emotional labourers use to decrease the pressures of constant emotional performance are varied.[31] They go backstage and blow a fuse, or they defy the rules in tiny little ways that assert their individuality. They share the irony of their situation with sympathetic customers. But sometimes these ways of coping are inadequate in the face of continuous and unsupported demands for emotional labour. The price of irony is sometimes alienation and burnout.

The example of emotional labour encapsulates the two-sided nature of the Crusade-Play metaphor. For many people, helping customers or clients or serving the public is a genuine motivation, and they do not generally have to motivate themselves to perform. And this is true of men as well as of women, who are, of course, 'naturally' predisposed to be nurturant![32] When enthusiastic leaders help them express for themselves why it is that their service is so worthwhile, so much the better. To call it a Crusade may be a bit over the top, they feel, but they certainly do it for much more than the money.

The flip side rapidly appears when employees discern attempts to engineer commitment to the organisation. They may have developed a commitment to customers and clients, to their occupation or profession, and to their immediate workmates and manager. But when those at the top of the organisation seek to control hearts and minds, it becomes a different matter altogether. Real Crusaders are reduced to toy soldiers, and both they and their organisation suffer as a consequence. This decline is summarised in Table 4.

Table 4 From Crusade to Play-acting

Crusade	Flip	Play-acting
Employer: Mission, vision, values leadership, charisma	Narcissism	Corruption Abuse of power
Employee: Commitment, authenticity	Collusion	Disillusionment, cynicism, pretence

Metaphor fix

So where does your organisation stand on the True Crusader versus Toy Soldier metaphor? The following questions may help you get a fix on its position.

* Could you provide without too much thought one or two reasons why it is that your organisation is engaged in the sort of activity that it performs? Do these reasons refer solely to the need to make a profit? If the answer is no, perhaps there is a vision waiting to be expressed.
* If such a vision exists, why has it survived? Has the organisation done anything to ensure its survival? Can you identify any organisational leaders who have embodied it?
* If the vision has faded, why has it done so? Has the organisation done anything to contribute to its loss?
* Has your organisation engaged in any initiative aimed at changing attitudes, mindsets, or culture? Did this initiative(s) give a new vision? Confirm and strengthen the existing vision? Contradict and devalue the existing vision? Have no effect whatsoever ? Have an effect which was not that intended?
* When top management engage in such initiatives, to what do employees attribute their actions?

References

1 Peters, T. and Waterman, R. (1982) *In Search of Excellence: Lessons from America's Best-Run Companies.* New York: Harper and Row.
2 Institute of Management (1996) *Managing the Management Tools.* London.
3 Barley, S. R. and Kunda, G. (1992) Design and devotion: surges of rational and normative ideologies of control in managerial discourse. *Administrative Science Quarterly*, 37, 3, 363–399.
4 Bryman, A. (1996) Leadership in organisations. In S. R. Clegg, C. Hardy and W. R. Nord (eds) *Handbook of Organisational Studies.* London: Sage.
5 Conger, J. A. (1989) *The Charismatic Leader: Behind the Mystique of Exceptional Leadership.* San Francisco: Jossey Bass.
6 Kouzes, J. M. and Posner, B. Z. (1993) *Credibility: How Leaders Gain and Lose it, Why People Demand it.* San Francisco: Jossey Bass.

7 Ghoshal, S. and Bartlett, C. A. (1998) *The Individualised Corporation*. London: Heinemann.
8 Sankowsky, D. (1995) The charismatic leader as narcissist: understanding the abuse of power. *Organisational Dynamics*, Spring, 57–71.
9 James, B. (1994) Narrative and organisational control: corporate visionaries, ethics, and power. *International Journal of Human Resource Management*, 5, 4, 927–952.
10 O'Reilly, C. and Chatman, J. (1986) Organisational commitment and psychological attachment: the effects of compliance, identification, and internalisation on pro-social behaviour. *Journal of Applied Psychology*, 71, 492–499.
11 Rentsch, J. R. (1990) Climate and culture: interaction and qualitative differences in organisational meanings. *Journal of Applied Psychology*, 75, 668–681.
12 Schein, E. (1993) *Career Anchors: Discovering Your Real Values*. London: Pfeiffer.
13 Sankowsky (op. cit.).
14 Conyon, M. J. (1995) Directors' pay in the privatised utilities. *British Journal of Industrial Relations*, 33, 2, 159–171.
15 Conyon, M. J. and Leech, D. (1993) Top pay, company performance, and corporate governance. Warwick: University of Warwick Economic Research Papers no. 410.
16 Sankowsky (op. cit.).
17 Argyris, C. (1998) Empowerment: the emperor's new clothes. *Harvard Business Review*, 76, 3, 98–105.
18 Cunningham, I., Hyman, J. and Baldry, C. (1996) Empowerment: the power to do what? *Industrial Relations Journal*, 27, 2, 143–154.
19 Harris, L. C. and Ogbonna, E. (1998) Employee responses to culture change efforts. *Human Resource Management Journal*, 8, 2, 78–92.
20 McCabe, D. and Wilkinson, A. (1998) The rise and fall of TQM: the vision, meaning, and operation of change. *Industrial Relations Journal*, 29, 1, 18–29.
21 Gill, J. and Whittle, S. (1992) Management by panacea: accounting for transience. *Journal of Management Studies*, 30, 2, 281–295.
22 Huczynski, A. A. (1993) Explaining the succession of management fads. *International Journal of Human Resource Management*, 4, 2, 443–464.
23 Jackson, B. G. (1996) Re-engineering the sense of self: the manager and the management guru. *Journal of Management Studies*, 33, 5, 571–590.
24 Hopfl, H. and Maddrell, J. (1996) Can you resist a dream? Evangelical metaphors and the appropriation of emotion. In D. Grant and C. Oswick (eds) *Metaphor and Organisations*. London: Sage.
25 Kets de Vries, M. F. R. (1993) *Leaders, Fools, and Impostors*. San Francisco: Jossey Bass.
26 Willmott, H. (1993) Strength is ignorance; slavery is freedom: managing culture in modern organisations. *Journal of Management Studies*, 30, 4, 515–552.
27 Fineman, S. (1996) Emotion and organising. In S. R. Clegg, C. Hardy and W. R. Nord (eds) *Handbook of Organisation Studies*. London: Sage.
28 Noon, M. and Blyton, P. (1997) *The Realities of Work*. London: Macmillan, p. 124.
29 Hall, E. (1993) Smiling, deferring, and flirting: doing gender by giving good service. *Work and Occupations*, 20, 4, 452–471.
30 Linstead, S. (1995) Averting the gaze: gender and power on the perfumed picket line. *Gender, Work, and Organisation*, 2, 4, 190–206.
31 Noon and Blyton (op. cit.).
32 Hochschild, A. R. (1983) *The Managed Heart: Commercialisation of Human Feeling*. Berkeley CA: University of California Press.

Chapter 3

Contract and Jungle

Doing deals

'I pledge you – I pledge myself – to a new deal for the American people,' promised Franklin Delano Roosevelt during the Great Depression. And doubtless prime minister Blair consciously sought to echo that great US president when he recently set up his New Deal scheme for unemployed people in the UK.

There is no doubt that the notion of a deal or contract between parties is an attractive one. It implies that they are free agents who can choose whether or not to enter into a contractual relationship; and if they decide to do so, agree mutually acceptable terms. Then there is the promissory nature of the contract: each party undertakes to fulfil their own obligations to the other which they have contracted. And they have contracted with each other because they depend on each other. The concept is attractive because it appeals to two fundamental features of human behaviour: *agency*, the perception that we have some capacity to influence our environment by our actions; and *reciprocity*, the mutuality which is the social glue which ensures that relationships endure.

The key element of the Contract metaphor, then, is that of *mutual obligations*. The employment relationship is being described as a contractual arena in which employers and employees make promises to each other and try to keep them. There is, of course, no implication that this is an altruistic activity. On the contrary, the metaphor sits well with the economists' view of people as maximising their own interests. The picture presented is one of a win–win situation, in which each party meets certain of the other's needs provided that the other meets certain of theirs. It is a rational and calculative view of the employment relationship which is consistent with a rationalist view of organisations and business.

The psychological contract

Much recent attention has been devoted to the concept of the psychological contract,[1] defined here as the perception of the two parties, employee and employer, of what their mutual obligations are towards each other. The term 'psychological' distinguishes the contract from the legal contract of employment, and puts it firmly into the perceptual and social spheres of activity. It raises all sorts of interesting questions. For example:

- How do the parties find out what the other wants so that they can make appropriate offers?
- How explicit is the deal; does it spell out the terms in great behavioural detail, or leave them vague?
- If in detail, where is there room for behaviour which is over and above that contracted, such as employees 'going the extra mile'?
- If vaguely, how much room is there for different perceptions of what the deal is, and thence mistaken allegations of violating it?
- How is the contract to be monitored as to whether it is being kept, whether it is still fair, and whether it still meets the needs of both parties?
- If there are violations, inequities, or inappropriate terms, how is the deal renegotiated and what prompts such renegotiations?

So the original definition has a snapshot quality about it, which tends to fix a particular contract at a point in time. The questions we have just raised point to the changing nature of contracts. 'The most powerful contracts of all are those that can be both changed and kept.'[2] Organisations' needs change as the business environment changes, and so do those of employees as their lives develop in varied ways. So it is probably preferable to use the metaphor as a verb, 'Contracting', rather than as a noun referring to 'the Contract'.

Contracting works

Now the benefits of psychological contracting appear obvious. If employees or their representatives do an employment deal with the organisation, they will:

- generate a sense of agency, avoiding the feeling of helplessness that ensues when deals are imposed
- develop a degree of confidence and trust, provided of course that the organisation honours its side of the bargain
- be personally motivated because it is their personal needs that are met.

And the organisation in turn will benefit from responsible and committed employees,[3] who feel an obligation to do what the organisation needs them to do.

Recent research on the psychological contract supports this analysis.[4, 5] A large stratified sample of respondents from the UK working population demonstrated two things. First, that appropriate HR (Human Resources) policies and processes lead to better psychological contracts in terms of mutual trust and perceptions of equity, and this in turn leads to higher commitment and motivation. And second, that only some 20 per cent were dissatisfied with their psychological contract so defined.

When we do seek to take a snapshot measure of the content of the psychological contract from a representative sample of managers and other employees, there seems to be little disagreement between the two parties as to what their obligations to each other are.[6] Managers and others believe that employees' obligations are to:

- work contracted hours
- do work of good quality
- deal honestly with customers and clients
- be loyal to the organisation
- treat its property properly
- dress and behave correctly
- go beyond one's job description when necessary.

The organisation's obligations in return included: training, fair procedures, equity in discipline and pay, consultation, a degree of autonomy, support, recognition, safety, and a degree of job security.

Here is an example of the psychological contract working well for both parties, with a high level of reciprocity:

> I have been made redundant three times before I came to Smith's, which is a small injection moulding shop where I now work. The wages are not as high as many other factories, but the firm does seem to protect the employees' living. Most factories, and certainly others where I have worked, resort to layoffs when there is a shortage of orders. This used to cripple me. . . . Our firm seems to spread its risk over different customers. They put us on maintenance and painting if production work is short. It is so much better to have peace of mind with a steady job, rather than high wages and then periods of nothing and frequently getting made redundant. . . . When the local buses went on strike, the lads hired a mini-bus and together with their private cars, they worked out routes and pick-up points and got everybody to work to time. All the other factories on our industrial estate had massive absenteeism. We kept going at full strength.[7]

Forms of contract

We can, perhaps, distinguish two sorts of contract:[8] *transactional* contracts, which are fairly specific and economic in nature, and basically to do with rewards for hard work; and *relational* contracts, which are both economic and social/emotional in nature. These are less clearly specified and to a degree open-ended. In a successful contractual relationship, it is possible that we come to trust the other party's reliability because they regularly fulfil a transactional contract. As a result, a more relational contract develops, whereby parties are willing to go beyond the contract trusting that the other will do the same for them when the need arises.[9]

However, that is not to say that organisations do not benefit from several sorts of contract.[10] Relatively short-term and specific transactional contracts can meet the need for flexibility and reliable performance. Longer-term and open-ended relational contracts may help organisations which need loyalty and good citizenship from their employees. Specific but longer and potentially renegotiable contracts combine some of the advantages of the previous two. As organisations diversify the range of contracts which they offer, the existence and use of these alternatives becomes increasingly attractive.

What is also clear is that whilst organisations' needs are varied, and the contracts they offer are increasing in number and variety, so too are the needs of employees. The increased diversity of the workforce has resulted in a much broader set of preferred deals. Some organisations are working hard to ensure that the two sets of needs are matched as far as possible. So, for example, a large organisation in the finance sector took the trouble to discover the current perceptions and future expectations of different employees at different levels. Figure 1 shows the current psychological contracts of clerical staff and newly appointed graduate recruits:

Having discovered that different groups of staff both perceived different

Organisation offers	Employee offers
Clerical staff	
A job today	Performance
Less punishment for mistakes	Hard work
Reduced promotion opportunities	More of his/her life
Good pay	More responsibility
Graduates	
Individualised training	Challenge to the organisation
Marketable skills	Rapid learning
Early career structure, later choice	Entrepreneurship
Undelivered promises	

Figure 1 Psychological contracts of clerical staff and newly appointed graduates

current contracts and expected different future ones, the organisation took steps to change the 'one size fits all' assumptions that had previously guided its contractual policies.[11] No longer was it assumed that everyone wanted a progressive career within the organisation, for example. Moreover, discretion was extended to local units so that, in its call centres, shifts are designed and allocated to match the outside role demands of employees.

The transactional trend

So the metaphor holds in many cases. Mutual obligations are honoured, and Contracts are kept. But as with all the other metaphors, Contract too has a few potential worms at its core. The first is the currently increasing concentration on transactional deals.[12, 13] Deals with employees are over a shorter term, as lifetime employment is no longer assumed. Employment contracts are now more often fixed-term, projects or functions are contracted out, and movement between jobs is more frequent. The outputs expected by the organisation are spelt out in greater detail, together with cost limits, quality parameters, and completion dates. What the contractor, be they internal or external, receives in exchange is also spelled out.

I have already alluded to one of the likely consequences of an increased emphasis on transaction. It is that the parties will neither give nor receive more than the deal requires. Good citizenship from the employee or goodwill from the employer is less likely than in more relational psychological contracts. This is bad news for companies which promise service which goes the extra mile. It is also bad news for employees whose career anchor is one of service.

But the second consequence is equally profound: increased fear in top management that employees will not produce what they are contracted to produce. At the root of this fear lies the economists' assumption about human nature. The economic theory of agency asserts that agents (employees) are by definition opportunistic and seek to shirk. Unless contracts are spelled out in detail and closely policed, employees will not fulfil the terms of the deal.[14]

This fear leads to a felt need to inspect, monitor and control. Typically, bureaucratic procedures are put in place, such as clocking in for workers to ensure that they are giving the time which they are contracted to give. Appraisal processes require the setting of highly specific targets and regular monitoring to check that they are being achieved. Everything that it is possible to measure is measured, and so are some that are not. Things which cannot be measured are assumed either not to exist, or certainly not to matter. If they cannot be checked and proved to have happened, then it is not worth paying attention to them. And the reason for all this checking is so that employees can be held accountable for the obligations which they have incurred in their transactional contract.

For all the talk in management books about empowerment and the need for top management to trust employees to do their jobs, the reality has often been the retention or enhancement of tight control. Achievement of output targets is what matters, and the recent stress on performance management has been more about rewarding people for achieving targets than for managing how they achieve them.

In sum, the trend towards more transactional contracts has increased employers' needs to *control*. The problem of control has always been the same: its costs. Ironically, the attempt to cut costs by more transactional contracts has resulted in increased transaction costs. And these can become insupportable, especially in hard times. Consequently some employees take the opportunity to fulfil all the gloomy self-fulfilling prophecies about them, and exploit the loopholes. So do some organisations, which brings us on to the second worm at the core of the Contract apple.

Perceived violation

Psychological contracts are the perceptions of both parties to the employment relationship, employer and employee, regarding what their mutual obligations are to each other. This leaves room for a lot of misunderstandings. If the terms of the deal are spelt out in excessive detail, then we have fewer misunderstandings but we are left with all the problems of the transactional trend described above. If the terms are left somewhat vague, then employers can believe one version of the deal and employees a different one.

For example, the employee may believe the Contract to be a much more relational one than does the organisation (a case of under-investment by the organisation).[15] It follows that one party could believe it was keeping its side of the bargain when the other perceives a violation. An employee might have believed that the deal included a degree of job security in exchange for the long service they had given, while this element did not feature in the employer's version at all. Indeed, some of the very HR processes that organisations use may give off the wrong signals.[16] The regular receipt of an annual bonus may be taken to imply that the Contract is to always receive a bonus; or regularly favourable appraisal assessments to indicate security of tenure.

However, perceived violation is not always the result of a mutual misunderstanding of what the deal is. On the contrary, employees frequently believe that the organisation has violated the contract knowing perfectly well what that contract was. And of course the reverse is also true; employers often believe, for example, that graduate recruits who leave after their initial training period have purposefully broken their side of the recruitment deal. And this is where emotions start shattering the cool and rational realm of contract.

One of the reasons why Contract is currently such a popular metaphor is that it offers an explanation for employees' reactions to redundancy. If they believed that their deal included security of employment, then, it was thought, this would explain why they felt so angry and disillusioned.[17] For the deal which they thought they had, and upon which they had based their working lives, was reneged upon by their employers. Even when this did not happen to them but to their colleagues, employees recognised that once the deal had been broken, it could be broken again. Redundancies have, indeed, become a regular feature of organisational life.

Anger and disillusion were only two of the profound responses to perceived Contract violation, however. Some employees felt bereaved,[18] guilty,[19] and distrustful of top management.[20] Management consequently sought to persuade them of the inevitability of redundancies due to the increasingly competitive environment; in other words, they tried to persuade them to attribute the cause of downsizing to uncontrollable external events rather than to conscious internal decisions. However, employees' attributions of causality were often to top management themselves, and in particular to their self-interest.

Contract violation is not perceived only in respect of major events such as redundancies. Over half of a sample of MBA graduates reported violation of their psychological contract two years into their employment. They were particularly disappointed in their employers' failure to deliver on perceived promises regarding training and development, compensation, promotion, job description, job security and feedback. The more they felt the deal had been reneged upon, the more likely they were to leave the organisation and the less trust and job satisfaction they felt.[21] What is more, they were less likely to engage in organisational citizenship behaviour.[22] Pay, in particular, is a fruitful source of perceived violations, with special anger being reserved for pay cuts made on people who are in a vulnerable position (for example, about to retire).[23]

So too is a general lack of recognition:

> We had a super lady, who as a matter of course was never late. She worked hard well before and after office times. The thing that made her behaviour more than to be expected was that she did it despite the organisation's attitude towards her. It did not deserve that dedication. Working beyond hours is not of itself abnormal, provided there is recognition from the organisation. I mean encouragement, thanks, and in due course financial reward and career advancement. This lady was all but ignored. No acknowledgement, no matter how hard she worked. Sad to say, at the end of the day she just upped and left.[24]

So contract violation by the employer often hurts both parties. The employee may suffer directly, but the employer suffers indirectly as a consequence of the impact of the violation. And we must not forget that the reverse is sometimes true. Employees may violate the contract, usually hurting their employer thereby; but they may lose long-term employability if they gain a reputation for unreliability.

Power inequality

The third, and by far the most devastating worm in the apple relates to the respective power of the parties. The Contract metaphor implies two parties as human agents with the power and opportunity to engage in negotiating behaviour and doing deals with each other. If one party imposes a deal upon the other through use of its superior bargaining power, then the Contract metaphor is inappropriate. For its central feature is the voluntary under-taking of mutual obligations.

Now many employees will have a degree of labour market power which ensures that their organisation needs them. It would find them difficult or costly to replace. Indeed, in some cases their organisation needs an employee far more than that employee needs their employer. But there are many more who have little or no labour market power. As far as many employers are concerned, the situation here is perfectly simple. They dictate the terms of the deal on offer, and employees take it or leave it. It is of little consequence if they leave it: there are always willing volunteers.

Parties with power who exercise it in this way have several advantages. Power affects external perceptions, with the powerful party being granted a degree of legitimacy.[25] It has the power to give accounts of its actions which seem acceptable and reasonable.[26] The powerless party, on the other hand, feels helpless, frustrated, and angry, or becomes decreasingly involved. The result is non-directed conflict or passivity and alienation. This is what happens when Contracts are not negotiated but imposed.

However, it is still perfectly possible to negotiate effectively when parties are of unequal power (as they nearly always are when labour markets are segmented as at present). The more powerful party will hold the balance of power, and the deal concluded will reflect this. But the dealing process may have enabled conflict over issues to be resolved, and the parties are more likely to be committed to the deal.

The free market ideology of the 1980s and early 1990s has removed some of what few legal constraints there were in the UK and the USA, and also in several countries in continental Europe (e.g. France). Moreover, it has reduced the power of the trades unions to negotiate effectively on behalf of their members. The rhetoric implies that this benefits both parties, since there is now no hindrance to their negotiating whatever deal they want. However, where there is an imbalance of power, it is necessary to restrain the complete freedom of one party to impose its desired 'deal' in order for the other to have any freedom at all. In countries such as Germany, however, legal constraints have generally been more extensive.

In the Anglo-American context,[27, 28] deals are more likely to be imposed, and the Contract metaphor often becomes inappropriate. If an employee's choice is between an unattractive job and no job whatsoever, the choice is no choice at all. What those organisations which impose contracts unilaterally fail to realise is that by doing so, they are depriving themselves of the major motivational benefits of contracting. These are the feeling of agency among employees and the matching of their outcomes to their needs. On the contrary, such organisations are risking demotivation through alienation, helplessness, and inappropriate rewards.

Litigation

Litigation used to be the last resort when contractual relationships were at risk. Mediators would seek to reconcile the parties rather than engage in costly legal process. In our increasingly litigious society, however, recourse to the law is often had much earlier in the process of the break-up of a contractual relationship. Perception of a violation can lead straight to the courts.

The metaphor holds for the employment relationship. Here too, there have always been a wide variety of options open to those who perceive their psychological contract to have been violated by the other party. Given the degree of ambiguity around the contract, a logical first response would be to seek to discover whether the other party has the same perception of what the deal is as you do. They may have broken your version of the deal unintentionally, believing that they were keeping their version. Explicit re-negotiation would then follow.

However, emotional responses to the breaking of psychological contracts are usually far too strong to allow such a rational approach. Where the contract has primarily been a relational one, implying trust, the response to violation is going to be in terms of profound feelings of betrayal, and thence of anger or grief. If, however, the deal is more transactional and spelt out, then the response may be much more in terms of a desire for redress. Specific promises have been broken, specific agreements disregarded; the other party must be forced to comply.

Of course, again there are alternative responses to running immediately to the rule book, the complaints procedure, the disciplinary procedure, the company lawyer, or one's union representative. There may be several different reasons for the violation which might explain or even excuse it in the complainant's eyes. However, the insistence on rights and redress, and the immediate recourse to 'litigation', prevent these reasons from coming to light until too late; too late, that is, for the sake of the relationship.

For if there is one type of event which is guaranteed to sour relationships, it is formal procedures. They usually result in an increased polarisation of the parties involved, even though they may in the end be necessary if justice is to be done. Thus, paradoxically, the attempt to spell out mutual obligations and accountabilities which results in a transactional form of contract relationship has a potentially damaging outcome. For the more the terms are spelt out, the easier it is to engage in 'litigious' activities about them. Whilst individual parties may benefit by gaining redress, the relationship may have been severely damaged.

Thus an employment relationship which is low trust, and therefore trans-actional, is open to further deterioration, because by its very transactional nature it encourages perception of violation. If rules, terms, and conditions are there to be cited, then they will be. Litigiousness of this nature is by definition an indication of the breakdown of a relationship. However, it is important to note that it occurs within the rules of the game. The assump-tion by the one 'going to law', whether employer or employee, is that it is worth their while to do so. The procedures still mean something; there is at least the possibility of justice being done; the rule of law still operates.

Litigiousness is therefore half way between Contract and the law of the Jungle. The parties are still playing within the contractual rules of the game. The law of the Jungle, on the other hand, is a different language completely. It is the language of social Darwinism, the survival of the fittest. There are no contracts there.

Beasts of the jungle

So Contract, like our other metaphors so far, contains within it the potential seeds of its own subversion. And those seeds, as before, are born of excess: too much control, or too much power. The law of Contract finally gives way to the law of the Jungle when these excesses become full blown. Too much control results in the dam bursting when the system becomes overstretched and collapses. Too much power inevitably results in its abuse.

Just as Contract becomes subverted to its opposite, so the accompanying rhetoric reflects this subversion. The current rhetoric around the psycho-logical contract denigrates the 'bad' old contract of security in exchange for loyalty, and exalts the 'good' new contract of employability in exchange for flexibility. The latter is presented as inevitable, so employees had better get used to it or perish in the Jungle. And it is indeed a Jungle out there, so inevitably it is going to be a Jungle in here too, runs the rhetoric.[29]

The second rhetorical line is that of social Darwinism. It is the survival of the fittest out there in the business Jungle (see Chapter 15). Self-interest is the only criterion for action, because if you fail to look after yourself, nobody else will. It is a win–lose game with the devil take the hindmost; win–win is just a figment of the refined liberal imagination. So treat yourself as Me plc[30] and toughen yourself up so that you are truly resilient.[31] 'The new career contract', we are told, 'is not with the organisation: it is with the self and one's work.'[32]

The organisation itself becomes part of the Jungle. Politics are around survival and power, and the needs to cultivate powerful allies, acquire a patron, and gain visibility are paramount. If you are a little beast in the Jungle then you will have to use all your natural cunning to survive. If you are a big beast, then throw your weight about to good effect; it is only natural.[33]

Big beasts are consumed by the desire to get even bigger. The finance centres of the world are noted for the unrestrained use of power by the stars of the dealing room. Such stars not only continuously seek to move jobs for an even higher salary. They also try to take their teams with them. As Ivan Boesky infamously said, 'Greed is indeed good when it is a zero-sum game.'

The ring masters

Some top managers treat their organisations as Jungles. Not least amongst them are those founders of family dynasties who set up their children to compete against each other for the right of succession. In these cases, the Family and the Jungle metaphors coexist.

Survival of the fittest in the organisational Jungle is adopted as a mode of 'developing' their brightest and best by a lot of companies:

> You're put through the mill. It's like being attacked by the dogs. They're looking out for pitfalls all the time. A truly chilling experience [referring to the 'developmental' experience of being allowed to present to the Board].

> The spotlight is on you; if you don't perform you're in trouble. They use difficult assignments to test the metal. Survival of the fittest if you like.[34]

But more often, the scene in the Jungle is simple and straightforward abuse of power. Deregulation in the UK dockyards led to cost-cutting and casualisation. Here is the experience of a casualised docker:

> You know your shift times in advance. But say you're on days – 7am to 7 pm – you could work the shift on Monday, but then be told to come in the next day at 3pm instead of 7am. Then you might get 7pm to 7am on Wednesday. Thursday is your day off, but by then your body clock is all over the place. You never know whether you should be sleeping or what. With flexible start times, you'd end up waiting by the phone half the time to be called in for your shift. Sometimes you might be at home for only 4 or 5 hours before you got a call to go in again. If you weren't in, they sent hand-delivered messages to your house or your neighbour's, and you'd get quizzed about where you were the next time you came in if they couldn't get hold of you. You know, as if you're supposed to be accountable 24 hours a day.[35]

So, as usual, cool and rational language, this time of contract, has been

Table 5 From Contract to Jungle

Contract		Flip	Jungle
Employer:	Promise, obligation	Ambiguity, power	Domination
	Reciprocity	Violation	Abuse
Employee:	Agency	Anger	Survival
		Litigation and redress	Fear and greed

replaced by the emotive language of anger and disillusion, of fear and greed. Table 5 shows the flip from Contract to Jungle. I will further address abuse of power and resistance to that abuse when I examine the Democracy metaphor. In the meantime, here is a *metaphor check* for the Contract metaphor:

- What do you believe to be the terms of your organisation's basic grade employees' psychological contract: what do you offer them and what do they offer you back? On what grounds do you base that belief?
- To what extent is their contract negotiated, or is it entirely imposed? If it is negotiated, how was that negotiation conducted and by whom?
- Has the organisation by and large kept to the terms of the contract? Have the employees?
- How has the organisation monitored employees' adherence to the contract? How have they monitored its adherence?
- If violations have occurred, who has been responsible for them? To what do you attribute these violations? What did employees feel about them at the time? Subsequently? How has their attitude and behaviour towards the organisation changed as a result?
- To what extent has the organisation renegotiated the original contract which it formed with employees? What prompted these renegotiations?

References

1 Rousseau, D. M. (1993) The contracts of individuals and organisations. In L. L. Cummings and B. M. Staw (eds) *Research in Organisational Behaviour*, 15. Greenwich CT: JAI Press.
2 Rousseau, D.M. (1996) Changing the deal while keeping the people. *Academy of Management Executive*, 10, 1, 50–59, quotation at p. 58.
3 Shore, L. M. and Tetrick, L. E. (1994) The psychological contract as an explanatory framework in the employment relationship. In C. L. Cooper and D. M. Rousseau (eds) *Trends in Organisational Behaviour*, 1. Chichester: Wiley.
4 Guest, D., Conway, N., Briner, R. and Dickman, M. (1997) *The state of the psychological contract in employment*. London: IPD Press.
5 Guest, D. and Conway, N. (1997) *Employee motivation and the psychological contract*. London: IPD Press.
6 Herriot, P., Manning, W. E. G. and Kidd, J. M. (1997) The content of the psychological contract. *British Journal of Management*, 8, 2, 151–162.
7 Manning, W. E. G. Unpublished PhD thesis, Birkbeck College, University of London.

8 Rousseau, D. M. (1990) New hire perceptions of their own and their employer's obligations: A study of psychological contracts. *Journal of Organisational Behaviour*, 11, 5, 389–400.

9 Herriot, P. and Pemberton, C. (1996) Contracting careers. *Human Relations*, 49, 5, 757–790.

10 Rousseau, D. M. and Wade-Benzoni, K. A. (1994) Linking strategy and human resource practices: How employee and customer contracts are created. *Human Resource Management*, 33, 3, 463–489.

11 Herriot, P. and Pemberton, C. (1997) Facilitating new deals. *Human Resource Management*, 7, 1, 45–56

12 Emmott, M. and Hutchinson, S. (1998) Employment flexibility: threat or promise? In P. Sparrow and M. Marchington (eds) *Human Resource Management: The New Agenda*. London: Financial Times and Pitman.

13 Guest, D. M. (1998) Beyond HRM: commitment and the contract culture. In P. Sparrow and M. Marchington (eds) *Human Resource Management: The New Agenda*. London: Financial Times and Pitman.

14 Kalleberg, A. L. and Reve, T. (1993) Contracts and commitment: economic and sociological perspectives on employment relations. *Human Relations*, 46, 12, 1103–1132.

15 Tsui, A. S., Pearce, J. L., Porter, L. W., and Tripoli, A. M. (1997) Alternative approaches to the employee–organisation relationship: does investment in employees pay off? *Academy of Management Journal*, 40, 5, 1089–1121.

16 Rousseau, D. M. and Greller, M. M. (1994) Human resource practices: administrative contract makers. *Human Resource Management*, 33, 3, 385–401.

17 Herriot, P. and Pemberton, C. (1995) *New Deals: The Revolution in Managerial Careers*. Chichester: Wiley

18 Noer, D. M. (1993) *Healing the Wounds*. San Francisco: Jossey Bass.

19 Brockner, J., Greenberg, J., Brockner, A., Bortz, J., Davy, J. and Carter, C. (1986) Layoffs, equity theory, and work motivation: further evidence for survivor guilt. *Academy of Management Journal*, 29, 2, 373–384.

20 Andersson, L. M. (1996) Employee cynicism: An examination using a contract violation framework. *Human Relations*, 49, 11, 1395–1418.

21 Robinson, S. L. and Rousseau, D. M. (1994) Violating the psychological contract: not the exception but the norm. *Journal of Organisational Behaviour*, 15, 2, 245–259.

22 Robinson, S. L. and Morrison, E. W. (1995) Psychological contracts and OCB: the effect of unfulfilled obligations on civic virtue behaviour. *Journal of Organisational Behaviour*, 16, 3, 289–298.

23 Lucero, M. A. and Allen, R. E. (1994) Employee benefits: A growing source of psychological contract violations. *Human Resource Management*, 33, 3, 425–446.

24 Manning (op. cit.).

25 Kabanoff, B. (1991) Equity, equality, power, and conflict. *Academy of Management Review*, 16, 416–441.

26 Bies, R. J. (1987) The predicament of injustice: the management of moral outrage. In L. L. Cummings and B. M. Staw (eds) *Research in Organisational Behaviour*, 9. Greenwich, CT: JAI Press.

27 Noon, M. and Blyton, P. (1997) *The Realities of Work*. London: Macmillan.

28 Legge, K. (1995) *Human Resource Management: Rhetorics and Realities*. London: Macmillan.

29 Marchington, M. (1990) Analysing the links between product markets and the management of employee relations. *Journal of Management Studies*, 27, 2, 111–132.

30 Bridges, W. (1995) *Jobshift: How to Prosper in a Workplace without Jobs*. London: Nicholas Brealey.
31 Waterman, R. H., Waterman, J. A. and Collard, B. A. (1994) Toward a career-resilient workforce. *Harvard Business Review*, 12, 4, 87–95.
32 Hall, D. T. and Moss, J. E. (1998) The new protean career contract: helping organisations and employees adapt. *Organisational Dynamics*, Winter, 22–37, quotation at p. 30.
33 Jackall, R. (1988) *Moral Mazes: The World of Corporate Managers*. New York: Oxford University Press.
34 Pemberton, C. and Herriot, P. (1994) *Getting on Board*. London: Careers Research Forum.
35 Saundry, R. and Turnbull, P. (1996) Mêlée on the Mersey: contracts, competition, and labour relations on the docks. *Industrial Relations Journal*, 27, 4, 275–278.

Chapter 4

Club and Outsider

Belonging

Boswell, according to Dr Johnson, was a very clubbable man. He could move around in those quintessentially English institutions, the gentlemen's clubs of London, with practised ease. He clearly had an appreciation of all the unspoken and implicit rules about how gentlemen behaved. He shared, or at least pretended to share, all of the assumptions of that social class which gentlemen's clubs served. He fitted in so well that, had he wanted to become a member of any one of them, he would have run no risk of being black-balled as an undesirable, not really a gentleman in every sense of the word.

To characterise the employment relationship as Club is to emphasise belonging as its key feature. We belong because we feel an affinity with fellow members. In Boswell's London, the affinity was one of social class, or rather, the subtle distinctions and nuances of social class which distinguished one club from another. In organisations, that feeling of affinity usually takes one of two forms. The first is simply that of *longevity*. We have all been here quite a long time, we know each other pretty well, and we have developed ways of operating with each other that enable us to get along without too many crises. Club members sit in comfortable leather armchairs wearing their tweed jackets with elbow patches and gossip happily. The second bond is that of *shared knowledge* rather than shared experience. We are all professionals here, we have had the same professional training and apprenticeship, we can trust any colleague to do a good job for a client.

Longevity is becoming less and less likely to form the basis for membership of the organisational Club. Average length of employment in an organisation has been decreasing slowly but steadily for many years now.[1] Indeed, the reinvention of the wheel is a daily danger where there is no-one left who can remember what happened last time round the economic cycle. Whilst the dangers of longevity are well known, its benefits do not get an airing so often.

Shared professional knowledge, however, is increasingly likely to be the membership card of the future. As Peter Drucker has argued:

The basic economic resource – 'the means of production' to use the economist's term – is no longer capital, nor natural resources (the economist's 'land'), nor 'labour'. It is and will be knowledge. . . . Value is now created by 'productivity' and 'innovation', both applications of knowledge to work.[2]

Knowledge-based professionals

So the knowledge-based professional should be in a very favourable position within such an organisation, we might conclude. But it all depends. Organisations and the development of technology both create and also destroy work activities.[3] It has long been a truism that the old-fashioned clerk has been rendered obsolete by information technology, as have the ledgers in which he wrote. But areas of work which used until recently to be the task of professionals are now performed by expert software. Telesales operatives take decisions on insurance premiums on the basis of software systems derived from the knowledge base of insurance professionals. These latter often have no job. Accounts are today audited by accountancy technicians using software capturing the knowledge of chartered accountants.

As their existing knowledge is extracted from them by their organisation and systematised, professionals have to innovate if they are to continue adding value.[4] They can no longer rely on their supposedly exclusive knowledge and qualifications. Yet provided that they meet the requirement to create new applicable knowledge, their future is assured. For they provide knowledge-based organisations with their core competences: the areas of knowledge which give those organisations their competitive advantage, which are hard for their competitors to imitate, and which add value for the customer.[5] Their confidence in their value to the organisation is what gives Club members that sense of belonging.

They have normally served a long and hard initiation which has provided them with a degree of exclusivity. They assume as a consequence that all their professional colleagues are fully aware of the rules of behaviour that go with being a professional. These include not merely technical expertise, but the reliability and integrity to which professionals lay claim. They are willing to accept that a certain degree of socialisation into the organisation is appropriate for young new entrants, but they still think that their fundamental values and attitudes have been acquired during their professional formation.

Professionals value especially the approval of Club members more senior than themselves with a high professional profile, wherever they may work. However, despite all their professional commitment, it does not follow that they have a correspondingly low commitment to their employer. Provided that the organisation demonstrates that it appreciates their professionalism, high professional and high organisational commitment can go hand in hand.[6, 7]

This Club ambience is especially likely in professional organisations, such as accountancy and law firms, where the company is owned by the senior professionals, the partners. But it can also be found in companies with a high number of specialists, for example, pharmaceuticals, software houses, aerospace and chemicals. Many public sector organisations, too, consist of one or several groups of professionals. The armed services and the police, for example, are just about the only organisations open for those seeking a military or a law enforcement career. The professional formation here is within the services or the police forces themselves. Thus in these cases both professional development and organisational longevity push strongly towards a Club model.

Club benefits

Club has some immense strengths as a model for the employment relationship:

- employees are motivated by the work itself; there is little need for supervisory zeal, merely professional mentoring
- employees are keen to engage in their own professional development, thereby adding to the organisation's intellectual capital
- employees trust in and rely upon colleagues' competence; major conflicts about how best to do things and whether they have been done properly are usually avoided
- top management will probably consist of professionals too, increasing the confidence of Club members in their leadership
- so long as the organisation provides the opportunity to exercise and develop professional competence, the loss of knowledge to competitors through turnover of key individuals becomes less likely
- values are likely to be shared, and hence value-based disagreements are less likely
- stories, myths, and rituals will develop, and will serve to maintain and enhance these values.

By way of an example of a Club, consider the British Army. Even today to a certain extent, entrants to a regiment have ties of locality with their colleagues before they even join. Their professional formation is identical in the beginning, but subsequently differs according to their speciality. Nevertheless, until relatively late in their career, all are trained so as to be capable of operating in armed combat.

Officers are regularly and frequently moved to new postings, in which it is important that they rapidly get up to speed. They have to form relationships with new colleagues and at the same time master the technical requirements of the new job. Yet because of the excellence of the training and the uniformity of the leadership and command system, units can be assembled for demanding missions with a complete assurance that soldiers will trust each other sufficiently to risk their lives.

Clubs can generate instant trust of this nature.[8] Surgical teams, aircrew, police teams, fire teams are all prepared to undertake the difficult and dangerous tasks that their employers expect of them because of their confidence in their colleagues. The training support and the development of the organisation's culture and ethos have ensured such trust.

The benefits of good Clubs are not limited to the organisation and the clients. Club members themselves usually find the situation extremely congenial. They are working with and for colleagues who are like themselves, and we tend to feel more comfortable with people who are like ourselves. Moreover, they do not need to spell out what is expected by way of performance and behaviour: they all share the same professional standards and the same assumptions; they know the rules. It feels very good to be able to trust the competence of their colleagues and be trusted in return. And if they take the opportunities for their own development, which are handed to them on a plate, their employability is unlikely to suffer.

Quality or cloning

So the benefits for individuals who belong, who fit in comfortably, are considerable. For example, accountants are already likely to share a particular value orientation, regarding accuracy, cost control, etc. Yet research showed that eight accountancy firms each had their own culture with respect to the value priorities that they held; and that individual accountants who more closely matched these values were more likely to adjust more quickly at entry, to be more satisfied with their job, and to stay longer in the organisation.[9] Moreover, they were also more committed to the organisation.[10]

Organisational processes relentlessly ensure comfortable fit (see Chapter 12). Organisations attract, select, and retain people who most resemble those already there.[11] Misfits are not normally attracted; if they are, they are not usually selected; and if they succeed in getting in, they are made to feel so unwelcome that they soon leave. The result is a cloned organisation, consisting of people getting on very well together, satisfied with their work, and committed to the organisation: but less capable of adapting to change and being innovative.[12] In particular, at senior levels where strategic direction in response to the environment is a major task, there may be a degree of groupthink which is dysfunctional.

Now it is easy to see why professional skills and competence should form the basis for inclusion. It is possible to admit that shared value priorities will help the organisation move forward in a single direction. But it is impossible to justify a shared biographical history that results in a common personal formation as well as a common professional one. This is practically guaranteed to produce groupthink. For example, it was found that in 93 top management teams in US corporate banks, the overall rate of turnover in the teams over a four-year period was positively related to the heterogeneity of the group. As far as individuals were concerned, the more different from the others they were, the more likely they were to leave. But what is important is the nature of the biographical details that formed the index of heterogeneity: age, job tenure, education level, degree subject, university attended, military service and a job in another industry or not.[13] Clearly, it was not professional competence alone that was determining the composition of these teams.

Add two final ingredients to the mixture: the pressure for so-called excellence, and the nature of retrenchment. First, *excellence*. Particularly in France and the UK, excellence at entry is assessed by reputation. Certain big accountancy firms, consultancies, and merchant banks in the UK, for example, use Oxford and Cambridge Universities and a handful of others as proxy for excellence. They recruit only from these institutions, which are themselves recognised to be strongly biased towards the upper socio-economic groups in society. Similarly, large French organisations may recruit professionals and managers only from the hautes écoles.

Second, *retrenchment*. When restructuring occurs and redundancies and outsourcing leave organisations stripped down to their core, who constitutes that core? Why, those most typical of the organisation in the first place![14] So the tendency is all towards uniformity.

Us and them

The apple is now ripe for the Club metaphor's maggot to start gnawing away at its core. And the maggot in question is that well-known social psychological phenomenon of 'Us and Them'.[15] The more exclusive the Club becomes, the narrower the population from which it draws its members, and the more demanding the eligibility requirements, then the higher grow the barriers between the in-group and the rest. The in-group defines itself by its distinguishing features, and its members make their membership ever more central to their identity.[16]

So not only are they accountants or merchant bankers; they are accountants out of the very top drawer, and they feel very good about themselves as a consequence. And the notion of 'top drawer' may have more to do with the gentlemanly qualifications for Dr Johnson's London clubs than with sheer professional excellence.

Now this exclusive professional identity automatically sets up oppositional inferior identities. 'They're only support staff,' imply the professionals by their actions if not by their words. Or, 'If only we could get those anoraks in IT to get some sort of understanding of the business.' Of course, these other identities are in relation to, rather than in opposition to, the dominant professional identity.[17] But such is the dominance and assertiveness of the latter that non-professionals are often construed as second-class citizens. As we shall see, these too can use stereotypes as an effective weapon.

That is not the end of the story, though. When professionals or any dominant group have selected in their own personal as well as professional image, other elements of their identities besides the professional one will be prominent and valued. Nationality, ethnicity, gender, educational background and so on will be clearly visible, though not necessarily verbally explicit. Hence people who may come to the organisation with different elements prominent in their identity, for example, mother, French, etc, will also find themselves excluded, even though they may share the fundamental professional identity. Thus they too will become Outsiders, who note their obvious differences with the in-group, interact with them less, and are soon excluded from recognition and reward.[18]

Other events may make them feel yet further outside the pale. The Club members are so conscious of their difference from all outsiders, and so eager to maintain that distance, that they invent obscure rituals and terminologies.[19] There are rites of initiation, for example, aimed at making the entrant feel small and humiliated, but in the end intensely proud at being admitted after having gone through hell. Entrants have to serve their time, doing hard and sometimes menial jobs on the pretence that they have to learn from the bottom. The learning process is often far longer than it need be, and can contain learning that is utterly irrelevant to the job. There is also a whole new language to learn, the mystifying jargon of the profession.[20] They are in fact being bound psychologically ever tighter into the Club, since after a while it is very hard to justify to themselves why they are willing to be treated so badly. The prize of belonging must be worth it, they reason, or we would not have put up with all this rubbish for so long. But the process itself is often intensely alienating.

Examples abound. Perhaps most noteworthy are the organisations where organisational membership is necessary for professional development: the armed services and the police. Initiation rituals and a subsequent harder time for recruits who fail to fulfil the gender or ethnic unofficial criteria for entry can be severe. Instead of bowing to the expectation to undergo even worse treatment than others, some leave and blow the whistle.

But these are dramatic examples. Consider instead those many organisations where the real Club is composed of the professional core. In accountancy firms, for example, the trainee accountants may get many boring audit assignments when they join, but they know that they stand a good chance of qualifying as a chartered accountant, and a fair chance of ultimately becoming a partner and getting a stake in the business. All the support staff, on the other hand, be they administrative or IT, frequently feel themselves to be second-class citizens. So do the support staff in merchant banks. Indeed, in many organisations today the picture is one of a huge segmentation of the employment relationship within the same organisation.[21] For some, the professional or managerial core, Club membership eases their path, while the contract and part-time workers find themselves treated worse and trusted less than their full-time colleagues.[22]

Exclusion and powerlessness

The in-group have a huge advantage in power. Apart from the obvious sources of power such as inside information, credibility, prestige, and rewards insiders have another secret weapon. In effect, it is they who define what is organisational reality.[23] It is they who can define their own interests as organisational needs. It is they who can legitimise their own actions by reference to professional autonomy. It is they who can construe the organisation's structure in terms of demanding masculine professional and managerial work versus nurturing feminine support and technical work.[24] Such definitions ultimately become accepted as fact, as the 'natural' state of affairs.

The Outsider initially feels alienated and isolated. Most keenly felt of all is the loss of collegiality. Outsiders expect a welcome, mutual support and respect, and even perhaps friendship.[25, 26] Soon, though, it becomes evident that while others are treated as colleagues, they are not. They may even be physically banished from their place of work altogether. This is what has happened in several professions: they have essentially been casualised.

Take publishing, for example.[27] In the increasingly competitive publishing scene of the 1980s, freelance editing work became the norm. Management's purpose was to reduce overheads and other costs and to match the supply of professional labour exactly to peaks and troughs in the workload. It was left to full-time commissioning editors to decide whether or not to employ casuals, some of whom do get regular work, whilst others are simply stopgaps for crises. Many of these casuals are former full-time employees made redundant and re-employed on a casual basis.

So by creating an Us and Them situation with Club members as the Us, Clubs inevitably create another, oppositional, Us. In fact, the more ways that Club members distinguish themselves from the rest, the more oppositional groups grow up. For they have more ways of defining their groups. As well as support staff or IT, they can be women or blacks, non-graduates or socialists, humorous or introverted; in fact any sort of excluded or unclubbable individuals we care to think of. From being isolated powerless aliens, they gain another membership, they march to another drumbeat. Now they have allies, now they belong again.

Soon they in turn have developed their stereotypes of orthodox Club members. In response to being stereotyped as possibly necessary, but certainly unwelcome costs, Outsiders start biting back. 'Young doctors straight from medical school who know it all and think they're God's gift,' they snort. 'Snooty Ivy League types who don't know their arse from their elbow; but of course, Daddy's got connexions.' 'Loose cannon who don't stay long enough in any one job to have to deal with the consequences of their own stupid mistakes.' 'Selfish careerists who don't give a damn about the rest of us; and then have the cheek to call us a drain on their profits.' Forming stereotypes about Them strengthens Outsiders' own alternative identities.

And having reaffirmed their alternative identity to that of Club membership, the new groups of Us start to think about power and interests. Having defined Club members as Them, Outsiders now see how much They benefit from being the in-group. Freed from the need to follow the rules and work towards their initiation and acceptance, they see how ridiculous the whole immense fabrication really is. And having achieved a sense of the ridiculous, they spot its soft underbelly, its weak points. They realise that their own interests were totally ignored, and determine to ensure that it will not happen again. They become a fifth column.

So the Club metaphor follows the pattern of Family, Crusade, and Contract. In each case, the flip side of the metaphor is prompted by the accumulation and abuse of power and the failure to understand how others will respond. Employees expect top management to care about them. When they start to see it as an excessively demanding parent, or when it appears to care more about its own interests than those of the organisation or the employees, then Feud develops. Charismatic leaders set out to lead Crusades, but unless they are squeaky clean in their conduct, and unless they involve the troops in the mission, then cynicism and Play-acting are the responses. The psychological need to check up and control is the worm at the core of Contract. So many controls are put in place to ensure that Contracts are kept that employees seize the opportunity to break the rules when management finds that the burden of checking up is too great. And as we have seen in this chapter, the power to include or exclude from the Club often leads the professionals, perhaps unconsciously, to alienate enough Outsiders to form a real opposition. The Club Committee failed to understand that there are deep and powerful alternative identities to their own. The slide from Club member to Outsider is depicted in Table 6.

Table 6 From Club to Outsider

Club		Flip	Outsider
Employer:	Formation, belonging standards	Exclusivity, cloning Groupthink	Stereotype Devalued
Employee:	Knowledge, value, collegiality, belonging	Exclusion, powerlessness Isolation, polarisation	Organised opposition

Metaphor check

1 Apart from being good at the job, what other spoken or unspoken entry requirements are there for your organisation?

2 Think of someone who got in without fulfilling one or some of these. What happened to them?

3 What are the initiation rituals in your organisation? If they happened in the street, would a criminal offence have been committed? When you underwent them, how did you feel? How do you think today's entrants feel about them?

4 Is there a single profession, or perhaps two or three different professions, central to your organisation? What are their relationships like with others in the organisation?

5 Look at the top management team. How many of them are members of the core profession? And how many of them are accountants? What other similarities do you detect amongst them? Now look at those waiting to succeed to the Board: how similar to each other are they?

6 Perhaps you have noted some similarities. Write them down, and think of their opposites. Some will have obvious opposites (e.g. male/female), others less obvious ones (e.g. long serving/new recruit).

7 Now think of any disaffected individuals and groups in your organisation. Do they have any similarities? Do they have something positive in common (e.g. they are young)? Or are they defined negatively, by opposites (e.g. they are not lawyers)?

8 How long do you think your Club will last in its present form? If it changes the rules, how should it change them and why?

References

1 Gregg, P. and Wadsworth, J. (1996) A short history of labour turnover, job tenure, and job security, 1975–1993. *Oxford Review of Economic Policy*, 11, 1, 73–90.

2 Drucker, P. F. (1993) *Post-capitalist Society*. Oxford: Butterworth-Heinemann, p. 7.

3 Abbott, A. (1988) *The System of Professions: An Essay on the Division of Expert Labour*. Chicago: University of Chicago Press.

4 Child, J. and Fulk, J. (1982) Maintenance of occupational control: the case of professions. *Work and Occupations*, 9, 155–192.

5 Prahalad, C. K. and Hamel, G. (1990) The core competence of the corporation. *Harvard Business Review*, 90, 3, 79–91.

6 Bartol, K. M. (1979) Professionalism as a predictor of organisational commitment, role stress, and turnover: a multi-dimensional approach. *Academy of Management Journal*, 22, 3, 815–821.

7 Gerpott, T. J., Domsch, M. and Keller, R. T. (1988) Career orientations in different countries and companies: an empirical investigation of West German, British, and US industrial R&D professionals. *Journal of Management Studies*, 25, 5, 439–462.

8 Meyerson, D., Weick, K. E. and Kramer, R. M. (1996) Swift trust and temporary

groups. In R. M. Kramer and T. R. Tyler (eds) *Trust in Organisations: Frontiers of Theory and Research*. Thousand Oaks CA: Sage.

9   Chatman, J. A. (1991) Matching people and organisations: selection and socialisation in public accounting firms. *Administrative Science Quarterly*, 36, 459–484.

10 O'Reilly, C. A., Chatman, J. A. and Caldwell, D. F. (1991) People and organisational culture: a profile comparison approach to assessing person–organisation fit. *Acadamy of Management Journal*, 34, 3, 487–516.

11 Schneider, B. (1987) The people make the place. *Personnel Psychology*, 40, 437–453.

12 Schneider, B., Kristof-Brown, A., Goldstein, H. W. and Brent Smith, D. (1997) What is this thing called fit? In N. Anderson and P. Herriot (eds) *International Handbook of Selection and Assessment*. Chichester: Wiley.

13 Jackson, S. E., Brett, J. F., Sessa, V. I., Cooper, D. M., Julin, J. A. and Peyronnin, K. (1991) Some differences make a difference: individual dissimilarity and group heterogeneity as correlates of recruitment, promotions, and turnover. *Journal of Applied Psychology*, 76, 675–689.

14 McKinley, W., Sanchez, C. and Schick, A. (1995) Organisational downsizing, constraining, cloning, and learning. *Academy of Management Executive*, 9, 3, 32–44.

15 Kelly, J. and Kelly, C. (1991) Them and us: social psychology and the new industrial relations. *British Journal of Industrial Relations*, 29, 1, 25–48.

16 Tajfel, H. (ed.) (1987) *Social Identity and Inter-group Relations*. Cambridge: Cambridge University Press.

17 Nkomo, S. M. and Cox, T. (1996) Diverse identities in organisations. In S. R. Clegg, C. Hardy and W. R. Nord (eds) *Handbook of Organisation Studies*. London: Sage.

18 Triandis, H. C., Kurowski, L. L. and Gelfand, M. J. (1994) Workplace diversity. In H. C. Triandis, M. D. Dunnette and L. M. Hough (eds) *Handbook of Industrial and Organisational Psychology*. Palo Alto CA: Consulting Psychologists Press.

19 Noon, M. and Blyton, P. (1997) *The Realities of Work*. London: Macmillan.

20 Noon and Blyton (op. cit.).

21 Hirsh, W. and Jackson, C. (1996) *Strategies for Career Development: Promise, Practice, and Pretence*. Brighton: Institute for Employment Studies, Report 305.

22 Pearce, J. L. (1993) Toward an organisational behaviour of contract labourers: their psychological involvement and effects on employee co-workers. *Academy of Management Journal*, 36, 5, 1082–1096.

23 Hardy, C. and Clegg, S. R. (1996) Some dare call it power. In S. R. Clegg, C. Hardy and W. R. Nord (eds) *Handbook of Organisation Studies*. London: Sage.

24 Calas, M. B. and Smircich, L. (1996) From 'the woman's' point of view: feminist approaches to organisation studies. In S. R. Clegg, C.Hardy and W. R. Nord (eds) *Handbook of Organisation Studies*. London: Sage.

25 Korman, A. K., Wittig-Berman, U. and Lang, D. (1981) Career success and personal failure: Alienation in professionals and managers. *Academy of Management Journal*, 24, 2, 342–360.

26 Sheridan, J. E. (1992) Organisational culture and employee retention. *Academy of Management Journal*, 35, 5, 1036–1056.

27 Stanworth, C. and Stanworth, G. (1997) Managing an externalised workforce: freelance labour use in the UK book publishing industry. *Industrial Relations Journal*, 28, 1, 43–55.

Chapter 5

Resource and Discard

Human assets

We owe our next metaphor to the economists, a profession not noted for its sophisticated understanding of human nature. Reflecting upon the French Revolution, Edmund Burke lamented 'the age of chivalry is gone. That of sophisters, economists, and calculators has succeeded; and the glory of Europe is extinguished for ever.' The metaphor of Human Resources is another example of economists talking and thinking about people at work as though they were just another type of asset.

At least, some would argue, this is an improvement on the usual financial approach, which is to treat them as costs. At least you conserve, develop, nurture and grow assets, whereas all you do with costs is try to cut them. This is doubtless true, but there are other connotations of the Resources metaphor as well as the tender loving care ones. For example, although some might hope that we treat resources as though we were stewards of them, the reality is that we often behave as though we own them: witness our ecosystem. What is more, we do not only grow them; we also use them, deploy them, and exploit them.

The ambiguity of 'exploit' is an excellent example of the tensions underlying the use of the Resources metaphor. It is considered morally neutral or even praiseworthy to exploit physical or capital resources to their maximum potential, but usually blameworthy to exploit people. But we do not only use resources; we use them up, as though they were simply commodities. Or, in another revealing double meaning, we exhaust them. Then when they are used up or burned out, we discard them or dispose of them. So the flip side of the Resource metaphor is always lurking just out of sight.

The central element of the Resource metaphor, then, is *value*. We are in business, so we would be stupid not to value our assets and therefore conserve or enhance them. But should we fail to value our human assets, or should we start to construe people as commodities, then we will before too long arrive at the flip side of the Resource metaphor: Discard.

The company is its resources

However, as usual, we start out with our shiny new rational metaphor borrowed from the economists. Its popularity is guaranteed. For not only does it take for granted that the employment relationship is capable of being managed rationally in the strategic interests of the business. It also chimes in with the times. When the market environment is volatile and the old market-based approaches to organisation strategy are difficult to apply, what more appropriate than a resource-based theory of the firm? It is its resources, and especially its knowledge-based resources, that will give companies the competitive advantage, runs the argument:

> when the external environment is in a state of flux, the firm's own resources and capabilities may be a much more stable basis on which to define its identity. Hence, a definition of a business in terms of what it is capable of doing may offer a more durable basis for strategy than a definition based upon the needs (e.g. markets) which the business seeks to satisfy.[1]

And if 'what it is capable of doing' depends to a considerable extent on an organisation's employees, then they are to be seen as its human resources, its human assets. Indeed they, just as much as its market positioning, may be the key to the firm's competitive advantage. The organisation may have a unique history of events in which individuals' capabilities have been developed and shared; it may have embedded these individual and social processes into the way it is managed; and it may have integrated this human capital with other forms of capital such as information, culture, and finance.[2] The Club metaphor reflected the importance of professional knowledge assets; the Resource metaphor can embrace human capital in its entirety, social and emotional as well as intellectual.[3]

Measuring resources

Now the first thing a prudent business will do is to quantify its assets. How can it possibly work out how to use them to the best business advantage if it fails to discover how much it has of them? How then should it quantify its human assets? How can it measure its intellectual, motivational, and social resources? An immense effort is currently being put into measuring people's capabilities: their aptitudes, competencies, motivations, and personality. Assessment technology has developed in leaps and bounds recently, and now interactive and dynamic assessment is possible as a result of the use of information technology. Traditionally, psychological assessment has been used mainly for purposes of selection. Now, however, a whole range of further uses is available:[4]

- assessment centres assess competencies, giving an indication of appropriate placement
- personality inventories permit teams to be composed in such a way that suitable people fill the main team roles
- development centres allow individuals to discover their training and development needs
- self-administered questionnaires help individuals to manage their own careers within the organisation
- personnel information systems allow these data and an employee's employment history to be called up instantly.

Moreover, the current psychometric orthodoxy maintains that it is characteristics of persons which determine their performance (and therefore their value to the organisation), regardless of the organisation within which they work.[5] Thus it is the individual, with his or her aptitudes and qualities, who is mistakenly taken to be the basic unit of the human resource; and it is these basic characteristics which will enable them to adapt rapidly and perform well wherever they are employed. The definition of human resources as those unique intellectually and socially based organisational capabilities which give a firm its competitive advantage has given way to a definition which assumes that individual people are the units of Resource.

Hard and soft human resource management

However, even though we may have succeeded in quantifying some of the basic elements of the human resource, the task remains of using it to the greatest business effect. How are we to get most added value out of the human resource? How are we to use it most effectively in the interests of the business? Two different approaches have been distinguished, so-called 'hard' and 'soft' Human Resource Management.[6]

The *hard approach* uses hard metaphors. Human Resource (HR) 'architecture' is put in place. The whole of this architecture is designed to support the organisation's business strategy. Human Resource philosophy, policies, programmes, practices, and processes are all integrated with each other and fitted to the business strategy to ensure its most effective and efficient achievement.[7] So, for example, we would expect to find different forms of Human Resource approaches in organisations with different strategic intent,[8, 9] as follows:

- Organisations for whom innovation is the source of their competitive advantage are likely to concentrate on designing work around teams and groups; rewarding longer-term achievements; placing employees in developmental roles, etc.
- Organisations set on enhancing quality are more likely to have detailed

job descriptions, high employee participation, a high emphasis on short-term results, and extensive training.

- Organisations seeking to compete through cost reduction will have narrowly designed jobs with little ambiguity or autonomy; career paths encouraging specialisation, expertise, and efficiency; short-term results-oriented performance appraisals; and minimal training and development.

The *soft approach* to Human Resource Management, on the other hand, concentrates on getting the most out of the human resource by harnessing its own motivational power. If employees can internalise the values and objectives which top management deems necessary to achieve the business goals, then control can be exercised by employees themselves. Hence internal self-control and self-motivation will supplement or maybe even supplant external processes such as appraisal and reward. Indeed, there is psychological evidence[10] to suggest that such behaviour as good organisational citizenship and staying loyally with the organisation only occurs when there is internalised commitment. The hard approach, which often results in mere behavioural compliance, is not enough. Hearts and minds matter too.

Do organisations do it, and does it work?

So to what extent is Human Resource Management, in its hard or its soft forms, practised? And if it is, does it work? The answer to the first question is that it is practised only patchily.[11] Quite a large number and wide variety of Human Resource processes are in use, but they seem to have been adopted in a piecemeal fashion rather than specifically designed to support business strategy. Human Resource professionals themselves believe that most of them were an attempt to deal with the results of restructuring.[12]

More recent radical change in organisations has resulted in a concentration on hard-nosed and shorter-term processes such as objective setting, performance measurement, performance-related pay, and short-term training. Softer, longer-term measures such as leadership development, workforce development, and organisational development are less frequent. Furthermore, it is the harder processes which are more closely linked to business strategy and its implementation in performance.[13]

Does it work? As we might expect, the answer is that it all depends. One or two HR processes on their own are unlikely to have much effect. But a bundle of processes certainly does. A bundle is a set of processes which reinforce each other, and bundles can improve bottom line benefits astonishingly. In a very large sample of US organisations, those organisations which fell into the top third in terms of their use of bundles of processes enjoyed higher sales per employee of $27,000, higher profits of $3,800, and higher market value of $18,600.[14] In a long-term UK study of small and medium-sized manufacturing companies, it was found that nearly 20 per cent of the variance in productivity and profitability could be explained by the number of HR processes which they had in place. Such favourites of business text books as strategy, quality, and technology, and even research and development, had far less effect. Particularly influential amongst the HR processes were the acquisition and development of skills, and job design. An emphasis on employee welfare, job satisfaction, and organisational commitment were especially predictive of productivity.[15]

One of the most recent and powerful examples of the importance of people management has been provided by the retailer, Sears.[16] Sears have established clear connections between employees' attitudes about the job and the company and their behaviour towards customers: Sears appeared to employees to be a compelling place to work. Employee behaviour made it a compelling place to shop for customers, who formed an overall impression on the basis of the helpfulness of the service they experienced and the value of the merchandise. This impression resulted in retention of that customer and recommendations to other potential customers. As a consequence, Sears became a compelling place to invest, in terms of return on assets, operating margin, and revenue growth. So powerful has Sears' measurement of performance indicators become that they look forward to examining the data for each individual salesperson and conducting performance reviews based upon them.

The jury is still out on whether one best bundle of HR processes fits all or whether different bundles are better for different organisations, but the weight of evidence suggests the latter. The research which advocates one best way tends to concentrate on one particular sector only,[17] and when the range of organisations is broader, different bundles are best. However, a recent influential text[18] sums up the situation as demonstrating clearly that the following seven HR activities/objectives are key to improving business performance:

- job security
- careful recruitment and selection
- decentralising and teamwork
- good pay, contingent on collective (not individual) performance
- training, and lots of it
- low differentials in status and pay
- systematic sharing of information.

Managing through people is hard work and it is a long-term project: but it works.

So the news is good, and personnel professionals can claim to be as beneficial to the business as the best of them. But we still need to ask *why* the HR processes have their beneficial effect. It would be easy to invoke a mechanical metaphor by way of explanation. Pull this combination of levers and out pour the benefits; invest in your human capital and you will reap the rewards. The explanation may lie, however, not in the direct effect of processes on people, but rather on a changed relationship with management. They must value us, think the employees; look how much effort, time and money they are spending on us. Feeling valued may be the main reason for adding value. Or, as I will argue (see Chapter 14), the use of HR processes is simply a symptom, a consequence of long-established and well embedded relationships within the organisation.

Using Human Resources to the full

Given that human resources are so productive and profitable, the argument sometimes runs, we should get as much value out of them as we can and utilise them to the full. We must exploit them (but in the nicest possible way), so we had better use them more flexibly.[19, 20]

Governments vary in the extent to which they permit employers to operate without the constraint of various social protections to employees. However, regardless of the degree of governmental regulation, organisations everywhere are trying to enhance *flexibility*. This is especially true of sectors where competition is particularly intense and efficiency and productivity is of the essence. The German automobile manufacturer BMW, for example, agreed to continue to maintain their Rover subsidiary in the UK only on the basis of an agreement that annualised hours are used to smooth the peaks and troughs of demand. Even flexibility proved in the end insufficient to ensure the survival of Rover within the BMW group, however.

This is an example of *temporal*, or working time, flexibility, which refers to management's use of variable hours to match demand fluctuations. However, working time flexibility can also be viewed from the employee's perspective, as permitting the meshing of their work role with other roles they play (parent, sportsperson, councillor, etc). If temporal flexibility can meet the needs of both employer and employee, then clearly the human resource is being used well rather than being used up.

Some of the temporal flexibility which firms will require is highly predictable. Supermarkets know the periods of high customer demand. Call centres are aware of the requirement for a 24-hour-a-day, 7-day-a-week service. Even automobile manufacturers have some idea of when demand peaks habitually appear. As a consequence, the opportunity is there to plan ahead so that employer and employee needs can both be met. Some companies have been wise enough to delegate right down to local level the freedom to do deals with employees. In some call centres, young employees work long hours for a month, then take off for a fortnight, while others who are parents work part-time shifts geared to school hours and school holidays.

Another form of flexibility is *numerical* flexibility: reducing or increasing the number of employees to match demand. Traditionally, hiring and firing has been the most common way to achieve numerical flexibility, but other ways of achieving it are becoming more common. Companies are sub-contracting (and not just their peripheral services such as catering), so that deals can be established and terminated at short notice when demand changes. Fixed-term and temporary contracts, too, permit a degree of numerical flexibility not possible with permanent contracts.

Numerical flexibility also offers potential benefits to both parties. By working for a contractor or an agency, employees can develop a degree of employment security which they may not have enjoyed with their original employer. Further, they may acquire a variety of skills and a more stimulating working life as a consequence of their different assignments. And fixed-term or temporary contracts may suit some who are at transition points in their lives or careers, or who want to try out a new occupation without committing themselves to it fully.

Functional flexibility means that employees engage in a greater variety of tasks, often as a result of the breaking down of various demarcation boundaries between occupations. The modern requirement to work in project teams rather than from within functional silos has also increased functional flexibility. At all levels of organisations, from semi-skilled assembly workers in automobile plants, through craft and technical employees, to managers and professionals, functional flexibility has increased. Indeed, the trend towards creating general managers in the 1980s has even resulted in greater attention now being paid to careers for technical specialists, with dual career ladders coming once again to the fore in some large organisations.

However, the overall benefits of functional flexibility to organisations are abundantly clear. It enables different tasks to be undertaken without employing new staff, but rather, with fewer people doing more tasks. A new customer or client can have their different requirements met more quickly. And employees can be motivated by the greater variety of the work they are doing. What is more, the broader their range of skills and the wider view they obtain of the business, the more employees are likely to use their skills in the business interests.

As with the other forms of flexibility, there are potential benefits for employees. The quest for added skills forces organisations to invest in training, and hence allow employees to enhance their internal and perhaps their external employability. This last caveat must be entered, since some multi-skilling may be company specific, or it may result in employees losing their cutting edge in their speciality which might encapsulate their real labour market value.

Finally, *wage* flexibility in principle allows organisations to relate earnings to output. With the decrease in the degree of collective bargaining in many countries, organisations have seized the opportunity to engage in a variety of pay arrangements at local levels. Unit or individual performance can be rewarded by performance-related pay or bonuses, and rewards can be commensurate with local rather than with national industry rates. They can also be varied to accord with fluctuations in the supply and demand of specific sorts of labour. Whether or not performance-related pay has fulfilled organisations' aspirations to manage performance and motivate staff is a moot point. However, what is certain is that wage flexibility has enabled them to match their wage costs more closely to their profits. There is greater uncertainty where the organisation is not a profit-making one, e.g. a school.

Once again, employees can benefit. Hard-working, ambitious and able workers can achieve recognition and reward for their performance; they do not have to wait for status and seniority to bring them these benefits. Overall, employee benefits, especially in terms of the work–life balance, training and development, and job variety, are examples of possible win–win outcomes of the more flexible rules of the employment game.

Using up Human Resources

When flexibility is a conscious strategy aimed at using human resources to the full, it can add value to the Human Resource (to continue with the metaphor). Employees can become more valuable to the organisation, and can themselves benefit in a wide variety of ways. However, Resources can also depreciate in value; they can be used up rather than used to the full.

Short-term targets and the ratcheting up of performance to achieve them can easily become the norm. This is particularly true of economies such as those of the USA and the UK, where shareholder pressure for short-term dividends is strongest. Moreover, the global nature of the business enterprise has emphasised the need for cost competitiveness and productivity gains everywhere. Hence, achieving relatively short-term financial targets has assumed added importance, and those elements of flexibility which can assist are selected for use in the employment relationship.

There is, therefore, a danger that functional flexibility, which has the capacity to add value over the longer term, may be downgraded whilst the boosting of performance and the cutting of costs in the short term become the main aims. A recent review of the HR management policies and practices of several blue chip UK companies noted for their degree of commitment to HR indicated that corporate rhetoric and employees' experience did not always coincide. Implementation rather than intent was the issue.[21]

And when short-term performance and the cutting of costs become the overriding aims of a business, then control mechanisms come to the fore: the control of manufacturing or business processes by technological means; and bureaucratic control through rules, targets, budgets and reporting structures. By the constraints they put upon initiative and learning opportunities, these controls are unlikely to lead to any added value accruing to the human resource. On the contrary, by their emphasis on immediate bottom line outcomes, they tend to prevent employees from spending any time on doing things better or on doing new things.

Indeed, such strategies not only fail to add value to the human resource; they actively devalue it. Much service sector work has overtaken the manufacturing assembly line in the degree of work intensification and dehumanisation imposed. This is despite the obvious fact that service work usually entails a degree of contact with the customer or client. But when that contact is itself regulated and segmented, the dehumanisation becomes more apparent and harder to bear. Managerial surveillance and intense pressure for speed are hardly likely to help McDonald's staff or supermarket checkout operators to add to their value to the business. Rather, they lose their capacity to be anything other than human cogs in a machine-like process and will doubtless shortly be replaced by technology.[22, 23]

Not all jobs are so designed as to de-skill people and actually reduce their value as human resources. Indeed, most employees claim to have added to their skill range and degree of responsibility in recent years.[24] The most reasonable conclusion to draw is that there are some sectors and some levels of employee where deskilling and devaluing has occurred, and others where upskilling is mainly the order of the day. However, upskilling and deskilling are not the only ways whereby value can be added or subtracted. Employees may be used up, exhausted and burned out however many or however few skills they may have acquired.

For control mechanisms are not all hard-nosed and explicit. The softer versions of Human Resource Management have also come up with a variety of ways of improving productivity and intensifying work. Like the demanding parent of Chapter 1, management can seek to ensure that employees have internalised the business values to the extent that they put themselves under pressure.[25] In manufacturing industry, employees may become inspectors of themselves and each other, so rendering supervisors superfluous.[26] In order to provide the data to inform this monitoring, individual performance and errors can be publicly displayed.[27] Or if you are a professional or a manager, the 'long-hours culture' can hold you in its grip:[28] in order to show your commitment, you have to work as long if not longer than the others (especially the boss).

Whether hard or soft HR control mechanisms are used to get the most out of employees in the interests of short-term profit, the result is often the degradation or destruction of human Resources. Instead of adding value to the business and to themselves, employees lose any value which they originally brought with them. Particularly if their job demonstrates a combination of high demands and low discretion and control, they are likely to succumb to stress and perform irrationally when they are healthy enough to get to work.[29] Or else they preserve their health and wellbeing by doing as little as they can get away with in the face of hard methods of control, or by paying lip service only to the soft ones. Either way, they may suffer corrosion of character: the inability to sustain any long-term purpose of their own or form trusting relationships.[30]

And when Resources are used up and exhausted, or else merely surplus to current requirements, they get jettisoned. When the number of redundancies achieved becomes something to parade proudly in the annual report, it is hardly surprising if employees take the lesson to heart and make their own survival their first concern. Feelings of guilt about their redundant colleagues, anger with the organisation and insecurity about the future are to be found among the survivors.[31, 32] This downward spiral is shown in Table 7.

So even the business-friendly Resources metaphor has its flip side. Employees can gain in value, add value, and feel valued; or they can lose whatever value they had. What is your experience? Here's a *metaphor check* for your own organisation:

1 Does your organisation have a 'Personnel' function or a 'Human Resources' function? Does it make any difference in practice?
2 What methods does your organisation use of quantifying its human resource? To what purposes is this information put? What would you like to know which your present HR information system cannot tell you? What business purpose would this added information serve?
3 Would you characterise your HR processes as primarily of the hard or the soft variety? Are they explicitly related to the business direction? To what extent can they be shown to add value? What are the good and bad outcomes of your hard (or soft) processes?
4 Are there any examples of flexible working practices/employment contracts in your organisation which were designed to meet employees' as well as organisation's needs? If so, what have been the outcomes?
5 Do short-term targets always/mostly/sometimes/seldom/never take precedence over training and development activities? Are managers rewarded for facilitating their subordinates' learning and development?
6 Do you, consciously or unconsciously, foster a long-hours culture by your own working habits?
7 Have you ever conducted a stress audit in your organisation? If not, why not? If so, did the results surprise you? What did you do about them?

Table 7 From Resource to Discard

Resource		Flip	Discard
Employer:	Value, conserve, deploy	Exploit, control	Use up, exhaust
Employee:	Contribute	Perform	Stress, survival
	Develop	Driven	

References

1 Grant, R. M. (1991) The resource based theory of competitive advantage: impli-cations for strategy formulation. *California Management Review*, 33, 3, 114–135. Quoted in J. Purcell (1995) Corporate strategy and its link with human resource management strategy. In J. Storey (ed.) *Human Resource Management: A Critical Text*. London: Routledge.

2 Purcell, J. (1999) Best practice and best fit: chimera or cul-de-sac. *Human Resource Management Journal*, 9, 3, 26–41.

3 Nahapiet, J. and Ghoshal, S. (1998) Social capital, intellectual capital, and the organisational advantage. *Academy of Management Review*, 23, 2, 242–266.

4 Anderson, N. and Herriot, P. (eds) (1997) *International Handbook of Selection and Assessment*. Chichester: Wiley.

5 Schmitt, F. L., Hunter, J. E., Pearlman, K. and Hirsch, H. R. (1985) Forty ques-tions about validity generalisation and meta-analysis. *Personnel Psychology*, 38, 697–798.

6 Hendry, C. and Pettigrew, A. (1990) Human Resource Management: An agenda for the 1990s. *International Journal of Human Resource Management*, 1, 1, 17–44.

7 Schuler, R. S. (1998) Human resource management. In M. Poole and M. Warner (eds) *The Handbook of Human Resource Management*. London: International Thomson Business Press.

8 Williams, A. P. O. and Dobson, P. (1997) Personnel selection and corporate strat-egy. In N. Anderson and P. Herriot (eds) *International Handbook of Selection and Assessment*. Chichester: Wiley.

9 Purcell, J. (1995) Corporate strategy and its link with human resource strategy. In J. Storey (ed.) *Human Resource Management: A Critical Text*. London: Routledge.

10 O'Reilly, C. and Chatman, J. (1986) Organisational commitment and psycho-logical attachment: the effects of compliance, identification, and internalisation on pro-social behaviour. *Journal of Applied Psychology*, 71, 492–499.

11 Storey, J. (1993) The take-up of human resource management by mainstream companies: key lessons from research. *International Journal of Human Resource Management*, 4, 3, 529–553.

12 Ezzamel, M., Lilley, S., Wilkinson, A. and Willmott, H. (1996) Practices and practicalities in human resource management. *Human Resource Management Jour-nal*, 6, 1, 63–80.

13 Gratton, L. and Hope-Hailey, V. (1997) Human Resource Management on the line? *Human Resource Management Journal*, 7, 4, 12–29.

14 Huselid, M. A. (1995) The impact of Human Resource Management practices on turnover, productivity, and corporate financial performance. *Academy of Man-agement Journal*, 38, 3, 635–672.

15 Patterson, M. G., West, M. A., Lawthom, R. and Nickell, S. (1997, 1998) Impact of people management practices on business performance. IPD Research Reports nos 21 and 22.

16 Rucci, A. J., Kirn, S. P. and Quinn, R. T. (1998) The employee–customer–profit chain at Sears. *Harvard Business Review*, 76, 1, 82–98.

17 Delery, J. E. and Doty, H. D. (1996) Modes of theorising in strategic Human Resource Management: tests of universalistic, contingency, and configurational predictions. *Academy of Management Journal*, 39, 3, 802–835.

18 Pfeffer, J. (1998) *The Human Equation: Building Profits by Putting People First*. Boston MA: Harvard Business School Press.

19 Blyton, P. (1998) Flexibility. In M. Poole and M. Warner (eds) *Handbook of Human Resource Management*. London: International London Business Press.

20 Emmott, M. and Hutchinson, S. (1998) Employment flexibility: threat or promise? In P. Sparrow and M. Marchington (eds) *Human Resource Management: The New Agenda*. London: Financial Times and Pitman Publishing.
21 Gratton, L., Hope-Hailey, V., Stiles, P. and Truss, K. (1999) *Strategic Human Resource Management: Corporate Rhetoric and Human Reality*. Oxford: Oxford University Press.
22 Ritzer, G. (1993) *The McDonaldisation of Society*. Thousand Oaks CA: Pine Forge.
23 Legge, K. (1995) HRM: rhetoric, reality and hidden agendas. In J. Storey (ed.) *Human Resource Management: A Critical Text*. London: Routledge.
24 Gallie, D. (1991) Patterns of skill change: upskilling, deskilling, or the polarisation of skills? *Work, Employment, and Society*, 5, 3, 319–351.
25 Willmott, H. (1993) Strength is ignorance; slavery is freedom: Managing culture in modern organisations. *Journal of Management Studies*, 30, 4, 515–552.
26 Delbridge, R. (1995) Surviving JIT: Control and resistance in a Japanese transplant. *Journal of Management Studies*, 32, 6, 803–817.
27 Wilkinson, B., Morris, J. and Munday, M. (1995) The iron fist in the velvet glove: management and organisation in Japanese manufacturing transplants in Wales. *Journal of Management Studies*, 32, 6, 819–830.
28 Kodz, J., Kersley, B., Strebler, M. and O'Regan, S. (1998) Breaking the Long Hours Culture. Brighton: IES Report no. 352.
29 Payne, R. (1995) Stress. In N. Nicholson (ed.) Encyclopedic Dictionary of Organisational Behaviour. Oxford: Blackwell.
30 Sennett, R. (1998) *The Corrosion of Character: The Personal Consequences of Work in the New Capitalism*. London: Norton.
31 Brockner, J. (1988) The effects of work layoffs on survivors: Research, theory, and practice. In B. W. Staw and L. L. Cummings (eds) *Research in Organisational Behaviour*, vol. 10. Greenwich CT: JAI Press.
32 Noer, D. M. (1993) *Healing the Wounds*. San Francisco: Jossey Bass.

Chapter 6

Democracy and Dictatorship

Of the people, by the people, and for the people

Ever since the Greeks threw out the tyrants and established democracy in the sixth century BC, the role of the citizen within the government of the state has been a central issue for nations and societies. So small were the Greek city-states (Athens, the cradle of democracy, boasted only 45,000 (male) citizens) that government could indeed, in Abraham Lincoln's words, be 'of the people, by the people, and for the people'. In Athens, power was vested in the public assembly of the people, which met every ten days and voted on proposals for laws or policy. There were more than 1,000 elected offices to be filled each year, yet citizens conceived it as their honour and duty to perform them without pay.

This radical combination of *rights* and *responsibilities* has underpinned our notions of democracy ever since. When St Paul boasted that he was 'a citizen of no mean city', he was asserting his rights as a Roman citizen to protection and status wherever he went. Of course, the direct government of the people by the people has been replaced in modern democratic states by representative government. But both citizens' rights and citizens' responsibilities remain fundamental to our ideas of political and social governance. Indeed, at the end of the twentieth century, both of the dominant political ideologies which over-emphasised one or the other, rights or responsibilities, have been rejected. Communism collapsed in a mere moment of historic time, whilst we are more slowly recognising the downside of unfettered free market capitalism.

It is hardly surprising, then, that ideas from our political heritage and experience should transfer across to employees' experience of the employment situation. It is when people are trying to emphasise the *social* contract implied in the employment relationship, as opposed to the individual employment deal, that they use the Citizen metaphor.[1, 2] Thus in organisations, too, the language of rights and responsibilities has found a place amongst the other metaphors that we use. And what a rich vocabulary that language offers! Amongst the rights that democrats have fought for is that of *voice*. To quote John Stuart Mill, 'If all mankind minus one were of one opinion, and only one person were of the contrary opinion, mankind would be no more justified in silencing that one person than he, if he had the power, would be justified in silencing mankind.' Or consider the *accountability* which the sovereign people's representatives owe to those who have elected them. We hold our representatives to account for their exercise of the power entrusted to them, especially when they come up for re-election. *Justice*, too, features strongly among the goods which citizens claim as of right, and is construed as existing in the abstract, above partisan interests and immediate issues.

Of course, to the extent that employers are subject to the law of the land in respect of employment law, equal opportunities legislation, etc., Democracy and Citizenship are more than mere metaphors. Indeed, the extent to which employers treat legislation as anything more than irritating and unwarranted state intervention is perhaps some indication of the degree to which those metaphors are applicable in their case.

However, the rights of citizens have featured more strongly in the recent political discourse of modern democracies than have their responsibilities. This is hardly surprising given the circumstances of the birth of those democracies. The USA and India were establishing their independence from British colonial rule; France and Britain, before them, were throwing out the remnants of feudalism; Spain was more recently ridding itself of a fascist dictator. The power of the few was being overthrown, and the rights of the many were a natural preoccupation. Yet a look back in history to the first democracy indicates the importance of the reciprocal responsibilities of the Athenian citizen to the state.

In the Western democracies, however, the most fundamental responsibility of all, that of exercising the vote to select one's representatives, is becoming decreasingly exercised. Participation and faith in the democratic process is falling away. Moreover, it is argued[3] that the social glue which holds civil society together is also under threat. Fewer people are engaging in good citizenship behaviour in their local and national communities, and as a consequence the fund of social capital on which democracies depend may be decreasing. There may be a number of underlying reasons for this decrease: the increased individualism and consumerism of Western societies and the weakening of societal institutions such as the family have been cited amongst many others. However, the fundamental point is that the responsibilities of citizenship are not close to the top of the political or personal agendas of many today. As a consequence, the metaphor of the good corporate citizen may carry less resonance for today's employees.

Voice and accountability

Nevertheless, basic concepts of democracy resonate still, especially three on the rights side of the democratic equation: voice, accountability, and justice. *Voice* means exercising influence on one's own and others' behalf: 'having a say' in what goes on. The purposes of the exercise of voice are to affect outcomes and to generate a sense of agency (the belief that what we say or do does have an effect). Voice, of course, can be expressed in various ways: the formulation of proposals for action; the critique of others' proposals; and assent to others' proposals. The absence of voice is often taken to indicate assent, whereas, of course, it may conceal mere acquiescence and conformity, apathy or downright but fearful rejection.

Moreover, the expression of voice by itself is seldom satisfactory. Indeed, when employees are encouraged to give voice through opinion surveys, but nothing happens as a consequence, the solicitation of their voice is often counter-productive. It is only when employees perceive that their voice has been heard and acted upon, or at least seriously considered, that they are willing to take joint responsibility for the consequent decision and its outcomes. Indeed, 'It is a challenge of management to persuade employees that their interests were considered when no formal or informal mechanism has been used for ascertaining what those interests are.'[4]

The *accountability* of the executive to the citizens is also at the back of our minds when we think of the metaphor of the Democratic Citizen. The civil executive is there because we the sovereign people put them there. Yet employees are only too aware that top management is there because various parties other than themselves put them and maintain them there. Employees may or may not feel that they are counted as stakeholders (together with shareholders, customers and the community). Yet there is still a sense in which they are very willing to hold top management accountable, both for how the organisation is run and also for the outcomes which befall it (and them).

Indeed, when things go wrong, employees will start to make attributions regarding the reasons for such failure. They assume that top management have the overall responsibility for the organisation's governance, and so are apt to attribute unfair outcomes or processes to management. At the least they will expect explanations, justifications, or maybe even apologies;[5, 6] they will hold management accountable. Management may offer good causal explanations, for example in terms of the severity of the competition and the need for a speedy decision. Or they may justify outcomes by taking personal responsibility, but saying that they were driven by an overriding value: for example, the very survival of the business. Or they may take personal responsibility, admit error and apologise. The chief executives of bankrupt Japanese corporations recently expressed public and tearful remorse to employees and to the cameras. The point is that however they deal with the situation, top management is expected to give an account of their activities. If they are in the least concerned about rights and responsibilities in their organisations, then they will do so.

Three forms of justice

Voice and accountability are crucial rights in a democratic society. Yet they can be better understood in the organisational context if they are incorporated into an overall view of organisational *justice* and fairness. Three forms of organisational justice have been distinguished: distributive, procedural, and interactional.[7]

Distributive justice is about the fairness with which the outcomes of the organisation's activities, both positive and negative – the pleasure and the pain – are distributed. The presence or absence of such perceived fairness has been shown to affect job performance, involvement or withdrawal, co-operation with colleagues, quality of work, honesty or theft and stress.

Procedural justice, on the other hand, is about the fairness of procedures. Are the organisation's processes fair in their design and implementation? Are they transparent, consistent, and unbiased? Are they correctable in case of error? Do employees have a voice in their design and use? Procedural justice has been shown to affect employees' commitment to their organisation, honesty or theft, intentions to leave, job performance and organisational citizenship behaviour. If employees perceive their rights to have been honoured, they reciprocate as good organisational citizens.

Finally, *interactional* justice concerns treating people with dignity and respect. A top management interested in interacting fairly with employees will give an account to them of its actions. It will not merely ensure that procedures are fair, but it will concern itself with the manner in which they are executed. And it will seek to be honest and sincere with employees: consider this example. Recent redundancy programmes may have given good outplacement packages (distributive justice). Those made redundant may have been chosen fairly (procedural justice). But if they were not given a reason for the redundancies or thanked for their contribution to the organisation, then they suffered interactional injustice. Indeed, interactional justice would permit them to express their anger in such a situation.

There are some interesting and important research findings regarding these three forms of organisational justice. Distributive justice affects attitudes towards more personal outcomes, such as pay and job satisfaction; whereas procedural justice affects attitudes at the organisational level, such as organisational commitment and evaluation of one's supervisor.[7] Moreover, procedural justice can considerably decrease the harmful effects of distributive injustice.[8] Organisational justice as a whole is about outcomes and procedures working together in the experience of employees to influence feelings of fairness. Whether the management action was making redundancies, freezing pay, relocating employees, or introducing drug testing or a smoking ban, the research results were always the same: procedural and interactive justice was crucial in moderating the effects of these measures on employees' commitment and performance.

Why? Perhaps because employees think that if procedures are fair, they stand a good chance of reward in the long run. Or possibly because their self-esteem is enhanced because they infer that they must be valued if they are treated well. Or perhaps it is down to trust: top management's intentions must be sound, think employees – they must care. Whatever the reasons, employees reciprocate, often with 'good organisational citizen behaviour'. Such behaviour is characterised by altruism, courtesy, sportsmanship and conscientiousness.[9] Specific behaviours of a good organisational citizen might be:

- assisting colleagues with their work, or with personal matters
- going the extra mile for customers
- being committed to the organisation's values
- making suggestions for improvements
- making extra efforts, or volunteering
- demonstrating loyalty and representing the organisation favourably to outsiders.[10]

Many organisations treat organisational justice as important, and have good organisational citizens as a consequence. All such organisations have recognised that the employment relationship cannot be seen in isolation from civil society. If people enjoy justice rights as citizens in the rest of their lives, they will expect something not too different in their working lives as well.

Cracks in the shield of justice

Yet there are many potential cracks in the Democratic edifice which can lead to its downfall and to its flip side: Dictatorship. As we consider the forms of justice, we can see how easily the coin can flip.

Take distributive justice. Here the issue concerns which comparisons are appropriate to serve as a basis for judgements about equity. US and UK directors, for example, are reportedly astonished at the degree of anger which their salaries and share options arouse in their employees. They believe that the appropriate comparisons to be made are with the directors of other similar organisations, and their remuneration committees concur. Yet employees may be making other comparisons. They may reflect on the gap between their own salaries and those of their directors. They may note that this gap has steadily widened over the past two decades. And they may compare the situation in Germany and Japan where the gap between top and median salaries is far smaller than in the US and the UK. They may also reflect that the process for setting directors' remuneration is itself a positive feedback loop; the higher the award to one, the higher the overall comparison point for all the others.

Or consider procedural justice. It is only too easy for processes which are fairly designed to lose some of that fairness in their execution. For example, open job advertisements and transparent procedures for internal selection may be in place; yet in practice they may sometimes be by-passed because of urgency or patronage. Careful succession plans may be formulated, yet half of the vacancies are filled with people other than those earmarked.

Finally, interactional justice may be breached by managers being unable or unwilling to treat people personally. External outplacement consultants, for example, may say the right words, but cannot do so with sincerity and credibility. Those made redundant want an explanation and some thanks for their contribution from those for whom they made that contribution.

Appraisal: a case study in procedural justice

The common personnel process of *appraisal* demonstrates how attempts at procedural justice may come to fail.

From the employee's perspective, appraisal may affect their performance-related pay, or their promotion prospects. At a deeper level, it may impact upon their self-esteem. From the employer's perspective, appraisal is primarily a tool for performance management; the motivation of good performance by reward and its improvement by the identification of training needs. The outcomes matter to both parties.

Considerable effort has been put into making appraisal fair.[11] The accuracy and reliability of appraisal ratings has been addressed by such means as behaviourally-anchored rating scales, which are supposed to force the appraiser to recall specific behaviour which they have observed rather than rely on general impressions. Yet research demonstrates that there is still considerable variability in ratings of the same person, and that this is due to differences between appraisers.

Moreover, appraisals are not always conducted in a professional way. There is often insufficient time spent on them, appraisers are untrained, and there is usually immense leniency bias. I recently consulted with an organisation which had four points on the rating scale, the top one being 'excellent'. This rating contained the largest number of appraisees. The organisation then divided the 'excellent' rating into three sub-ratings. Most appraisees fell into the uppermost of these.

Clearly, the ideal of accurate and objective measurement is honoured more in the breach than in the observation, and so is the attempt to implement the process properly. Why should this be? Essentially, employees are concerned about outcomes, and they seek to manage the impression they make upon the appraiser. Appraisers may need to enhance the employee's performance so that they can achieve their own demanding targets; but they may well also be concerned to ensure that they can work in a congenial relationship for the future.

Given the unequal distribution of power in the appraisal relationship, it is argued that only if the employee trusts the appraiser not to use this advantage to secure their own ends can fairness be achieved. Yet the whole process of cascading down objectives from the business plan ensures that it is the appraiser's objectives that are legitimised (they need their subordinate to perform well in order to achieve the targets that have been set them by their own appraiser).

Thus radical theorists argue convincingly that it is the exercise of power that dominates appraisal in its present predominant form.[12, 13] We should perhaps be asking whether the process itself is inherently unjust, since it gives little opportunity for the interests of the employee to be addressed. The injustice may be distributive rather than procedural.

Rhetoric, whistleblowing, and surveillance

So reality may fail to approach the ideal of Democratic justice in organisations, just as it has so often failed to do so in politics. Even in Western democracies, we sometimes experience elective dictatorships. However, some would go further and say that the very metaphor of Citizenship is a *rhetorical device*.[14] That is, it is an attempt to persuade people that there is a degree of universally applied justice in organisations which simply does not exist nor is ever likely to. From this perspective, the citizenship metaphor is merely an attempt to conceal the extreme differences in how people actually are treated within the same organisation.[15] The organisation has taken away the individual voice of the employee by annexing it and incorporating it into a single and universal 'voice'. Trade unions have been known to do the same.

The presence of rhetoric has always been a warning sign, both politically and organisationally. Demagogues were would-be dictators in ancient Greece and Rome and have been ever since. Rhetoric in organisations, too, is usually to be interpreted as an attempt to manage meaning so as to gain or retain power.[16] Where redundancies have been made, for example, the situation may be rhetorically represented as favourable by making comparisons with other organisations where they were even more severe.

When employees see through the rhetoric, when their own experience tells them that it cannot be true, then they are more likely to be on the alert for injustice. If they have a strong sense of justice, they may blow the whistle on acts they perceive as wrong. *Whistleblowers* are typically highly competent and principled individuals with a strong set of values. They gradually come to see that the actions about which they are concerned are often not isolated behaviour, but rather a systemic part of the way an organisation operates.[17] They gain much more political awareness, and begin to act politically rather than simply ethically. Indeed, it is generally those who have been more committed to the organisation who are more outraged by its injustices.[18] Whistleblowers act to their own cost. Of 87 US whistleblowers, only one did not suffer some form of retaliation at the hands of their company; 16 lost their homes, 14 divorced, and nine attempted suicide.[19]

When organisations act unjustly, employees may respond heroically by whistleblowing, because they are morally outraged; or quiescently, because they interpret it as a part of the natural order; or cynically, perceiving that they could do nothing about it anyway and would suffer if they tried. However, there are some organisations in which injustice is endemic. Power is exercised ruthlessly and often capriciously, resources are seized and appropriated for personal and political purposes, and people are treated with contempt and disdain rather than with respect. Democracy is dead; Dictatorship has taken its place. The coin has flipped.

Typical of dictatorships and the ruthless exercise of power is the use of techniques of *surveillance*. Dictators seek to ensure that their demands, however unreasonable, are met, and believe that they can do so by continuously checking on people – the all-seeing eye. They may also be afraid of what employees may be hatching up. Sophisticated electronic techniques make such surveillance feasible,[20] but it can equally well be achieved by the old-fashioned telephone. All the long-hours culture boss has to do is to phone an employee at the office at 7.30 (morning or night). In Japanese manufacturing transplants in Wales, employees were constantly monitored and their errors publicly noted and recorded, as was absence and timekeeping.[21, 22] Bogus shoppers check up on supermarket check-out clerks,[23] and supervisors monitor the length of time spent away from their phone by telesales staff.

Surveillance is just one type of Dictatorial behaviour which demonstrates a lack of respect for employees. There are many others, but surveillance is of particular interest at the moment. This is because additional means of surveillance have recently become available, but the uses to which they will be put are still unclear. Electronic data can be owned and used as tools for surveillance by those with power; or they can be employed by the workforce themselves to add value and learn by means of the instant feedback which they provide and the information which they contain.[24] All the evidence suggests that it is the former rather than the latter use which is gaining the upper hand.[25]

Resistance movements

How are employees to react when they find themselves inside a Dictatorship? For many the prime concern is survival with as much dignity as they can muster. A huge variety of survival techniques have been developed over the years.[26] One approach is to try and find ways round the domination, to beat the system in some little way whilst still existing within it, and so level up ever so slightly the unbalanced scales of justice. So employees can engage in *fiddles*, thus levelling up what they see as distributive injustice.[27, 28] They can steal time back by taking unauthorised or legitimate but unnecessary breaks. Or they deal with their anger, frustration, or contempt for management by *jokes*, a historic weapon against tyranny. They may even engage in *sabotage*, the possibilities for which have multiplied in the digital age, but which is a direct challenge to management. Even middle managers can engage in sabotage too.[29] But the most common survival mechanism is to withdraw into one's own inner world, to keep most of one's self for oneself rather than give it all to the job. Survivors of this type are not anti-social. They simply *comply*, and hitherto their compliance has offered little challenge to management. However, when top management believes that good organisational citizenship behaviour by employees is necessary for competitive advantage, mere compliance ceases to be enough. For good Citizenship by definition goes beyond compliance, since it actively searches out opportunities to help.

Two forms of resistance

Two of these forms of resistance were observed in two case studies,[30] located in an engineering employer and in an insurance company. The first was a classic resistance ploy used by male shopfloor workers since the industrial revolution began. In response to a takeover by American owners, and various initiatives such as a corporate culture programme and a bonus system, these workers exercised their intimate knowledge of the production process in their own interest. They were able to pace their work without management understanding how they did so, and exercise their own control over production. They kept their knowledge, and themselves, to themselves: 'resistance through distance', although still in effect granting management its 'right to manage'.

The second example demonstrates 'resistance through persistence'. Here a pregnant employee confronted the organisation regarding an issue of procedural justice (the fairness of a promotion procedure). She persisted in obtaining information from local management and used it to play them off against corporate HR management. Concentrating on the conduct of the process alone, she insisted on outlasting the local manager in face-to-face discussion, partly through threatening to be sick on his carpet when he called the meeting at 9.00 a.m! She used to the full both her personal power as a persistent pregnant woman, and also her legitimate power as having suffered procedural injustice which contravened the organisation's code of fair practice. With the aid of her union representative, she used the firm's own procedures against itself.

The power to outflank

Dictatorial organisations have not overlooked these forms of resistance, however. Rather, they have often engaged in a variety of *outflanking movements*,[31] using their superior power to overcome the resistance movement. They may employ a variety of strategies:

- keeping employees ignorant about the organisation itself, the true sources of power, the rules that exist, and how to get support
- the isolation and scapegoating of resisters
- the separation of work life and home life into separate watertight compartments, so that the norms of everyday life are not seen as applicable
- the use of the job market to instil fear, or more generally, the clear evidence of the dangers in resisting
- the provision of routines and rituals to put management's meaning on to a meaningless job.

To take another case study:[32]

Management imposed a new system on to clerical workers in a utility. Its poor design indicated to these employees that managers did not grasp the degree of complexity involved in their jobs. Its simplicity also indicated that management was interested in becoming less dependent on these workers for their firm-specific knowledge. Despite management statements to the effect that customer service was paramount, employees drew the conclusion that such a poor system was designed to save money. This was particularly annoying, since most of the staff were strongly motivated by a desire to serve the customer better.

Employees' attempts to resist, however, were outflanked. Their union was male-dominated and its bureaucratic procedures were alien to the mainly female clerical staff. Attempts at sabotage and at working to rule were thwarted by the capacity of the system to exercise surveillance, and dismissals resulted. And the implicit threat to replace them by a compliant part-time workforce was enough to keep the majority in line.

Now the transition from Democracy to Dictatorship can happen for a variety of reasons. A specific act of injustice or deceit on the part of management can trigger the flip of the coin. Or equally, an act of anti-citizenship behaviour by employees can cause management to react repressively. The absence of voice, the loss of control over one's destiny, or the experience of distributive, procedural or interactional injustice can turn the good corporate citizen into the resisting rebel. Just as Families can turn to Feuding and Contracts to the law of the Jungle, so Democracy can descend into Dictatorship. Table 8 summarizes the flip from Democracy to Dictatorship.

So here is a *metaphor check* for the Democracy metaphor to estimate your position on the top or the flip side:

Table 8 From Democracy to Dictatorship

Democracy		Flip	Dictatorship
Employer:	Distributive, procedural, interactional justice	Rhetoric Power	Surveillance Repression, outflanking
Employee;	Rights, responsibilities, voice	Acceptance Compliance	Resistance Fear

1 What are employees' responses to top management's remuneration?

2 What is your impression of the degree of transparent implementation of organisational processes such as appraisal: 90%; 75%; 50%; 25%?

3 How happy are you with the way in which colleagues were made redundant at the last restructuring?

4 Is regularly going beyond the call of duty a frequent, occasional or rare behaviour?

5 Does your organisation have a published policy regarding whistleblowing? What happened to the most recent whistleblower?

6 What is the more frequent use of information technology: to keep a check on employees or to inform them?

7 How frequent is sabotage of any sort in your organisation? What forms does it take, and to what do you attribute it?

References

1 Parker, M. (1997) Organisations and citizenship. *Organisation*, 4, 1, 75–92.

2 Organ, D. W. (1997) The motivational basis of organisational citizenship behaviour. In B. M. Staw and L. L. Cummings (eds) *Research in Organisational Behaviour*, vol. 12, pp. 43–72. Greenwich CT: JAI Press.

3 Fukuyama, F. (1995) *Trust: The Social Virtues and the Creation of Prosperity*. London: Hamish Hamilton

4 Folger, R. and Cropanzano, R. (1998) *Organisational Justice and Human Resource Management*. Thousand Oaks CA: Sage, p. 47.

5 Bies, R. J. (1987) The predicament of injustice: The management of moral outrage. In L. L. Cummings and B. M. Staw (eds) *Research in Organisational Behaviour*, vol. 9, pp. 289–319. Greenwich CT: JAI Press.

6 Brockner, J., DeWitt, R. L., Grover, S. and Reed, T. (1990) When it is especially important to explain why: Factors affecting the relationship between managers' explanations of a lay-off and survivors' reactions to the lay-off. *Journal of Experimental Social Psychology*, 26, 389–407.

7 McFarlin, D. B. and Sweeney, P. D. (1992) Distributive and procedural justice as predictors of satisfaction with personal and organisational outcomes. *Academy of Management Journal*, 35, 3, 626–637.

8 Brockner, J. and Siegel, P. (1996) Understanding the interaction between procedural and distributive justice: The role of trust. In R. M. Kramer and T. R. Tyler (eds) *Trust in Organisations: Frontiers of Theory and Research*. Thousand Oaks CA: Sage.

9 Moorman, R. M. (1991) The relationship between organisational justice and organisational citizenship behaviours: Do fairness perceptions influence employee citizenship? *Journal of Applied Psychology*, 76, 845–855.
10 Brief, A. and Motowidlo, S. J. (1986) Prosocial organisational behaviours. *Academy of Management Review*, 11, 710–725.
11 Folger and Cropanzano (op. cit.).
12 Coates, G. (1994) Performance appraisal as icon: Oscar-winning performance or dressing to impress? *International Journal of Human Resource Management*, 5, 1, 167–191.
13 Townley, B. (1993) Performance appraisal and the emergence of management. *Journal of Management Studies*, 30, 2, 221–238.
14 Hancock, P. G. (1997) Citizenship or vassalage? Organisational membership in the age of unreason. *Organisation*, 4, 1, 93–111.
15 Hirsh, W. and Jackson, C. (1996) *Strategies for Career Development: Promise, Practice, and Pretence*. Brighton: Institute for Employment Studies, Report 305.
16 Hardy, C. and Clegg, S. R. (1996) Some dare call it power. In S.R. Clegg, C. Hardy, and W. R. Nord (eds) *Handbook of Organisational Studies*. London: Sage.
17 Rothschild, J. and Miethe, T. D. (1994) Whistleblowing as resistance in modern work organisations: The politics of revealing organisational deception and abuse. In J. M. Jermier, D. Knights and W. R. Nord (eds) *Resistance and Power in Organisations*. London: Routledge.
18 Brockner, J., Tyler, T. R. and Cooper-Schneider, R. (1992) The effects of prior commitment to an institution on reactions to perceived unfairness: The higher they are, the harder they fall. *Administrative Science Quarterly*, 37, 241–261.
19 Winfield, M. (1990) *Minding Your Own Business*. London: Social Audit.
20 Lyon, D. (1994) *The Electronic Eye: The Rise of Surveillance Society*. Cambridge: Polity Press.
21 Wilkinson, B., Morris, J. and Munday, M. (1995) The iron fist in the velvet glove: management and organisation in Japanese manufacturing transplants in Wales. *Journal of Management Studies*, 32, 6, 819–830.
22 Delbridge, R. (1995) Surviving JIT: Control and resistance in a Japanese transplant. *Journal of Management Studies*, 32, 6, 803–817.
23 Ogbonna, E. and Wilkinson, B. (1990) Corporate strategy and corporate culture: The view from the check-out. *Personnel Review*, 19, 4, 9–15.
24 Zuboff, S. (1988) *In the Age of the Smart Machine*. Oxford: Heinemann.
25 Ford, M. (1998) *Surveillance and Privacy at Work*. London: Institute of Employment Rights.
26 Noon, M. and Blyton, P. (1997) *The Realities of Work*. London: Macmillan.
27 Greenberg, J. (1990) Employee theft as a reaction to underpayment inequity: The hidden costs of pay cuts. *Journal of Applied Psychology*, 75, 561–568.
28 Greenberg, J. (1997) The steal motive: Managing the social determinants of employee theft. In R. A. Giacalone and J. Greenberg (eds) *Anti-social Behaviour in Organisations*. Thousand Oaks CA: Sage.
29 Lanuez, D. and Jermier, J. M. (1994) Sabotage by managers and technocrats: Neglected patterns of resistance at work. In J. M. Jermier, D. Knights and W. R. Nord (eds) *Resistance and Power in Organisations*. London: Routledge.
30 Collinson, D. (1994) Strategies of resistance: power, knowledge, and subjectivity in the workplace. In J. M. Jermier, D. Knights and W. R. Nord (eds) *Resistance and Power in Organisations*. London: Routledge.
31 Clegg, S. (1994) Power relations and the constitution of the resistant subject. In J. M. Jermier, D. Knights and W. R. Nord (eds) *Resistance and Power in Organisations*. London: Routledge.

32 O'Connell-Davidson, J. (1994) The sources and limits of resistance in a privatised utility. In J. M. Jermier, D. Knights and W. R. Nord (eds) *Resistance and Power in Organisations*. London: Routledge.

Chapter 7

Partnership and Conflict

Partners are an icon of our time. Police series on television feature pairs of cops who brave the mean streets together, relying on each other to watch their backs and save their lives. Police partnership is so well-established a cliche that it now needs to be spiced up by introducing a love interest with a mixed gender pair, or a gender interest with two female cops.

Comedians gain fame in partnerships: Laurel and Hardy, Morecambe and Wise, and countless others. The Chaplinesque Laurel nevertheless needed the straight man Hardy, just as Morecambe needed Wise. The combination was far more than the sum of its parts.

Partnership has entered our personal experience too. Such is the ambiguity of family and marriage that we now use the word partner to describe all those in an intimate relationship. This now seems infinitely preferable to the demeaning 'boyfriend' or 'girlfriend', especially when used to describe grandparents aged 55!

All of these examples are of pairs of individuals who associate with each other because they have shared interests in common. The dictionary quotes *association* and *joint interest* as two of the three defining features of partnership, although not specifying that it refers only or primarily to couples. The third is *participation*.

Partnership has also had a longstanding business denotation. A partner in a professional firm is 'a principal or a contributor of capital in a business or a joint venture, usually sharing its risks and profits';[1] a stakeholder in a very literal sense. Note that partnership in a professional firm is an elite position. Only one in ten of the already elite young graduates who join the top-flight accountancy firms will make it to partner. The term as used in the professional context certainly does not refer to the employment relationship enjoyed by all employees.

What is partnership?

The Partnership metaphor for the employment relationship faithfully incorporates the three features of the dictionary definition: association, joint interest, and participation. It also carries clear echoes of three of our previous metaphors: Citizen, Contract, and Resource. The Partnership concept of industrial democracy is based on the assumption that the *citizen's* democratic right of self-determination applies in the workplace as much as in the state. The idea of mutuality encapsulated in Partnership is reflected in the mutuality of obligations implied by *contract*. And how can we possibly be making best use of the knowledge and experience of our human *resources* if we fail to allow them a degree of participation in the organisation's decisions?

So what is Partnership? The most recent attempt at definition[2] forces us to distinguish three different levels of analysis. The first level is that of *processes*. We will know whether Partnership is being practised, and how well, by investigating the extent and quality of direct communication (e.g. by team briefings); upward problem solving (e.g. by employee attitude surveys); financial involvement (e.g. by profit sharing); and employee representation (e.g. by joint consultative committees).

The second level of analysis is in terms of the holding of certain *values* which relate to other stakeholders, and their expression in behaviour. These concern management's recognition of employees' right to contribute to at least some decisions; and employees' recognition that management has a right to expect certain levels of performance and flexibility. Trust that mutual obligations will be honoured, and an element of constancy and consistency in the employment relationship, are also implied.

Finally, there are some *personnel practices* which assist Partnership rather than being central to its definition. These include single status employment contracts, a commitment to a degree of security of employment, and investment in training and development.

Such a definition rescues the metaphor from being just another way of referring to all progressive employment practices. It applies to some more than others, with the emphasis on joint decision-making. It is summed up by the Involvement and Participation Association[3] as follows:

- a commitment to working together to making the business more successful
- understanding the employee security conundrum and trying to do something about it
- building relationships at the workplace which maximise employee influence through total communication and a robust and effective employee voice.

So Partnership is a concept with strong emphases on what employees have to offer and on management's responsibility for ensuring that they have the resources and the opportunity to offer it. Historically, Partnership has been sought in three main ways:

1 *Industrial democracy*, whereby employee representatives have a place in the decision-making structures and processes of the organisation

2 *Economic democracy*, in which employees have a financial stake in the organisation

3 *Participation*, involvement, and empowerment processes which are acted out in a wide variety of ways.

Of these Partnership modes, the first clearly has strong links with Citizenship and is supported on the basis of employees' rights, usually at governmental level. The second and the third, however, are granted by top management within the organisation.

Industrial democracy

Historically there have been examples of industrial democracy every bit as democratic as ancient Athens. In the former Yugoslavia, for example, workers were management, while at Mondragon in Spain there was a network of producer co-operatives. There still are in certain wine-growing regions of France. However, the main forms of industrial democracy to be found at present on a large scale fall into four categories:[4, 5, 6]

- *codetermination*, where employee representatives sit on the company board – in Germany forming up to half of the board
- *works councils*, which function at plant level and which vary considerably across nations in terms of their powers and the range of issues they address
- *joint consultative committees*, which have no power to take decisions and mostly are information channels both upward and downward
- *shop-floor programmes* which seek improvements in the work process of a specific team or assembly line.

These forms are widely practised in Europe, and some (e.g. works councils) are required by the European Union, with the United Kingdom somewhat unwillingly acquiescing. In the United States, however, industrial democracy projects tend to be isolated and focus on quality and productivity only.[7] These US initiatives are either at the level of work teams, following the Japanese example, or they involve strategic business planning at business unit level. These latter initiatives at major US companies (e.g. Dow Corning, Xerox) have mostly fallen by the wayside in the 1990s.

The key current issue regarding industrial democracy appears to be the following: is it possible to have both jobs and justice?[8] In other words, can firms which use institutions of employee representation to remove insecurity of employment survive in an increasingly competitive environment? Or do we assume insecurity, and expect individuals to become resilient (as in the

UK and USA)? What is clear is that the institutions of industrial democracy depend upon legislative support for their continued existence. When German firms locate subsidiaries in the UK, they do not normally recognise unions or engage in employee involvement.[9] Even where works councils and other institutions survive in multinational corporations, they are likely to be paternalistic, marginalised, and emasculated.[10]

Economic democracy

Employees typically enjoy two forms of financial stake in their companies: profit sharing and share ownership.[11] *Profit sharing* can take several forms. Employees can be presented with the profit share that they have accrued at the end of the financial year, and it can take the form of a cash payment or shares. Alternatively, payment can be delayed for tax purposes until the employee retires or leaves. Some or all employees may benefit, and the size of the profit share may depend on salary or seniority, or alternatively all may receive the same amount. Usually, profit share schemes only kick in above a certain profit margin. Profit sharing has been made legally compulsory in some countries, notably France, India, Pakistan, Nigeria, and several South American countries. Others provide a degree of legislative support, e.g. the UK, Denmark, Germany and Greece.

The most common form of *share ownership* is where employees are minority shareholders. In some cases shares are presented to employees as a form of bonus. Alternatively, they may be given stock options, i.e. the opportunity to buy shares at a predetermined price at some point in the future. A final option is to offer staff shares now at a discounted price. In the USA, legislation supports employee stock ownership plans (ESOPs), whereby shares are either donated to a trust fund by companies or are purchased through leveraged support from financial institutions. By 1993, approximately 10 million US workers were involved in ESOPs. The UK, too, has legislated tax incentives for share ownership, and Australia, Argentina, Egypt, Poland, Belgium, Denmark, France, Germany, Greece and Ireland also offer varying degrees of legislative support.

Many organisations therefore practise these two forms of economic democracy because they are legally obliged to do so or because tax incentives have made it worth their while. In particular, profit sharing and share ownership may substitute for pension contributions, or even enable companies to keep basic wage costs lower than they would otherwise have been. However, they may also serve other than financial purposes:

- they can be used as part of an overall reward package to attract and retain good people
- they can act as effective motivators, since they are partly consequent upon the outcomes of individual effort and performance

- share ownership can serve to inform and educate employees about the business's performance in its commercial environment
- share ownership can give employees a sense of ownership of and identification with the business.

However the evidence is mixed. Certainly, financial democracy is associated with other forms of participation. Joint consultative committees, information sharing, collective bargaining and union density are higher in firms which practise it. But, there is little evidence for an impact on incentivisation and risk, performance, or performance monitoring.[12] Employee buy-outs, however, can enhance organisational commitment, involvement and integration of the workforce.[13] It is also worth noting at this point that whilst industrial democracy is strongly collective in nature, depending as it does upon effective representation of employees as a group, economic democracy is highly individual. Employee involvement in the latter is material in nature, and implies no participation in decision-making. It is perhaps no accident that in certain countries, e.g. the UK, economic democracy has been sponsored by governments interested in supporting 'management's right to manage' and the individualisation of the employment relationship.[14]

Participation and involvement

The terms participation and involvement are synonymous – with involvement perhaps currently more fashionable.[15] Empowerment practices are perhaps best understood as a subset of participation/involvement. A simple definition of participation (e.g. 'interaction between workers and managers which results in workers influencing decisions') obscures the essential features of the process. We need to ask about its depth and scope, its forms and methods, the organisational level at which it occurs and its purposes and outcomes.[16]

How much do employees influence the final decision? Do they merely receive information about it, are they consulted before management takes it, or do they actually exert influence upon it? The recent emphasis appears to be on the first two of these, with employee information the dominant purpose of the three.

What are the forms that participation takes when it is not a legislative requirement? Recent developments favour face-to-face participation at the lowest levels of the organisation. This may take the form of team briefings of a purely informative nature. Alternatively, quality circles, suggestion schemes, customer care or total quality programmes may involve employees in the allocation, scheduling, and improvement of tasks. However, process changes or even product changes and investment plans could all potentially benefit from employee involvement.

Given that involvement is in the gift of management, is it possible to speculate upon their motives in its introduction? The overwhelming emphasis on informing and consulting employees rather than jointly taking decisions with them suggests that management wishes to retain its decision-making power. However, it also indicates that management recognises that it cannot assume that employees are well motivated. Involvement is a potent added source of co-operative motivation. Similarly, in an era of ever intensifying competition, to ignore a potential source of competitive advantage – the knowledge of employees – is to handicap one's business unnecessarily. There are also suggestions that the involvement of employees at the levels of information and consultation with individuals or small groups can help to undermine the power of collective representatives (the unions). Whatever their motives, it is clear that, in the UK at least, managers are in general in favour of greater employee involvement.[17]

As for employees, they too favour greater participation, particularly in those decisions which directly affect their own working lives. They are keen that higher level, more strategic, decisions should be influenced by their representatives. Direct face-to-face participation can impact job satisfaction and absenteeism favourably, but these effects tend to wear off as such forms of direct participation as team briefings or quality circles become routine.

There are two further qualifications to the apparently benign organisational impact of involvement upon employees. The first is when nothing happens as a consequence of the consultation process. Attributions of motive are quickly made: 'They're only doing it to keep us happy.' The second is the often immense gap between organisational processes and the reality on the ground.[18] Processes of involvement may have been established corporately. However, unless local line managers actually put them into practice wholeheartedly, rather than going through the motions or ignoring them entirely, they will have an adverse impact, or at best no impact at all. One of the reasons why line managers often fail to buy in is that involvement processes have frequently been introduced as one-off initiatives rather than as part of an overall change of organisational strategy.[19]

The term *empowerment* has a slightly different meaning from participation and involvement. For a start, it is more rhetorical than these, since its users seek to persuade employees that some power is being surrendered and handed over by management to employees. It is much more explicitly aimed at hearts and minds, and is presented as one of the corner-stones of employee commitment.[20] In fact, however, it is more limited in its scope than participation and involvement, since it is used to refer to direct involvement of teams of workers in a limited range of issues. These are likely to relate to the production or service delivery processes.[21] Once again, unless empowerment is one of a bundle of human resource processes which themselves derive from and reinforce a participatory culture, it is unlikely to have any beneficial outcomes.[22, 23] What is more, the greater promise implied in the label 'empowerment' is likely to lead to greater cynicism if that promise is broken. In particular, if the added discretion offered by empowerment is offset by increased accountability and responsibility and no extra pay, the new empowerment deal may appear to be no more than a confidence trick.[24]

Partnership and conflict

So the overall picture seems mixed. Employees and managers have positive initial attitudes towards involvement and participation, and positive initial outcomes have been observed in terms of enhanced commitment and reduced absenteeism.[25, 26] Employees certainly have contributed valuable ideas which have improved quality and productivity.[27, 28] However, the practice is patchy, even when practice is inferred from policy statements rather than from observed reality on the ground.[29, 30]

In the major piece of research on Partnership in Europe, the following results indicate just how little progress has been made in the Democratisation of the employment relationship. The degree of employee involvement in decision-making was assessed by a 6 point scale, where 1 = not involved; 2 = informed beforehand; 3 = informed beforehand and can give opinion; 4 = opinion taken into account; 5 = take part with an equal weight being given to their opinion; and 6 = can take decision themselves. The mean score for employees at operative level was 2.0 in 1981; for supervisors, 2.6; for middle managers, 3.2; and for senior managers, 3.8. There was barely any change in these means by 1993.[31]

This may be because organisations are hesitant to surrender any real degree of decision-making power. Alternatively, they may be complying reluctantly with legislative requirements. Instead, there may be an insidious attempt to 'create the feeling of participation' on the assumption that the perception is as good as the reality if the desired outcomes ensue. Participation becomes nothing more than an internal marketing exercise, with different interest groups of employees forming niche markets for the target communications. Such 'participation' is inauthentic and creates cynicism or worse when the ploy becomes transparent.[32]

Hence *attributions* by employees are likely to be unfavourable towards management unless their experience matches the rhetoric:

- Employees may attribute management's tentative steps towards Partnership to their need to comply with legislation.
- They may infer that management is simply trying to get more work, responsibility and ideas out of them without increasing the support or reward it is prepared to give in return.
- They may note that their influence is limited to suggesting rather than participating in decisions; that it relates only to matters of day-to-day working practice; or that the 'consultation' seems to be occurring after the decision rather than before it.

- They may infer as a consequence that management is unwilling to surrender any of its real power.
- Or they may discern management's focus on the individual rather than on collective representation and come to the same conclusion.[33]

Whatever the attribution of management's motives drawn by employees, the consequent lack of trust is likely to shatter the assumption that Partnership will result in a win–win situation. Indeed, moves towards Partnership can result in Conflict rather than in co-operation. The reason for such a counter-intuitive outcome derives from one of the most fundamental features of the employment relationship: the *interests* of the two parties.

The intention of the Partnership movement is to emphasise the common interests shared by top management and employees. The foremost of these has to be the survival and success of the business. From both management's and employees' perspectives, this is a necessary condition for security of employment and a source of income (unless of course they are capable of getting another job without too much trouble). However there are other interests which may not coincide so neatly. For example, the employee's interest in maintaining their health and their personal relationships may not sit easily with management's desire to enhance productivity by intensifying the work process.

Thus while co-operation is the natural policy for both parties to follow when the focus is on shared interests, *Conflict* is the equally natural order of the day when it is on conflicting ones.[34] There are two ways in which Conflict may arise as a result of participation initiatives. The first is when top management's motive is perceived to be one of control rather than co-operation. Control is normally sought by those wishing to further their own interests at the expense of those of others. Hence employees who perceive an attempt to control them further will have their attention drawn to the conflicts of interest which require this added control to be exercised.

The second cause of Conflict in participation initiatives is what is termed a *dispute of right*. These disputes occur when one or other of the parties is perceived to have broken an agreement. If the rhetoric of Partnership is not matched by the experience, employees will feel in dispute with management. They will see the extended glove of Partnership as concealing the iron hand of control. A perceived contract will have been broken.

Thus there may be conflicts of interest and disputes of right. In modern organisations, these are less likely to take the florid form of strikes and lockouts, pickets and scabs. Rather, discord may evidence itself in absenteeism, sabotage, leaving the organisation, play-acting, or any other of the many forms of resistance which I have described elsewhere. Clearly these expressions of conflict are harmful to both parties. But it is such *expressions* of Conflict as these which are damaging, not the existence of conflict itself. Conflict is inevitable where the interests of parties are not identical, and it is the responsibility of top management to recognise its existence and address it openly (see Chapter 16).

If we look at other sorts of Partnership, it is clear that the way in which conflicts of interest, or indeed, conflicts about courses of action, are normally dealt with is by processes of dialogue and negotiation. If such processes are not available and used, then the imposition of one party's solution at the expense of the other's interest is much more likely. The conflict is likely to be internalised psychologically and privately rather than addressed socially and publicly.

Conflict internalised

The real flip side of the partnership coin is not conflict *per se*. Conflict is inevitable given that interests are not identical. Co-operation characterises the employment relationship where interests are the same, control where they differ. And the attempt to control both signals and engenders Conflict. Rather, the flip side occurs when Conflict is *internalised* in employees' minds.

The decline in union membership and power is a signal of the individualisation of the employment relationship.[35] It is individual employees who perceive themselves as one of the Family, sharing in the Crusade, a member of the Club, having a Contract, being a Resource, being a Citizen, and being a Partner. Hence it is only too easy to internalise conflict into one's own mind when its external expression becomes difficult. It is often very hard as an individual to express the conflict between wanting the organisation to succeed and wanting a life of one's own. Overt expression may result in damage to one's career within the organisation, or at worst loss of one's job in the next round of redundancies on the basis of being 'less than fully committed'.

There are some aspects of Partnership which actively encourage the internalisation of conflict. For example, empowerment often means taking on additional tasks at the behest of different managers so that no-one (except the person themselves) knows the overall workload with which they are tasked.[36] The 'freedom from rigid and constraining job descriptions' makes such overload possible. Again, however, any overt expression of a conflict between the organisation's and the individual's interest could gain them a reputation for lack of commitment.

Another element of empowerment which can result in the individual internalising conflict is the emphasis on *teamworking* by employees manufacturing the product or delivering the service.[37] Teamworking in practice can mean that employees feel that they are letting their workmates down if they fail to deliver the demanding targets set for the team by management. The expectations of significant others in their lives, or their own wellbeing, are in danger of being subordinated.

Furthermore, the internalisation of conflict by employees may damage

Table 9 From Partnership to Conflict

Partnership		Flip	Conflict
Employer:	Participation, shared interests, co-ownership	Rhetoric Retention of power	Assertion of own interest
Employee:	Commitment, quality, improvements	Attributions of motive, cynicism	Disputes, internalisation

them psychologically. If some salient elements of their selves are involved in their organisational commitment, whilst others are implicated in their own interests, there is a danger of overwhelming guilt, or of psychic splitting, or worse.

To conclude, the consideration of the Partnership metaphor has brought us face to face with some of the fundamental issues regarding the employment relationship. For example:

- To what extent are employees' and top management's interests identical?
- What implications does this have for the balance between co-operation and control, the fundamental management dilemma?
- To what extent is today's employment relationship a personal matter between employee and organisational representatives, unmediated by employee representatives?
- And what are the psychological effects upon individuals of these developments?

Table 9 summarises these dilemmas.

Finally, your *metaphor check* for Partnership asks you:

1 Using the scale described on page 92, what is the degree of employee involvement typical of your organisation? Should it be higher or lower if the organisation is to succeed? Why?

2 Consider your most recent employee attitude survey. Were the results fed back? Did any actions result? Were employees informed of these actions? Were the outcomes evaluated?

3 Do you think the top management of your organisation believe that they have the same interests as their employees? Do they act as though they believe it? How do they think and feel about conflict?

4 What was the last occasion of conflict in your organisation? Was it a conflict of interest? What were those interests? Was the conflict of interests acknowledged, and if so, how was it resolved?

References

1 Random House Dictionary (1987) New York: Random House.
2 Marchington, M. (1998) Partnership in context: towards a European model? In

P. Sparrow and M. Marchington (eds) *Human Resource Management: The New Agenda*. London: Financial Times and Pitman.

3 Involvement and Participation Association (1992) *Towards Industrial Partnership*. London: IPA.

4 Poole, M. (1998) Industrial and labour relations. In M. Poole and M. Warner (eds) *Handbook of Human Resource Management*. London: International Thomson Business Press.

5 Strauss, G. (1998) An Overview. In F. Heller, E. Pusic, G. Strauss and B. Wilpert (eds) *Organisational Participation: Myth and Reality*. Oxford: Oxford University Press.

6 Hammer, T. H. (1998) Industrial democracy. In M. Poole and M. Warner (eds) *Handbook of Human Resource Management*. London: International Thomson Business Press.

7 Heckscher, C. and Schurman, S. (1997) Can labour–management cooperation deliver jobs and justice? *Industrial Relations Journal*, 28, 4, 323–330.

8 Guest, D. E. (1997) Towards jobs and justice in Europe: a research agenda. *Industrial Relations Journal*, 28, 4, 344–352.

9 Guest, D. E. and Hoque, K. (1996) The influence of national ownership on human resource management in UK greenfield sites. *Human Resource Management Journal*, 6, 4, 50–74.

10 Ramsey, H. (1997) Fool's gold? European works councils and workplace democracy. *Industrial Relations Journal*, 28, 4, 314–322.

11 Long, R. (1998) Profit sharing and employee shareholding schemes. In M. Poole and M. Warner (eds) *Handbook of Human Resource Management*. London: International Thomson Business Press.

12 Pendleton, A. (1997) Characteristics of workplaces with financial participation: evidence from the Workplace Industrial Relations Survey. *Industrial Relations Journal*, 28, 2, 103–119.

13 Pendleton, A., Wilson, N. and Wright, M. (1998) The perception and effects of share ownership: empirical evidence from employee buy-outs. *British Journal of Industrial Relations*, 36, 1, 99–123.

14 Blyton, P. and Turnbull, P. (1998) *The Dynamics of Employee Relations* (2nd edn). London: Macmillan.

15 Marchington, M. (1995) Involvement and participation. In J. Storey (ed.) *Human Resource Management: A Critical Text*. London: International Thomson Business Press.

16 Blyton and Turnbull (op. cit.).

17 Poole, M. and Jenkins, G. (1996) *Back to the Line? A Survey of Managers' Attitudes to Human Resource Management Issues*. London: Institute of Management.

18 Marchington (op. cit.).

19 Huczynski, A. A. (1993) Explaining the succession of management fads. *International Journal of Human Resource Management*, 4, 2, 443–464.

20 Walton, R. (1990) From control to commitment in the workplace. *Harvard Business Review*, 90, 2, 89–106.

21 Wilkinson, A. (1998) Empowerment. In M. Poole and M. Warner (eds) *Handbook of Human Resource Management*. London: International Thomson Business Press.

22 Pfeffer, J. (1994) *Competitive Advantage Through People*. Boston MA: Harvard Business School Press.

23 Huselid, M. A. (1995) The impact of human resource management practices on turnover, productivity, and corporate financial performance. *Academy of Management Journal*, 38, 3, 635–672.

24 Cunningham, I., Hyman, J. and Baldry, C. (1996) Empowerment: the power to do what? *Industrial Relations Journal*, 27, 2, 143–154.

25 Strauss, G. (1998) Participation works – if conditions are appropriate. In F. Heller, E. Pusic, G. Strauss and B. Wilpert (eds) *Organisational Participation: Myth and Reality*. Oxford: Oxford University Press.

26 Guest, D. and Peccei, R. (1998) *The Partnership Company: Benchmarks for the Future*. London: Involvement and Partnership Association.

27 Sako, M. (1998) The nature and impact of employee 'voice' in the European car components industry. *Human Resource Management Journal*, 8, 2, 5–13.

28 Heller, F. (1993) The under-utilisation of human resources in industrial relations theory and practice. *International Journal of Human Resource Management*, 4, 3, 631–644.

29 Fernie, S. and Metcalf, D. (1995) Participation, contingent pay, representation, and workplace performance: Evidence from Great Britain. *British Journal of Industrial Relations*. 33, 3, 379–415.

30 Heller, F. (1998) Playing the devil's advocate: Limits to influence sharing in theory and practice. In F. Heller, E. Pusic, G. Strauss and B. Wilpert (eds) *Organisational Participation: Myth and Reality*. Oxford: Oxford University Press.

31 IDE Research Team (1981) *Industrial Democracy in Europe*; (1993) *Industrial Democracy in Europe Revisited*. Oxford: Oxford University Press.

32 Heller (op. cit.).

33 Wilkinson, A., Marchington, M., Goodman, J. and Ackers, P. (1993) Refashioning industrial relations: The experience of a chemical company over the last decade. *Personnel Review*, 22, 3, 22–38.

34 Edwards, P. K. (1998) Industrial conflict. In M. Poole and M. Warner (eds) *Handbook of Human Resource Management*. London: International Thomson Business Press.

35 Purcell, J. (1998) Employee relations, management of. In M. Poole and M. Warner (eds) *Handbook of Human Resource Management*. London: International Thomson Business Press.

36 Kunda, G. (1992) *Engineering Culture*. Philadelphia PA: Temple University Press.

37 Garrahan, P. and Stewart, P. (1992) *The Nissan Enigma: Flexibility at Work in a Local Economy*. London: Mansell.

Chapter 8

Customer and Rip-off

Consumerism rampant

Today even death is a consumer event. So permeated are our lives with the role of consumer that an event such as the death of Princess Diana is packaged for us. We can then consume it and make all the appropriate responses. Sold a spurious sense of personal relationship and intimacy, we are then given the appropriate models for our grief to take. We place flowers in piles, cry visibly, and feel a common bond of grief with total strangers. Those who refuse to buy the package are castigated as unfeeling and inhuman.

The same applies to those areas of experience previously considered so sensitive that they were not supposed to intrude into polite conversation: politics, religion, and sex. Each is packaged for our consumption by spin doctors, tele-evangelists and advertisers. Each is turned into a commodity, whereas in its authentic form it is a relationship.

The most audacious commodification of them all is that of our selves.[1] Various media sources and other expressions of our culture not only urge us to engage in a makeover of our appearance. They want us to reinvent our very selves as well. They seek to sell us new personas to try on and see how they fit. Just as politicians and stars of film and television reinvent themselves, so we too are supposed to become someone new. Our selves are to become our favourite project.

In a business-obsessed culture where everything has its price, there is only one really worthwhile self to cultivate: self as business, Me plc.[2] What product are we offering? Who is our Customer? How can we best market and sell our selves? Who can we benchmark our selves against? How can we research and develop our selves? How should we best manage our selves? The social world is seen as a market-place, and our self is both a business and a commodity, runs the newly marketised but age-old self-improvement message. The American Dream is alive and well, and reappears repackaged yet again.[3]

It would have been miraculous if consumerism had not provided a metaphor for the employment relationship, and indeed that miracle has failed to happen. Employee as *Customer* is one of the favourite metaphors of today's rhetoric, especially, as one might expect, in the retail sector.

There is potentially, as usual, a shiny top side to the metaphor. In a recent attempt to broaden the Anglo-American obsession with the shareholder as the only real stakeholder in a business, customers, employees, and the community have been incorporated as *stakeholders* too.[4] Metrics such as the Balanced Business Scorecard have been developed to ensure that outcomes other than shareholder dividends are monitored and rewarded. Employees are seen as equally important to the business as customers and shareholders; indeed they may sometimes be all three at the same time if they buy from their own company and own shares in it.

Cynics may argue that this sudden concern for employees was due to the manifest absurdity of asking employees to treat the customer as king when they themselves were being treated as wage slaves! Be that as it may, the development of balanced business scorecards and the like is an attempt by large corporations to recognise their wider responsibilities. Accepting the current mistaken but nearly universal assumption that if you can't measure it, it doesn't exist, such metrics are necessary to demonstrate a value placed upon employees and others.

Moreover, there is a business logic at work here. Much research by organisations seeks to establish what customers want. In particular, customers are interrogated about what they expect from employees. Organisations can then work out what employees need in order to meet these customer expectations. The *support* offered by the organisation may take the form of resources of one sort or another: learning opportunities, tailored systems, supportive supervisors, employee assistance programmes, or merely permission to be more flexible in their dealings with customers. Some organisations (e.g. Centrica) are beginning to put together a one-stop-shop support service for front-line employees. This is an employee assistance programme which goes far beyond the traditional meaning of this phrase.

Organisations which take this logic through to such a conclusion are, however, few and far between at present. Many use the language of *employee* as Customer in recognition that employees need support if they are to meet customers' expectations as far as is reasonable and good for business. However, they fail to explore what real practical support would involve, let alone provide it, and the metaphor becomes cheapened.

Employee as customer

It is but a small step from calling employees Customers because they need support in dealing with the real customers to calling them *internal business Customers*. As soon as this apparently small step is taken, however, the whole armoury of marketing concepts and techniques comes into play. Employees are marketed to, and the employment relationship becomes another branch of the marketing profession. They are persuaded that they have this need, or that they should view the organisation's situation in that way. They are surveyed to find out what they are likely to want and how they might react to an offer. The employee 'market' is then segmented, so that policies and practices can be tailored and 'sold' to each segment, whilst hopefully retaining an overall 'employer brand'.[5] In sum, employees are treated as though they are Customers to be presented with a choice to make; and employee communications becomes no more than an internal marketing exercise.

And this 'choice' (provided it is the 'right' one) will enhance the self and enlarge the identity. For employees who do 'buy into' their organisation will be able to identify their selves with its success.[6] If employees have defined their selves as businesses, then this is indeed a successful joint venture. They are in business in the corporation on their own behalf. Their own business success then derives not only from the success of the organisation as a whole, but more especially from those bits of it of which they can take ownership. A corporate culture, a major project, a product launch, all can be seen as acquisitions to their own 'business'; for all will bring them greater 'business' success. Hence added tasks come to be construed as entrepreneurial business successes; they are business which they have brought in for themselves.

But of course, internal Customers can become suppliers of services to other internal Customers. And as we all know, to succeed in business we have to treat the customer as king. So the pressure is on to delight our internal Customer as we get ourselves more internal 'business'.[7]

The Consumer metaphor is perhaps the most audacious of all our metaphors; after all, if anyone is a Customer within the employment relationship, it is the organisation purchasing the labour of the employee. The transformation from a benign view of employees as stakeholders in the business to the total engagement of their every moment in 'their own' business is one of the slickest conceptual conjuring tricks ever invented. Its results, when it comes off, must make cost-conscious top managements extremely happy, as in the following example:

> A store manageress regularly came in to work on Sundays, when the store was shut, bringing her boyfriend with her. Their purpose was not to make secret love in the aisles, but rather to do all of the tasks which the company would not pay to be done by the appropriate craftsmen. So her boyfriend and his brother-in-law sawed down the new cash desk to size and installed it on the floor; put fitting-room curtains up; and painted departmental panels. Why? 'I get so upset when it's not done, because I feel personally responsible. . . . I kept thinking they were judging me on it so it just became something that had to be done. It drove me barmy, so I asked my boyfriend. . . .'[8]

'Customers' ripped-off

The successful use of the customer metaphor to tie in employees to this astonishing degree actually depends upon the confluence of three different rhetorical streams. There is the *commercial* or *business rhetoric*, which assumes that every social context is a market, and therefore every action within it is a business action. There is the *self-reliance rhetoric*, which argues that each of us is on our own in this market, and there is no-one we can trust but ourselves. Hence we are 'in business for ourselves'. And there is the *Customer/Consumer rhetoric*, which insists that we treat everyone else as a demanding customer, and should expect to be so treated ourselves. Hence when we, in business for ourselves, deal with others, we should treat them well since they are our customer.

These three rhetorical streams have come to pervade our lives; they fill our waking consciousness. The platform announcer at the railway station calls us customers rather than passengers. We are urged to create our own web site on the Internet so as to market ourselves better. And if we are to succeed in our business enterprise, then we have to provide superlative service; we have to delight *our* customer. When the 'Customer' is our employer, then the circle is complete and there is no way out.

In their own way the Crusade and the Partnership metaphors tie in with the Customer rhetoric. In the Crusade, we are all on this huge enterprise together, an enterprise frequently characterised as providing uniquely excellent service to the customer. A delighted customer who returns time and again is the Holy Grail, the pursuit of which is the inspiring vision that spurs us all on. The Partnership metaphor, too, ties in neatly with the Customer rhetoric. Partners are in business together. In a sense, they each have their own business, which they are combining in order to maximise resources and effort, and therefore outcomes. Hence they need to serve each other well.

Yet just as the Crusade and Partnership metaphors frequently flip on to their downside, often suddenly and with a loud crash, so too Customers may realise that they have been taken for a ride. The whole thing has been one huge Rip-off. For Crusaders the light may have suddenly dawned when they realised that their leader was in it for baser motives than he or she pretended. For Partners, the risk, effort, and commitment may have been shared, but the profits certainly weren't. For Customers, the business relationship turns out to be all one way. It is they who are providing the service, and it isn't always to the real customer. It finally dawns upon them that they are serving the interests of top management rather than their own.

In all three metaphors, the realisation is likely to be sudden. The significance of a particular event suddenly becomes apparent, and the rhetorical bubble is pricked. The leader of the Crusade is caught out corrupting the vision. Top management as Partner takes a hugely disproportionate share of the end-of-year profits for itself. Top managers as Customers set impossibly increased targets, whilst employees as Customers are given minimal support as they desperately seek to meet them.

Reactions to these eye-opening events are likely to be highly emotionally charged. The first reaction of employee as Customer is likely to be one of anger at being Ripped-off. This feeling is, after all, what consumers are supposed to experience, since as customers we are entitled to expect only the best. The second reaction is the realisation that we have allowed ourselves to be taken for a ride, and the injured pride and self-esteem that that realisation brings. And the third, delayed, reaction may be of regret at the loss of our ambitions and of our sunk costs. As with the flip side of all the other metaphors, it is the emotional reactions which are likely to affect the employment relationship most profoundly.

People, relationships, and commerce

The overwhelming power of the streams of rhetoric, and the obvious relevance of the other metaphors, indicate the extent to which the concepts and values of the consumer, commerce, and the marketplace have permeated the whole of our language. One outcome of this trend has frequently been remarked upon. It is the assumption that every organisation is a business, and that market principles should therefore always apply. Everything is a product which is consumed, including health, education, social services, and government. The provision of services by public sector organisations has arguably suffered as a consequence.

However, there is another more profound consequence of the consumer revolution and the commercialisation of everything. This outcome lies embedded within organisations. It is the commercialisation of every part of the organisation and its activities, including all of the people elements of organisational life. The use of the Customer metaphor to describe the employment relationship is but one instance of this commercial imperialism.

Yet this conceptual and linguistic conquest is highly damaging. It requires us to talk about people and their relationships in business terms only. By reducing the very process of organising to the operations of the market place, it removes at a stroke most of the rich understanding of people and their relationships with which our language and social experience provide us. Fortunately for organisations, the triumph of commerce-speak is more in the public and rhetorical arenas than at grass roots levels. There, the importance of people and their relationships in getting things done together (which is, after all, the purpose of organising) is usually recognised.

It is therefore appropriate that the highly commercial Customer metaphor is the concluding chapter in the first part of this book. For I will argue in the remaining two parts that it is because fundamental aspects of people and their relationships have been downplayed in the employment relationship

Table 10 From Customer to Rip-off

Customer		Flip	Rip-off
Employer:	Stakeholder	Internal	Overstretch
	Support	Marketing	Abuse
Employee:	Initiative	Consumer	See through
	Identification	Total engagement	Anger, regret

that the shiny top side of our eight metaphors so often flips over to the downside. See the summary of the flip from Customer to Rip-off in Table 10.

Finally, a brief *metaphor check*. How dominated by market-speak and the language of consumerism is your organisation? In particular, to what extent are employees spoken of, and spoken to, as though they were Customers?

- Do top managers speak of 'selling' something, such as a policy change, to employees?
- Do your external marketers also manage internal communications?
- Has your organisation introduced a Balanced Business Scorecard?
- How has your organisation recently improved the support which it provides for customer-facing staff?
- Does your organisation have an internal billing procedure? What are its costs and benefits?
- Have you recently felt Ripped-off as a 'Customer' of your organisation? In what way? How did you feel about it?

References

1 du Gay, P. (1996) *Consumption and Identity at Work*. London: Sage.
2 Bridges, W. (1995) *Jobshift: How to Prosper in a Workplace without Jobs*. London: Nicholas Brealey.
3 Guest, D. E. (1990) Human resource management and the American Dream. *Journal of Management Studies*, 27, 4, 378–397.
4 Hutton, W. (1994) *The State We're In*. London: Jonathan Cape.
5 Hales, C. (1994) Internal marketing as an approach to human resource management: a new perspective, or a metaphor too far? *Human Resource Management Journal*, 5, 1, 50–71.
6 Willmott, H. (1993) Strength is ignorance; slavery is freedom: Managing culture in modern organisations. *Journal of Management Studies*, 30, 4, 515–552.
7 Garrahan, P. and Stewart, P. (1992) *The Nissan Enigma: Flexibility at Work in a Local Economy*. London: Mansell.
8 du Gay, op. cit., p. 163.

Introduction to Parts 2 and 3

The coin on its edge

By now you may be feeling somewhat let down. Most management books are relentlessly upbeat. They provide uplifting accounts of top managers or other organisational heroes who have led their organisations to outstanding success. They outline the way in which this has been done, and imply that readers can enjoy the same success if they follow the same methods. This genre has come to be known as the *excellence* literature, after the 1982 blockbuster by Peters and Waterman, *In Search of Excellence*.[1] Activist Anglo-Americans favour the approach of looking to see how it's been done elsewhere and then trying to do it themselves. Others have typically been somewhat more cautious.

On the other hand there exists another genre, which we might term the *oppression* literature. This comes from some academics, who offer a radical critique of organisational life derived from political, philosophical and sociological theory. This literature is written for other academics and for students, and it is highly unlikely to appeal to practising managers. Whilst the excellence literature is relentlessly upbeat, looking only at the top side of our metaphors, the oppression literature is equally resolutely downbeat, painting a gloomy picture of an unrelieved flip side.

So while the preceding chapters may have appeared pessimistic, balancing the top side with the flip side, they hopefully do some justice to our messy experience. And that experience surely encompasses both sides of the coin. For some the top side is their predominant experience, and, unsurprisingly, these fortunate people are more likely to be located higher up the organisation. For others, particularly those at the bottom and/or with flexible contracts, the flip side may dominate. For many more, the coin may balance infuriatingly on its edge, periodically falling on to one side or the other. Such a mixture of experience is entirely to be expected, if we accept that the employment relationship itself is an ambiguous and delicately balanced combination of control and co-operation.

However, there are far more potent drivers than books, even those written by famous gurus; and the most potent of them all is *experience*. Your own working experience may force you to take a resolutely upbeat stance. You have to believe that the next innovative management intervention will achieve its purpose; or, at least, you have to pretend to believe in it for public consumption.[2] For although you may have had little say in its choice and development, you will certainly be held responsible for its successful implementation. You may suspect that 'taking our people with us' requires more than a series of managerial innovations. You may feel that the overall quality of the relationship between management and employees is the real requirement for survival and success. But unless you put on a relentlessly optimistic and can-do performance, your organisational commitment and leadership abilities come into question. The consequence is that you act as though the top side wins out every time. You clearly recognise the existence of the flip side as well, but you keep that realisation to yourself.

However, the proper understanding of the employment relationship depends upon the acknowledgement that both sides of the coin exist in juxtaposition. So, therefore, does any attempt to improve that relationship.

A review of our metaphors in the first eight chapters suggests that there is a constant danger of the balance between control and co-operation being lost. Management needs to exercise control, since it wants its own interests to win out over those of employees where these do not coincide. However, it also needs to enlist the co-operation of employees to achieve its purposes.[3] Each metaphor demonstrates the potential to fall on to its flip side when too much control is exercised, and this is particularly true of those metaphors which are strongly co-operative in tone. So, for example, the Partnership metaphor promises co-operation and collaboration, yet management has usually been unwilling to surrender enough power to make true collaboration possible. The Contract metaphor implies mutually agreed obligations, but the supposed mutuality often consists of an offer which the employee cannot refuse. Alternatively, management subsequently unilaterally reneges on the deal.

In the case of other metaphors, control is exercised in order to engineer cooperation. So the Crusade and Customer metaphors are attempts to persuade employees to internalise the purposes of management. Power is exercised through the control of culture; the winning of hearts and minds has superseded direct supervisory control. Employees now 'control' themselves; external supervision has become internal monitoring.

The uses and users of metaphors

This takes us on to a question I have hitherto largely avoided: who uses metaphors, and what are their purposes in doing so? For metaphors do not exist in isolation, either floating around somewhere out there in the organisational ether, or locked inside the heads of individuals. They are rather part of the conversations that permeate organisational life. Indeed, some commentators would even define organisations as sets of conversations.[4]

In the Introduction, I suggested that the fundamental purpose of metaphor is to help people understand and express their *experience* of one situation in the light of another, which they understand better. The key situation is the employment relationship, and the metaphors are many and varied, although they are all in terms of some other relationship. People may express their experience in terms of the top side or of the flip side, and we require convincing evidence if we are to deny the authenticity of both of these forms of expression. The preachers of excellence have a hard task in arguing that all downbeat expressions are in some sense bogus or untrue, the products of a few bad apples in the organisational barrel. But the doom merchants of oppression have the same difficulties with affirmations by employees of the top side of the coin. Both are arrogant if they assume that all such expressions are false representations of employees' experience.

However, people may use the eight metaphors for other purposes than the attempt to understand and express their experience of the employment relationship. They may, for example, use them to express their *aspirations* for that relationship. Employees may use the Family metaphor to describe the degree of care and consideration they would like to receive from their employer. Top management in many professional firms would love them to become really convivial Clubs again, in which everyone felt comfortable and confident in their colleagues' competence. Human resource professionals in many large organisations aspire to having employees treated as valued Resources to be nurtured and developed rather than as costs to be cut. Unfortunately, one of the dangers of aspirations and prescriptions is that it becomes easy to confuse the aspiration for the experience. We want them to be true so much that in the end we ignore the gap between where we are and where we would like to be. Company Annual Reports, for example, frequently present aspirations for the employment relationship as descriptions of reality.

A third common purpose of metaphor is to persuade. Its use, in other words, is *rhetorical*, where rhetoric is defined as the attempt to persuade others to perceive their experience in the way in which the user of rhetoric wishes them to perceive it. It is no accident that leaders down the ages have used metaphor as their rhetorical stock in trade. For the provision of a metaphor allows the listener or reader to give a meaning to their experience in terms of other experiences with which they are familiar and about which they feel strongly. Where the situation is ambiguous, as it is in the employment relationship, such metaphors can help people make some simple sense out of what is inherently complex. But in this case, instead of generating metaphors for themselves out of their own experience, employees are provided with them by management. And top management's own purposes determine which metaphors it chooses. It may, for example, feel that only if it captures the imagination and enthusiasm of all of its employees does it stand a chance of prospering, so it talks in terms of a Crusade.

One of the signs that a particular use of metaphor is rhetorical is its simplicity. If the employment relationship within an organisation is always represented as a Crusade, or as a Family, or as a Club, we begin to suspect a rhetorical purpose. For we all know that our individual experience is complex and messy. Sometimes when a senior colleague gives us some valuable help we can think of it as a Club, whilst on other occasions the imposition of impossible targets leads us to view it as nothing short of tyranny, the flip side of citizenship. Likewise, we are fully aware that within most organisations, our own included, the employment relationship is highly segmented. Some employees enjoy Club privileges and are consistently treated as valuable Resources with whom Contracts have to be made and kept. Others feel themselves to be Outsiders, Discards, and subject to the law of the Jungle. Thus the rhetorical use of metaphor is revealed by an excessive simplicity and a failure to reflect the complexity of our own and others' experience. Rhetoric deals in all or nothing, either or; messy experience consists in both, and with a strong hint of maybe.

Now rhetorical attempts at persuasion can result in changed behaviour for three different reasons.[5] People may *comply*, because they see that the other party has the whip hand. They may *identify* with the persuader, and change their behaviour because they wish to follow them. Or they may be persuaded by the influence attempt, and *internalise* the words, and the beliefs and values which they represent, into their own minds. The fourth and final use of metaphor, then, is to *induce employees to act* according to management's wishes, preferably because they have internalised the view of the employment relationship provided for them. Taking the Crusade metaphor as an example again, employees may pretend to go along with it and play at being Crusaders because they have no other choice; they may comply. Or they may identify with the charismatic leader who uses the metaphor so effectively, and be willing to follow him or her (but only him or her) to the ends of the earth. Or they may come to actually believe in the vision and values of the Crusade and become true Crusaders. Of course, to determine whether this latter belief is 'authentic' is not an easy task; but if we find a somewhat overblown metaphor in universal and tiresomely repeated use throughout an organisation, we may have justifiable suspicions that it is not.

As I argued above, different types of employee tend to use more of the top side or more of the flip side of the metaphors when they are seeking to describe their experience, even within the same organisation. Organisations are often so segmented in terms of the employment relationship that experiences could not be more different.[6] The graduate fast tracker may be treated like royalty, the temporary word processor like dirt. Moreover, different types of employee may use the metaphors for predominantly different purposes. Aspirational and rhetorical uses may be favoured more by senior management; experiential and internalised ones by those lower down the organisational hierarchy. These differences in the uses of metaphor are, of course, not accidental. They reflect the distribution of power within the organisation, and in particular the use of that power to exercise managerial control and induce employee co-operation.

A psychological approach

So what are we to conclude? That the employment relationship is a unique product of capitalist society, representing a unique challenge to management? After all, to maintain control whilst fostering co-operation is a demanding task, even when management holds far greater power. Indeed, a large power differential may not be the advantage that it appears to be at first sight, since the temptation to use that power to coerce employees may be irresistible, but is ultimately self-defeating. This is the position taken by most writers about the employment relationship. They demonstrate the ways in which the social, economic, political, institutional and cultural differences between nations moderate the ways in which organisations conduct the employment relationship. They are suitably wary of making broad generalisations and of engaging in general prescriptions, even within nations or organisational sectors. Some go so far as to claim that all generalisations do unacceptable injustice to the richness of individual examples.[7]

I will take a diametrically opposite position. I will argue in the rest of this book that the employment relationship is but one of many human relationships. My emphasis will be on the employment *relationship* rather than on the *employment* relationship. It is no accident that the metaphors which people use to describe it are taken from a range of other relationships. For there are certain features of human relationships which apply more generally across the board. The employment relationship may appear uniquely difficult to manage and to experience, but there are other equally difficult relationships which we could all cite. The histories and current contexts of the employment relationship may differ across nations, but there are equally different contexts for other relationships. Fundamentally different cultural assumptions about people, such as whether human activity is basically individual or collective,[8] may result in different views of the employment relationship; but these fundamental differences permeate all relationships. A *psychological understanding of the employment relationship depends upon the understanding of relationships first and of employment second.*

I have, after all, invoked several psychological explanations already. The Family metaphor is permeated with psychoanalysis and developmental psychology. The exclusivity of the Club was analysed in terms of the theory of inter-group relations. The fundamental element of the Citizenship metaphor was people's perceptions of justice and equity. Whatever local forms the employment relationship takes, there are certain fundamental social psychological principles of which all such forms must take account. And these principles are not unique to the employment relationship. Rather, they are apparent in other relationships too. Hence, rather than the employment relationship being an esoteric field for experts, it is likely that we all appreciate its fundamentals. For we have all developed an intuitive psychological understanding of how relationships in general work.

However, the most powerful indications that a psychological approach is fundamental to understanding and managing the employment relationship are, once again, the metaphors that people use to describe it. Each of the metaphors points to a basic psychological need which the employment relationship is capable in principle of meeting:

- *Family* implies the need for *security* and *care*
- *Crusade* points to *purpose* and *meaning*
- *Club* emphasises *belonging*
- *Contract* is about *reciprocity* and *mutuality*
- *Resource* signals *being valued*
- *Democracy* and *citizenship* refer to *the expectation of justice*
- *Partnership* indicates *shared interests*
- *Customer* implies *service* and *choice*

In Part 2, Chapters 9 to 12, I will seek to establish what these psychological fundamentals are, whilst taking due account of the immense cultural differences in social behaviour in general and in the employment relationship in particular. For the fundamental elements of relationships are expressed in practice in profoundly different ways in different cultures and different organisations, and different people respond in different ways. My fundamental argument will be that relationships invariably both affect and are affected by the selves of the parties involved. The reason why so many employees experience the flip side rather than the top side of the metaphors is because selves are largely ignored in today's employment relationship. I will propose that the only proper process for any relationship, including the employment relationship, is one of dialogue.

Thus Part 2 is about trying to understand the employment relationship in particular from the perspective of a psychological understanding of relationships in general.

In Part 3, Chapters 13 to 16, I will seek to outline some of the key areas in which dialogue will need to occur. I will outline the reasons why three topics for dialogue are particularly important for the immediate future of the employment relationship: the *compliance* dialogue, in which the need for compliance from most of their employees will have to be argued by top management; the *difference* dialogue, in which they will have to explain why people within the company are treated so differently from each other; and the *change* dialogue, where changes initiated will need to be justified. Finally, and most important of all, the conditions for the establishment of dialogue in organisations are described, together with some of the changes which will have to be made if these conditions are to be set up and dialogue is to occur. The solution, I will argue, is essentially a *political* one.

References

1 Peters, T. J. and Waterman, R. H. (1982) *In Search of Excellence: Lessons from America's Best Run Companies*. New York: Harper and Row.
2 Knights, D. and McCabe, D. (1998) 'The times they are a changin'? Transformative organisational innovations in financial services in the UK. *International Journal of Human Resource Management*, 9, 1, 168–184.
3 Blyton, P. and Turnbull, P. (1998) *The Dynamics of Employee Relations* (2nd edn). London: Macmillan Business.
4 Broekstra, G. (1998) An organisation is a conversation. In D. Grant, T. Keenoy and C. Oswick (eds) *Discourse and Organisation*. London: Sage.
5 Aronson, E. (1981) *The Social Animal* (3rd edn). San Francisco: Jossey Bass.
6 Hirsh, W. and Jackson, C. (1996) *Strategies for Career Development: Promise, Practice and Pretence*. Brighton: Institute for Employment Studies, Report 305.
7 Grant, D., Keenoy, T. and Oswick, C. (1998) Introduction: Organisational discourse: Of diversity, dichotomy, and multi-disciplinarity. In D. Grant, T. Keenoy and C. Oswick (eds) *Discourse and Organisation*. London: Sage.
8 Triandis, H. C. (1995) *Individualism and Collectivism*. Boulder CO: Westview Press.

Part 2

Relationship psychology

Chapter 9

Relationships and the self

Selves are social

For far too long, economists' untested assumptions about people have dominated discussions and policies regarding the employment relationship. People in general, we have been told, are essentially shirkers, who will avoid work (which they find unpleasant) if they possibly can. And they are opportunists, rationally milking every situation to enhance their own interests.[1, 2] What does a psychological approach have to offer instead of these misleading generalisations?

The most fundamental difference is that psychologists do not discuss the employment relationship in terms of individual actors maximising their personal advantage in a social vacuum. Rather, theirs is an essentially social analysis, in which the employment relationship is no different from other relationships in its essential features. Psychologists insist that *our relationships are between our selves and others*.

You may be tempted to respond to this last sentence that whilst economists may be wrong, psychologists are merely banal. Yet the statement is more complex than it appears at first sight. A clue lies in the separation of the words 'our' and 'selves'. For the social psychologist, relationships are an ongoing process. They are not between two separate and independent parties, the individual and others, as common sense and our language would seem to indicate. Rather, both parties are partly defined by their relationship with the other.

Thus 'the individual' is not the independent actor mysteriously pre-programmed to maximise his or her own interests assumed by economists. Rather, individuals are people who use their notions of themselves to organise their understanding of the world and their actions. And these self-concepts are derived from their relationships with others. 'Individuals' construct their selves largely on the basis of how they perceive others reacting to them. Likewise these 'others' are not separate and out there. Rather, their influence upon the individual's self is exercised only through the individual's perceptions of them.[3, 4]

To put some flesh on to these somewhat abstract propositions, let us return to our metaphors. If employees perceive their current employment relationship to be like a Family, then it is likely that they will have the notion of being securely cared for as part of their self-concept. If the reverse is true, and their various dealings with their employer degenerate in their view into a family Feud, then they may well construe themselves as abandoned and insecure. Similar consequences for the self can be inferred from the other metaphors and their flip sides, as follows:

- Crusades persuade them that they have a vision, whereas Playing at soldiers makes them realise they are cynics
- Belonging to a Club gives them a clear social identity, but exclusion makes them feel Outsiders
- As Contractors with their employers they are proudly independent actors who exchange mutual obligations; out there in the lawless chaos, they are animals at risk in the social Darwinian Jungle
- If they are valued human Resources, their self-esteem goes up a notch or three; treated as used-up Discards, it plumbs the depths
- As Citizens, they see themselves as having a right to justice and equity; overpowered or outflanked, they become Prisoners or wage slaves
- Proud Partners have a share in the enterprise; Conflicted former partners often end up as mutual victims
- Customers perceive themselves as having a choice; deceived customers realise they are being Ripped off.

So for all the eight metaphors, the experience of the top and the flip sides has an impact upon the selves of the parties. The top sides tend to enhance the self, providing purpose, identity, and self-esteem; the flip sides provide less welcome identities and usually damage self-esteem. The fundamental point is that the parties' selves both affect, and also are affected by, their ongoing employment relationship. However much we may wish to represent employment as a rational and limited contract, our experience tells us that it is more often a highly emotive relationship in which our selves are intimately involved. For wherever selves are involved, emotions are heightened. Our employer may require us to do something which conflicts with our values; or we may find that our self-esteem has been enhanced as a result of completing a difficult project with which we had been entrusted. In both cases the self is involved; and where the self is involved, emotions are stirred.

What are our selves for?

So what is the nature of our selves? How does our self develop from our relationships? And of what elements does it consist? These questions need answering, but as posed above, they carry dangerously misleading connotations. The self-concept is not a construction in the sense that it is a permanent and completed psychic building made up of fixed blocks or elements. Rather, it is a *functional mental model* which we are continuously developing, and in which the elements frequently change their salience and sometimes their identity. Ask yourself how you would have responded five years ago to the request to write down the first five words that occurred to you to complete the sentence 'I am a . . .'. Now complete the sentence for today.

True, there are all sorts of ways in which we seek to defend and preserve our existing self-concept against the evidence with which others provide us (particularly if that evidence does not boost our self-esteem). But unless we adapt it to a degree, it will cease to perform its functions.

These functions are the things that make us human. We desperately search for *meaning* in our experience. Our eight metaphors for the employment relationship are just one attempt to find meaning. We are inveterate searchers after explanations, and have developed a complex framework of attributions to help us do so.[5] We seize upon the obvious explanation with glee if it is foolish enough to make itself conspicuous. We maintain our equilibrium and self-esteem by attributing good outcomes to our own qualities and bad ones to the rest of the world. We do not act as disinterested scientists when looking for explanations, for our concern is not usually to come to a disinterested conclusion. Rather we are searching for a meaning that enables us to tell ourselves and others a consistent story about events, especially when they are contrary to our expectations or threaten an important relationship.[6] New meanings and new stories, which we may develop on our own or in collaboration with others, may well change our mental frameworks. And that includes our self-concept.

This emphasis on meaning, and the stories which encapsulate it, directs our attention to the importance of *language* in forming and developing our selves. The symbolic nature of language makes it possible for the experience of others as well as our own to help to form our notion of our selves.[7] We are not dependent entirely upon social relationships in the here and now. Rather we can draw upon the knowledge, history and myths of others as they are passed on to us. My national identity, for example, is not based solely on how people of other nationalities react to me as a British person. It is based more upon a history and mythology passed on to me in a variety of symbolic ways.

Moreover, the social account of the development of the self does not argue against individual uniqueness. We each have engaged in our social relationships from a unique perspective, or point of view.[8] Such a point of view is a result of our genetic make-up, our social situation and our history of mutual obligations and commitments. So although our concept of our selves changes as a result of our social experiences and relationships, it is embedded in a unique personal history and biology which gives us a core of continuity. It is this core self which gives us a perspective on our experience from which we can give it a meaning.

But why do we search for meaning and explanation? Why do we have to make sense of our experience, and why do we so castigate postmodernist thinkers who resolutely refuse to do so? The answer may be that we seek not only to understand the past and the present, but also to predict the future. And we need to engage in this latter activity because we seek some degree of *control* over what happens to us.[9] If we can estimate what is going to happen, we can anticipate and prepare for it and thus moderate its effect upon us. Indeed, so motivated are we to maintain our view of ourselves as in charge of our lives that we vigorously defend our freedom of choice if we perceive it to be threatened.[10] We may, however, have largely lost that control element of our self-concept, if our experience has revealed little relationship between our actions and our outcomes. The Ethiopian suffering his fifth successive year's drought, or the American made redundant on each successive restructuring may both, in different degrees, experience this disconnect. They have both learned to see themselves as helpless.[11]

Some elements of the self

Our self-concept is the foundation for our sense of our ability to act so as to control what happens to us, and for any feeling of security that ensues. How does it succeed (or fail) in this function? One fundamental element in our self-concept is our *identity* (or rather, our identities). We perceive ourselves to be members of a variety of social categories, for example a family, an organisation, a gender, an occupation, a religion, a nation, a social class, or an ethnic group.[12] Our perception of ourselves as members needs to be shared by other members who are willing to include us; it needs, in other words to derive from relationships. Otherwise it is likely to be challenged by others' behaviour towards us. Literature is replete, for example, with 'social upstarts' being 'put in their proper place'.

Elements of our identities may be more or less salient. For some women, their identity as women is highly salient, whereas for others that of occupation or relationship is far more so. Moreover, different identities may become salient for us in different situations. Identity as woman may gain in relevance in a working environment where most people are men; identity as mother when family crisis hits.

The fundamental point, however, is that the identities that are incorporated into our self-concept enable us to make sense of our experience and perhaps to feel more in control of it. By incorporating social categories into our selves we feel ourselves supported by that membership, and evaluate ourselves more highly. We gain status. Gay Pride, for example, enabled those with a gay identity to challenge perceived prejudice and win greater control over their lives. Which brings us to a second profoundly important element of the self: our *self-worth*. Self-esteem refers to our general evaluation of ourselves; self-efficacy[13] to our beliefs about our capacity to succeed in particular situations. Both forms of self-evaluation are crucial to our capacity to feel in control. We are, again, dependent upon others for these elements of the self. However, we may defend or enhance our self-worth ourselves by:

- searching out those who will enhance it
- avoiding experiences where it might be damaged
- rationalising away any evidence which threatens it.

Perhaps the most important feature of our self-concept, however, is its *reflexivity*. We are aware of our selves, literally 'self-conscious'. Consequently we can monitor our own behaviour and our relationships,[14] and see how consistent they are with our view of ourselves, our values and beliefs. We can examine these same values, beliefs, attitudes, and aspirations, and ask ourselves whether they are consistent with each other. We can reflect upon our level of self-esteem, and ask ourselves how justified it is when we compare ourselves with others. We can reflect upon our relationships and represent them to ourselves, for example as metaphors. And we can even consciously seek to create new selves for ourselves,[15, 16] since we can compare our past and present selves and imagine new and different ones.

So the self-concept is profoundly important for our survival and happiness as human beings. It is primarily derived from our past and present relationships with others, and at the same time it impacts upon the relationships which we enter and maintain. This two-way commerce may well be unequal. For example, a mother's responses to her young child may affect the child's self-concept much more than the child's expression of himself or herself affects the relationship with his mother. Or, vice versa, an accountant who has changed her employer a dozen times may well find that her view of herself is not affected in the least by her thirteenth employer's treatment of her. But her self-concept as an independent and experienced professional who will take no nonsense may profoundly affect her relationship with that employer. Whatever the balance of influence, relationships with others and individuals' self-concepts are inextricably bound up together within the same continuing and dynamic social process.

Relationships are dynamic

We have reviewed the nature and importance of the self-concept as the mental model which guides the responses of the parties in a relationship to each other. However, we have not yet defined *the nature of relationships*, nor have we explored how it is that they affect, and are affected by, self-concepts.

A relationship can be said to exist when the parties interact with each other more than once, and previous interactions affect subsequent ones. 'Each interaction . . . is affected by past interactions and by expectations of future ones: thus the nature of the relationship affects the interactions within it, and those interactions affect the future of the relationship, though what happens between interactions may also play a role.'[17] We may have spent the interim reflecting upon previous interactions and talking about them; explaining them and interpreting their meaning; interacting with different people; changing our self-concept or engaging in other forms of learning, and so on. 'All this implies that relationships are virtually never static, that a changing pattern of interactions is likely to be the rule rather than the exception, and that such stability as they have is essentially dynamic in nature' (ibid).

Given their dynamic quality, it is hardly surprising that we spend so much time seeking to make sense of our relationships. We rehearse to ourselves and others the *narrative stories* of our relationships,[18] dividing them up into stages and explaining our own role in them. We may recall the early stages of growth in the relationship fondly, and construe its more recent history and the likely future as a series of ups and downs. Alternatively, we may fix upon a turning point, a defining moment, when the apple cart was upset and it all went horribly wrong. Either way, most relationships have a finite life, which may follow a pattern of acquaintance, growth, maintenance and decline. Or they may consist of a flux, which appears to start and finish by total chance however hard we try to put a structure and a meaning upon it. Nevertheless, we constantly try to create some sort of account of our relationships. And given that our relationships affect and are affected by our self-concept, then our accounts of them will tend to be consistent with it. An individual with a strong national identity is unlikely to describe his attendance at a public demonstration of patriotic fervour as the consequence of his being duped by the state-controlled media.

We ourselves create a huge variety of narrative accounts of our relationships, accounts which differ between individuals and across different sorts of relationship. Our individual experience is hard enough to make sense of; it seems an impossible task to make sense of the experience of others too. Any general model will inevitably be a huge over-simplification. Nevertheless, it will be useful to select one general framework, which categorises social behaviour into four fundamental forms.[19] These are labelled communal sharing, authority ranking, equality matching and market pricing, denoting four different principles upon which relationships are based.

Communal sharing

Communal sharing ignores individual differences and divides resources according to need. There is a strong sense of belonging to the group, and people derive their identity from their group membership. Gifts are given without the expectation of reciprocity, and decisions tend to be taken on the basis of consensus. A high value is placed upon relationships, altruism, generosity and concern for others. However, this is true only of the in-group, e.g. the family or the ethnic group. The response to other groups is likely to be one of the same degree of hostility as the degree of favour shown to one's own.

It is likely that communal sharing provides the best basis for mutual commitment and trust of the four forms of social behaviour, provided that the commitment and trust are between members of the in-group rather than between the in-group and other groups. When communal sharing is the basic relational principle, members are more likely to *commit* themselves to relationships in the sense of wanting, intending, and expecting to keep them going, and taking steps to ensure that they improve and last longer. The dependence of communal sharers upon their group renders strong commitment more likely, since they have few or no alternative relationships available. Moreover, since their identity is bound up with their group membership, the continued maintenance of that relationship is crucial to the integrity of their self-concept.

Given this common identity and their refusal to exploit each other, communal sharers are likely to *trust* each other strongly.[20] They may take risks or make sacrifices on each other's behalf without expecting any return, and this will result in trust reciprocated. Further, the sense of security that derives from belonging facilitates trust. But above all, empathy with each other's needs, taking those needs on board oneself, and acting in effect as agent for the other's interests leads to what writers on trust consider the highest form of trust: identity based trust.[21] So communal sharing enhances trust between individuals.

However, the flip side of this coin is that the deeper the trust, the more bitter the falling out when that trust is perceived to have been broken.[22] The most deeply trusted member of the family quickly becomes its black sheep. Thus the commitment and trust deriving from a communal sharing orientation can be of huge benefit to the in-group; but woe betide both those individuals who are ejected and also all other groups who are outside the charmed circle.

Authority ranking

Authority ranking, the second basic form of relationship, is based upon hierarchy. Resources are divided according to rank, and the inequality inherent in hierarchy is perceived as part of the natural order of things. Respect, deference, loyalty and obedience are expected of those ranking lower in the hierarchy, while those at the top are expected to protect them in return. Identification is with the leader or leaders rather than with the group, and reward and punishment are considered the appropriate tools for regulating the behaviour of those who fail to keep the rules.

The key underlying themes for authority rankers are likely to be the issues of *power* and *conflict*. In a hierarchical relationship, power is unevenly distributed. Those at or near the top of the tree exercise control over the rest.

They may delegate some of their authority to those further down, but they impose rules as to how it is to be exercised. However, power is seldom totally sovereign. There is a delicate balance of interests and perceived obligations. In exchange for obeying the rules and playing their designated roles, those lower in the hierarchy expect certain needs of their own to be met by those in power (for example, protection against external threat and the provision of the means to survive). Moreover there are some rules of the relationship which those in power are expected to keep. The retention of a degree of individual privacy is one such rule, which is why surveillance is so prominent an issue in nation states and in organisations.

Those in power have often succeeded in managing meaning so that their power and control are perceived as natural states of affairs to which there are no alternatives (or only perverse and unnatural ones). They have succeeded in defining social reality. The concept of the divine right of kings is a historic example of such management of meaning. When their subordinates have internalised hierarchy into their personal accounts of relationships, those in power have little need to impose the sanctions upon errant behaviour which they have at their disposal. For those subordinates police themselves through their internalised rules and roles and conception of hierarchy.[23]

Nevertheless, conflict can often occur in hierarchies. Those at the top can be perceived to be breaking the rules (as in the case of surveillance quoted above) whilst those lower down have been keeping them. Perhaps more important, people may start to feel that they have no control over what happens to them. While they may have tolerated their loss of autonomy when their interests were being met, they may not continue to do so if the pay-off balance is disturbed. People may start to mistrust the competence of those in power ('Do they know what they're doing any more?'); their reliability ('They don't keep their promises'); their motives ('They're only in it for themselves'); and even their integrity ('You can't believe a word they say nowadays'). Such mistrust is an almost inevitable precursor of conflict.

Of course, internal conflict is normally perceived as a disaster by those in power. Indeed, many try to generate external conflict in order to induce the feeling of a common fate within. The common interest of survival in the face of threat may submerge those internal conflicts of interest which were becoming apparent. But conflict may not necessarily damage the relationship in the long term. Some responses to conflict may be harmful, others beneficial. Four typical responses to conflict in relationships have been distinguished:[24] exit, voice, loyalty and neglect. The *exit* of 'troublemakers' may strengthen the hierarchy; their *voice* may result in issues being addressed which had been neglected; the *loyalty* of the majority may be reaffirmed in the face of dissension; and many may simply retreat into *neglect*, complying minimally rather than internalising the hierarchy's aims. Whatever the outcome of conflict, it is evident that power and conflict are the major issues in hierarchical relationships.

Equality matching

The equality matching form of relationship is based upon the ideas of reciprocity and fair exchange. People try to respond equitably to others' behaviour towards them, and when resources are being distributed, the guiding principle is that of equality. In contrast with communal sharing, equality matching does divide up the resource cake between individuals; but that division is on the basis of fair shares for all.

Equality matching is based upon a fundamental feature of relationships: *reciprocity*. Reciprocity is the tendency to respond with like for like. A reciprocal response may be returning a favour, but it may equally well be tit for tat, an eye for an eye and a tooth for a tooth. Of course, reciprocity can be delayed as well as immediate. If someone hits me, I may well hit them back instantly. However, if they are very much bigger, I may well get my retaliation in later and in a less physical way.

Likewise with benefits, although here the situation is more complex. I may not seek the returns on the good turn I have done another since I may prefer him to remain indebted to me. Or I may realise that the other party cannot at the moment afford to reciprocate a good turn I have done her, so I back off, realising that she may leave the relationship for another if I press my rights.[25] Or I may suspect the motives of someone doing me a good turn, and seek to avoid becoming indebted myself. In general, if the relationship is changing, the parties have to adapt to each other, so that if one starts becoming more generous, so does the other. On the other hand, this tendency to escalate can contain the seeds of its own destruction; the parties can ruin each other by outdoing the other's good turns or acts of revenge.

In equality matching relationships, reciprocity is a very dominant principle, unlike community sharing, for example, where need is more likely to be dominant, or authority ranking, where hierarchical position is the key factor. Given this centrality of reciprocity, *equity* and *justice* also become of central importance. For if reciprocity is expected as the norm, disputes are likely to arise over whether a particular action or benefit is commensurate with the original action to which it is a response. How are we to judge whether our outcomes from a relationship are equivalent to what we put into it? Equity theory[26] suggests that we do so by making social comparisons. We may compare our cost-benefit ratio with that of our partner in the relationship; or we may look at others whom we perceive to be in a similar relationship. If our cost-benefit ratio is less favourable, or indeed if it is more so, than these comparisons then we may feel either angry or guilty and seek to redress the balance accordingly. If we perceive our imbalance as unfavourable relative to our comparisons, then we will seek to redress it in a more favourable direction; if it seems too favourable, then we may, counter-intuitively, seek for a less favourable deal.

However, it is important to note that considerations of reciprocity and equity may be paramount in equality matching. Equality matching relationships are more likely to be at a moderate level of intimacy only, where the parties find themselves in similar circumstances to each other and have a degree of interdependence. Hence they are not at a high level of intimacy, where they identify and empathise with each other, and deal with each other on the basis of need and entitlement, often with altruistic motives. Nor on the other hand are they in an antagonistic or competitive relationship, where self-interest is the key factor. Rather, when equality matching relationships are between individuals, they are about parity and equality; when they are between people as incumbents of roles, for example in bureaucratic organisations, then equity alone is key.[27]

Of course, equity becomes an issue when norms of fairness start to be questioned. Why should this group be used for comparison purposes rather than another? Why should Directors' salaries be based on comparisons with those of the Directors of other companies rather than with those of other employees in their own? And any challenge to what is thought to be fair is usually a challenge to those in power, since they are likely to have had a considerable say in the development of fairness norms within a relationship. Such challenge is likely to be made when outcomes suddenly become salient, for example when top management awards itself a 15 per cent salary increase when others get a rate of inflation increment. It is also likely to occur when individuals' internal standards of fairness derived from their upbringing and experience are violated. In particular, individuals may need to believe in a just world in which there is some degree of relationship between actions and outcomes. They need to feel that the playing field is to a degree level, so that their efforts to control their own outcomes can succeed. Hence they will seek to maintain equity by complaining about unfairness and by acting equitably themselves.

Market pricing

The final form of relationship, market pricing, is a lot simpler. Here the elements of reciprocity and equality are a lot less prominent than in equality matching. Rather, outcomes are simply the consequence of how valued your inputs are in the social market place of life. What you get out is proportional to what you put in. Hence market pricers form their self-concept on the basis of those features which bring them social value. In industrial and post-industrial societies, occupation is one such feature, so that many people in such societies will define their selves by their occupational membership as their salient feature. Occupation is particularly likely to be a prominent feature of the self if the occupation is of high status in the market place.

Achievement in meeting the market place's needs is a prime value, and individuals will expect to receive the benefits the market place owes them.

The problems that arise from the market pricing model are, of course, those that bedevil pure market models in general. How are fluctuations in the social market place to be controlled so that their harmful effects upon individuals are mitigated? Suppose women in a particular culture have believed that the social market place has placed and will continue to place a high value upon their fulfilling their role as mother? The social market place, however, changes so that it now values engaging in paid employment more highly than motherhood. To the extent that a woman has invested a considerable part of her life in her motherhood role, the change in the social market place has rendered that investment of less value than she expected.

The four forms of social relationship and their associated features are summarised in Table 11. But it is important to stress that they are not mutually exclusive. I was, therefore, only using a figure of speech when I personalised people as communal sharers, authority rankers, etc. Rather, all four forms of relationship are to be found in any given society, and any one member of that society will probably engage in all four of them. Wherever they are found, they tend to give rise to the same key issues, which have to be addressed if they are to be conducted successfully.

This brings us on to a most important question. To what extent are the above ideas about the self, and about relationships and the forms which they take, universally useful? Or are they merely the perceptions of a British psychologist formed in the traditions of European and American psychology? I would argue that the following propositions are applicable everywhere, despite the immense cultural differences which pertain across the globe:

Table 11 Four forms of relationship

Relationship type	Values	Behaviour	Selves	Key issues
Communal sharing	Relationships Consensus	In-group Commitment and trust	Identify with group	Need and entitlement
Authority ranking	Hierarchy, reward and punishment	Respect Loyalty Obedience	Identify with leader(s)	Power Conflict
Equality matching	Reciprocity Fairness	Concern with outcomes	Individual with rights	Equity
Market pricing	Market needs and benefits	Self-promotion	Occupation, social value	Market regulation

- Everyone has a self-concept; it is our means as human beings of attempting to control our fate and make sense of our experience
- The self-concept is formed on the basis of social experiences and at the same time affects those experiences
- Social relationships in general can usefully be categorised according to their underlying principles.

Relationships, selves, and the employment relationship

The employment relationship is but one of the many different relationships undertaken by employees. It is, nevertheless, a relationship like any other relationship. In other words, it consists of a dynamic and ongoing process between individuals and their employer. To assert this is simply to indicate that I am approaching the employment relationship from a psychological perspective. It is not to deny the importance of societal institutions, or of the national or local history of industrial relations. Nor is it to advocate an individualist rather than a collective approach to the conduct of employment relations. Nor is it to deny that the employment relationship involves an unusual mix of control and co-operation, ambiguity, and uneven distribution of power.[28] Rather, I am arguing that *from a psychological perspective* the most important level of analysis is that of the individual employee in relation to the employer. As I will indicate in later chapters, social groupings such as the work group, the organisation, and the national culture of the individual are all of immense importance for the employment relationship. But from the psychological perspective, they have their effect primarily as a result of the ways in which they impact the individual's self-concept and identity.

Hence the same caveats apply to the constructs of 'individual employee' and 'organisation' as apply to every other instance of 'the individual' and 'the other'. That is, these two parties are *not* independent of each other and related only by employment. Rather, the individual is partly defined as such through his or her relationship with the organisation. And the organisation is not a separate external entity, but rather a perception of the individual, mediated through its various representatives whom that individual has directly or indirectly encountered.

Moreover, not only does the relationship itself partly define its parties; it is also a *dynamic ongoing process* in time, which changes the perceptions of both of them. The nature and identity of the change may vary between individuals and over time. In other words, some individuals will perceive their organisation in a completely new way as a consequence of their experiences in the employment relationship; they may meanwhile maintain a relatively stable self-concept unaffected by these self-same experiences. For others, however, the reverse is true. They may maintain roughly the same view of their organisation, but change their view of themselves (for example, by gaining in self-esteem and self-efficacy).

For example, evidence on the meaning of work for people in different countries suggests that work is a more central and salient part of life in some countries than in others.[29] We would expect that their relationship with their employer would consequently be less important for the citizens of these latter countries, and hence that it would in general have less impact upon their self-concept. Likewise, people at the beginning of their career might be more profoundly affected by their employment relationship than those at the end of it.[30] Either way, whatever the balance of influence, the point is that the relationship and its parties are in a constant process of dynamic change. Any investigation at one point in time can only be a snapshot.

Furthermore, from the psychological perspective, the employment relationship is to be analysed at the level of the *individual*. For if the relationship is a matter of perceptions of the self and perceptions of the organisation, the former are by definition unique, even if more of the latter may be shared across employees. Yet even perceptions of the organisation are likely to be unique in some elements. Although all will have experienced the same reward structure or the same culture change programme, for example, each will have had a different set of personal experiences with different organisational representatives. Thus in any organisation, any attempt at an aggregate assessment of the state of the employment relationship will by definition conceal more than it reveals.

What is more, even those experiences which are shared in common will be given different meanings and interpretations. For each employee will fit them into an *account* of their own experience of the employment relationship in order to try and make sense of what has happened to them. 'Construed realities constantly change as new facts arise and new questions are asked.'[31] Of course these accounts may be communally discussed and agreed amongst employees. However, employees will individually use their account to help them understand what is going on in the organisation and predict what might happen, thus helping them cope with change and uncertainty and feel a degree of control over their working lives. The underlying need to control one's experience and outcomes at work, rather than to be totally controlled by 'the organisation', underlies this striving for meaning. It also raises the possibility of conflict as being inevitable unless employees are satisfied with the degree of control which they enjoy.

A psychological perspective on relationships also forces us to face up to the fact that employees bring to their current employment relationship a *self-concept* derived from a multiplicity of other relationships, and also from previous employment experiences. Their identities, their self-esteem, their initial view of the relationship and of their own part in it, are all elements of their self-concept. All these features will affect the way in which each of them perceives and responds to the way they are treated. An element of their identity which apparently has nothing whatsoever to do with their working life may actually have a profound effect upon their employment relationship. For example, an employee's religion or lack of it is their own affair, we may believe; but if they are a pious Muslim or Christian and are unable to pray at midday or are forced to work on Sunday, it is our affair too. For unless organisations take account of this element of their selves, then, as far as they are concerned, their employer has become their persecutor.

Forms of the employment relationship

So much for some ways in which the general relational process applies to the employment relationship. I now reconsider the four forms of relationships and their relevance. Earlier in the chapter (see page 116) I have pointed to the ways in which the eight metaphors and their flip sides could influence elements of the self. Resource, for example might enhance self-esteem, while its flip side, Discard, could drastically damage it. Now I will relate the metaphors to the four forms of relationship in general. This analysis suggests that the employment metaphors do indeed encapsulate these forms, and that the same primary issues arise. To reiterate my argument: employment relationships are a subset of human relationships in general, and need to be analysed from this perspective. Therefore we should expect them to demonstrate the features of the four forms: communal sharing, authority ranking, equality matching, and market pricing.

Family and Club both clearly reflect *communal sharing*, with its emphasis on mutual commitment and trust. Family and Club both lead to the formation of a strongly focused identity, a particular feature of communal sharing. And both share the same danger, of becoming exclusive and intolerant of other groups. Crusade and Resource, however, clearly partake more of *authority ranking*. Both imply power exercised by, in the one case, a charismatic leader, and in the other, the management with its 'right to manage'. Both face issues of power, control, and conflict. Contract, Citizen, and Partner metaphors all ally closely with *equality matching*. All of them are concerned with equity of treatment: imposed contracts, the violation of citizens' rights, or unequal partnerships are seen as inequitable.

Finally, *market pricing* is reflected in the Customer metaphor, with its emphasis on the sovereign market and the maxim that the customer is always right. The danger of damage to the victims of the unfettered market is certainly highlighted in the Customer metaphor. So both in terms of the relational process which they imply, and in terms of the forms of relationship which they incorporate, our eight metaphors fit nicely within a psychological analysis of the employment relationship. Our own experience of employment can be explained in the same psychological terms which explain all relationships.

Summary

A psychological view of the employment relationship cannot view the employee as a rational independent economic actor. Rather, any relationship, including the employment relationship, has to be construed as an ongoing dynamic series of exchanges between the parties. The self-concept of the individual both affects and is affected by the relationship. The self is important because it enables people to feel that they have an element of control over their lives, and to make sense of their experience. Selves are dynamic, but contain elements of identity, self-worth, and reflexivity. This capacity for reflexivity enables people to create narrative stories of their relationships which make sense for them. Relationships may be characterised as falling into four categories: communal sharing, implying mutual commitment and trust; authority ranking, where the key issues are power and conflict; equality matching, implying reciprocity and justice; and market pricing, where value in the social market place is all-important. Different forms of employment relationship as described by the eight metaphors clearly each fall into one of these four categories.

References

1 Williamson, O. (1975) *Markets and Hierarchies*. New York: Free Press.
2 Kalleberg, A. L. and Reve, T. (1993) Contracts and commitment: economic and sociological perspectives on employment relations. *Human Relations*, 46, 12, 1103–1132.
3 Hinde, R. A. (1997) *Relationships: A Dialectical Perspective*. Hove: Psychology Press.
4 Markus, H. M. and Kitayama, S. (1991) Culture and the self: implications for cognition, emotion, and motivation. *Psychological Review*, 98, 224–253.
5 Kelley, H. H. (1971) *Attribution in Social Interaction*. Morristown NJ: General Learning Press.
6 Planalp, S. and Rivers, M. (1996) Changes in knowledge of personal relationships. In G. J. O. Fletcher and J. Fitness, (eds) *Knowledge Structures and Interaction in Close Relationships*. Hillsdale NJ: Lawrence Erlbaum.
7 Giddens, A. (1979) *Central Problems in Social Theory*. London: Macmillan.
8 Harré, R. and Gillett, G. (1994) *The Discursive Mind*. Thousand Oaks CA: Sage.
9 Deci, E. L. and Ryan, R. M. (1985) *Intrinsic Motivation and Self Determination in Human Behaviour*. New York: Plenum Press.
10 Brehm, J. W. (1976) Responses to loss of freedom: A theory of psychological reactance. In J. W. Thibaut, J. T. Spence and R. C. Carson (eds) *Contemporary Topics in Social Psychology*. Morristown NJ: General Learning Press.
11 Seligman, M. E. P. (1975) *Helplessness: On Depression, Development, and Death*. San Francisco: Freeman.
12 Nkomo, S. M. and Cox, T. (1996) Diverse identities in organisations. In S. R. Clegg, C. Hardy and W. R. Nord (eds) *Handbook of Organisational Theory*. London: Sage.
13 Bandura, A. (1986) *Social Foundations of Thought and Action*. Englewood Cliffs NJ: Prentice Hall.

14 Bem, D. J. (1972) Self-perception theory. *Advances in Experimental Social Psychology*, 6, 1–62.
15 Jackson, B. G. (1996) Re-engineering the sense of self: the manager and the management guru. *Journal of Management Studies*, 33, 5, 571–590.
16 Watson, T. J. (1994) Management 'flavours of the month': their role in managers' lives. *International Journal of Human Resource Management*, 5, 4, 893–910.
17 Hinde, op. cit., p. 477.
18 Bruner, J. (1990) *Acts of Meaning*. Cambridge MA: Harvard University Press.
19 Fiske, A. P. (1992) The four elementary forms of sociality: framework for a unified theory of social relations. *Psychological Review*, 99, 689–723.
20 Sabel, C. F. (1993) Studied trust: building new forms of cooperation in a volatile economy. *Human Relations*, 46, 9, 1133–1170.
21 Lewicki, R. J. and Bunker, B. B. (1996) Developing and maintaining trust in work relationships. In R. M. Kramer and T. R. Tyler (eds) *Trust in Organisations: Frontiers of Theory and Research*. Thousand Oaks CA: Sage.
22 Mishra, A. K. (1996) Organisational responses to crisis: the centrality of trust. In R. M. Kramer and T. R. Tyler (eds) *Trust in Organisations: Frontiers of Theory and Research*. Thousand Oaks CA: Sage.
23 Hardy C. and Clegg, C. R. (1996) Some dare call it power. In C. R. Clegg, C. Hardy, and W. R. Nord (eds) *Handbook of Organisation Studies*. London: Sage.
24 Rusbult, C. E., Zembrodt, I. M. and Gunn, L. K. (1982) Exit, voice, loyalty and neglect: responses to dissatisfaction in romantic relationships. *Journal of Personality and Social Psychology*, 43, 1230–1242.
25 Thibaut, J. W. and Kelley, H. H. (1959) *The Social Psychology of Groups*. New York: Wiley.
26 Adams, J. S. (1965) Inequity in social exchange. *Advances in Experimental Social Psychology*, 2, 267–299.
27 Lerner, M. J. (1981) The justice motive in human relations. In M. B. Lerner and S. C. Lerner (eds) *The Justice Motive in Social Behaviour*. New York: Plenum Press.
28 Blyton, P. and Turnbull, P. (1998) *The Dynamics of Employee Relations* (2nd edn). London: Macmillan Business Books.
29 Meaning of Working (1987) *The Meaning of Working*. London: Academic Press.
30 Isabella, L. A. (1988) The effect of career stage on the meaning of key organisational events. *Journal of Organisational Behaviour*, 9, 345–358.
31 Isabella, L. A. (1990) Evolving interpretations as change unfolds: how managers construe key organisational events. *Academy of Management Journal*, 33, 7–41.

Chapter 10

Cultures, relationships and selves

A cultural distinction: collectivism versus individualism

I argued in the last chapter that selves were intimately involved in every employment relationship. Selves both affect and are affected by the employment relationship, as they are in other forms of relationship. Thus if either of the parties fail to take account of the other's self, the relationship is likely to fail. For the other will respond in ways which derive from their selves, not in the ways which meet the needs of the first party. They will, for example, pay more attention to defending their existing self against what they perceive to be threats to it. Or they will change their selves in ways which make the relationship harder to conduct in the future.

The top management of an engineering company may require its professional engineers to reduce costs and thereby compromise quality, castigating them for their 'lack of business awareness'. The engineers' identity as professionals with standards is therefore threatened. They may defend this identity by banding together and enlisting their professional institution in their support; or they may change their self-concept to one of helplessness to resist, the abnegation of responsibility and heads below the parapet. The former response defends their professional identity; the latter changes their self-concept to something less useful to themselves and to their organisation in the long run.

The fundamental point is that in every relationship selves are involved, and how the parties' selves affect and are affected by the other's actions has a profound effect upon the course of the relationship. This is a universal feature of the process of forming and maintaining relationships in general and the employment relationship in particular. Whilst there is an identity of *process*, however, there is a vast diversity of *content*. Selves are extraordinarily varied, and therefore unless the parties to the employment relationship appreciate this variability, they will have little hope of forming a satisfactory relationship. We need, therefore, to consider the variability in the important elements of selves, and the different ways in which they are likely to impact the employment relationship.

Even if we had succeeded in avoiding it until recently, there is one issue which the globalisation of business has forced us to pay attention to. It is the extent to which culture affects selves. The culture within which employees originally formed and are currently developing their selves therefore demands our attention. For culture has a profound effect upon the self. It is the context for most of the social relationships from which our selves are derived. Since different cultures favour different forms of relationship over others, then the selves nurtured within each culture are likely to be different. I therefore make no apology in placing culture at the very forefront of the drivers of the employment relationship.

Cultures are unique, the outcome of a long history of experience within a particular ecological, economic, political, linguistic and social context. To give a flavour of a particular culture within a single book, let alone a single chapter, is a daunting task. To compare all cultures along a set of dimensions and then derive their implications for selves is totally impossible.[1, 2, 3] Instead of attempting the impossible, I will select a single distinction between cultures which has been made by scholars from different disciplines, simply by way of example. This is the distinction between *individualist* and *collectivist* cultures, which has been recognised as of particular importance and has been extensively researched.[4]

Thus I am using merely one example of cultural difference to demonstrate how culture impacts upon selves, and hence upon the employment relationship. I am certainly not claiming that the individualist/collectivist distinction encapsulates cultural differences in general. Moreover, another caveat needs to be entered at this early point. The translation of a feature of a culture on to the self of an individual member of that culture is anything but direct. A single set of individualist values is not shared by all members of an individualist culture. I am merely saying that an individual from one culture is more likely to share the values of that culture than an individual from another. When I refer to 'individualists' or 'collectivists', therefore, I am referring to notional 'typical' members of each culture. A final caveat relates to the false equation of culture with nation. Sometimes we refer to a national culture, sometimes to a supranational one, and sometimes to a subnational one.

Let us then consider the distinction between individualist and collectivist cultures as but one example of how cultures as a whole may impact upon selves and the employment relationship. *Individualism* values loose linkages between individuals 'who view themselves as independent of collectives; are primarily motivated by their own preferences, needs, rights, and the contracts they have established with others; give priority to their personal goals over the goals of others; and emphasise rational analyses of the advantages and disadvantages to associating with others'.[5] *Collectivism*, on the other hand, values close linkages between individuals, 'who see themselves as parts of one or more collectives; . . . are primarily motivated by the norms of, and duties imposed by those collectives; are willing to give priority to the goals of these collectives over their own personal goals; and emphasise their connectedness to members of these collectives' (ibid).

Individualist and collectivist behaviour

A large body of research clearly indicates the following behavioural differences:

- Individualists seek to be self sufficient and self reliant and to engage in aggressive competitive behaviour in order to achieve higher status than others. Collectivists try to maintain relationships, even when they may be disadvantageous to themselves, and emphasise reciprocal obligations.
- Individualists seek to maximise their own returns and improve their own position. Collectivists' main concern is to act so as to support the interests of the in-group to which they belong.
- Individualists value autonomy and freedom for themselves, and act independently when they can. Collectivists act interdependently, and conform to their group's norms; they do their duty and enjoy doing it.
- Individualists are prone to act on impulse, whilst collectivists control impulse by discipline, both self-discipline and social sanctions.
- Individualists may behave creatively and innovatively, whereas collectivists are more likely to be constrained by tradition.
- Individualists are likely to gain early independence from their family; collectivists value family integrity, not wishing to 'lose' a member.
- Individualists value their privacy; collectivists are more likely to enjoy sociability within their own group setting.
- Individualists have many transitory relationships; collectivists seek to maintain and continue relationships within their group.
- Individualists engage in clear, up-front and explicit communications; they seek to tell things as they are. Collectivists seek to maintain relationships by saving the other's face. They therefore communicate ambiguously or tell white lies in order not to embarrass a member of their in-group. Much of their communication is implicit and context dependent.
- Individualists believe in universal standards of right and wrong, and are much concerned about equity and justice. Collectivists consider actions to be right or wrong depending upon the situations in which they are carried out.
- Individualists value integrity, that is, a degree of consistency between one's values and attitudes and one's behaviour. Collectivists believe that attitude and behaviour should not necessarily be consistent. Indeed, there are many occasions when it is right, rather than merely expedient, to comply, even though you may not agree with what you are doing.

- Individualists see responsibility as incumbent upon individual persons, whereas collectivists believe it to be collective.
- Individualists are likely to have negative attitudes towards collectivists, and vice versa. However, the collectivists' attitudes may be more negative as a consequence of the strength of their loyalty towards their own group.

These gross generalisations are supported by a range of evidence from anthropologists, sociologists, and psychologists.[6, 7, 8] However, they must be qualified in several ways. First, much behaviour is situation specific, and the norms for these situations are roughly the same universally whatever the culture. So, for example, similar, basically collectivist, behaviour is expected in religious services everywhere in the world (although even in the case of religion, individualist or collectivist religious beliefs are typical of their matching cultures). And anywhere where there is a bureaucratic institution of some form or other, collectivism will win out in that institution's operations.

However, elements of cultures are not set in stone. A culture is the way of life which a social group has developed to help it survive in its environment. Culture embodies a set of assumptions, values, behavioural norms and artefacts which enable the social grouping to make sense of, and control, itself and its environment. Hence as the environment changes, cultures change too, although cultural change often appears to lag far behind technological and economic change.

The direction of many cultures has been away from traditional collectivism and *towards modernity*. Nations such as the USA, Germany, and the UK can be characterised as already possessing a culture of late modernity.[9] Cultures in late modernity are characterised by strongly individualist values. A wide range of options for styles of behaviour are visible (especially in cities), available and legitimised. However, given the uneven distribution of resources in many individualist cultures, the range of options for some is vastly greater than that for others within the same culture. In general, women and the poor have fewer options. Thus, the variety of options in late modern cultures is somewhat illusory. It is, furthermore, limited to a degree to the lifestyle options approved by consumerism.

In general, as nations industrialise and acquire information technology, it is easy to discern a trend towards individualist modernity and away from collectivist tradition. Such nations as Japan and the former East Germany are typical examples of previously collectivist cultures moving rapidly towards late modernity. On the other hand, it is certainly possible to argue that there are many cultures, especially Islamic ones, which maintain collectivist cultures with fundamentalist religion as the cultural glue, whilst being willing to benefit from technological advances.[10] In sum, while there may be a general move towards late modernity, this move may be only partial in the sense that those moving may not take on board all of its elements. And second, in the light of gross and growing inequalities,[11] the move may for many be aspirational rather than actual.

Relationships and selves: individualist, collectivist and on the turn

In terms, then, of the development of the self, the social relationships and situations typical of collectivist societies will result in the development of certain sorts of selves; those typical of individualist societies will result in quite different ones; and there is a movement from collectivism to individualism such that selves too are changing in the same direction.

Individualist relationships are often isolated, in the sense that they are not anchored in a wider social setting. The parties relate to each other as individuals, rather than as representatives of groups. Hence they have only each other, and expect only the other(s) to provide all the benefits of the relationship. The temporary nature of so many individualist relationships is due to the failure of one or both parties to achieve their expected outcomes. Given the high expectations engendered by the media in particular, frequent failure is hardly surprising. The outcomes which individualists desire from relationships are essentially personal ones, such as their own, and perhaps the others', happiness, pleasure or enjoyment. If there is a conflict between these personal goals and collective ones derived from one's group membership, the former tend to win out. Overall, individualists tend to belong to a lot of groups and form a lot of relationships; however, most are temporary and superficial.

Collective relationships, on the other hand, are usually with another as a representative of a group rather than as an individual. The importance of group relationships means that the norms for behaviour in the group and between groups are clearly specified. It is one's duty to observe them, since if they are broken, relationships may be threatened. Since the maintenance of relationships is of the utmost value, norms are powerful and internalised. One may get no personal pleasure or reward out of behaving properly, but one still does so however personally painful it may be. Collective relationships are apt to be fewer in number than individualist ones, but are more likely to be deeper and to be characterised by mutual trust. Perhaps this is because the parties have confidence that the norms for the relationship will be observed and its obligations met.

The nature of the relationships which predominate in individualist and collectivist cultures, respectively, influences the nature of the selves which individuals construct in their interactions with others.[12] Members of collectivist cultures define themselves more in terms of their group memberships: family, locality, religion and so on. They are part of something bigger than themselves; relationships are the element of which they are merely a part. They are happy to have done their duty, and their self-esteem varies little around an average since they do not wish to appear above others. Rather than having a great need to achieve, their major concern is fear of failure, where failure consists of letting others down (and therefore yourself). Adjectives that they would use to describe themselves favourably would be 'dutiful' and 'co-operative'. When they attribute the causes of favourable outcomes, they are less likely than individualists to attribute them to themselves, and if they do, they credit themselves with making the appropriate effort rather than with ability or aptitude. Given the stability of their relationships, and given that their relationships are the key elements of their selves, collectivists tend to have consistent selves which change relatively little over time. Hence they are described in terms of their character, that is, the degree to which their regular behaviour accords with the norms of their society.

Members of individualist cultures, on the other hand, tend to define themselves by their personal attributes: their name, their appearance and personality, their interests and achievements, their occupation. Their selves are central, and the social context merely contributes to those selves. They see themselves as independent and self-sufficient rather than as interdependent. Their self-description is apt to refer to their distinctiveness or uniqueness, the ways in which they stand out from others. They have high self-esteem, to the extent that they consistently rate themselves as well above average. They are particularly likely to attribute favourable outcomes to themselves, and in particular to their own abilities. Given the multiplicity of their relationships, their self-concept tends to be more complex and multifaceted. Given the temporary nature of those relationships, it is likely to change more frequently than that of collectivists. And given the relative unimportance of norms, and the differences amongst the norms of the many different groups to which they belong, individualists are likely to be described in terms of their personality rather than their character.

The single most defining feature of individualist selves, however, is their extreme *reflexivity*. Individualists are conscious of their selves, and believe that they can create new selves. They believe in the possibility, not only of self-development, but even of self re-creation. The self and its continuous re-creation, in other words, are a personal project to which they can devote themselves. One form of re-creation is to continuously revise the narrative story of one's life so that it gives a new and hopefully unique perspective on one's past, present, and future. Individualists need these narrative selves to make sense of their experience; and they need to maintain a lifestyle which supports their narrative. Provided that they can create and maintain some meaning, they can feel themselves to have some control over their lives. Collectivists have less need of such narrative selves; their selves are set secure in their social memberships.

We may summarise the differences between collective and individualist selves as shown in Table 12.

Table 12 Collective and individualist selves

Collective selves	Individualist selves
Dominant elements relational	Dominant elements personal
Self-esteem average	Self-esteem high
High fear of failure	High need to achieve
Dutiful and co-operative	Unique and distinctive
External attributions	Internal attributions
Self-attributions to effort	Self-attributions to ability
Consistent selves	Changing selves
Character	Personality
Taken for granted	Reflexive, narrative

Cultural selves and employment relationships

What, then, are the implications of cultural selves for employment relationships? This is so broad a question that we first need to emphasise the variety of relationships that constitute the employment relationship both between and within organisations.[13, 14] After all, our eight vastly different metaphors could not do justice to this variety. Granted this caveat, are there any general implications to be drawn from the cultural differences in selves that I have outlined?

We assume that when employees enter an employment relationship, they bring with them their existing selves, and therefore a set of dispositions to act in certain ways, hold certain values, etc. The main question, then, is this: are the major and salient elements in their self-concepts compatible with the sort of relationship which the organisation desires? If an employee from a collectivist culture seeks a strong identification and long-term relationship with their employer, whereas the employer desires only a brief, part-time and highly transactional form of deal, is there any future in the relationship? Or is the *degree of fit* between the self and the proposed relationship just too small for any hope of success?[15]

Returning to our metaphors, individualists seem more likely than collectivists to favour employment relationships based upon the Contract, Resource, Democracy, and Customer metaphors; collectivists may favour Crusade, Club, Family, and Partnership. Employers from individualist cultures may risk the coin turning on to its flip side if they seek to establish relationships in collectivist cultures based upon those metaphors which they themselves prefer.

Now of course the relationship between the self and the employer is not a static one, but rather, like other relationships, reciprocal and dynamic. The old phrase 'a square peg in a round hole' implies that both person and job are static entities. 'Fit' should rather be construed as a satisfactory ongoing employment relationship from the perspective of both parties.

This form of fit can be developed if the employee seeks to adapt their self to the relationship, or if they succeed in adapting the relationship to their self, or by a mixture of both. People from collective cultures are more likely to be willing to adapt their selves to the relationship; if the gap is just too wide, they may nevertheless comply behaviourally without changing their selves (an acceptable solution for collectivists). Individualists, on the other hand, are more likely to seek to change the relationship to suit their selves. They will exit if this solution is impossible and if they can find another job.

There are several likely areas of difficulty in forming a satisfactory employment relationship when primarily individualist and primarily collectivist cultures are both involved.[16] Such cross-culturalism is of course becoming more common as international organisations set up subsidiaries and seek to export HR management practices from their culture of origin into other cultures. It is also an issue for those corporate giants who can claim to be truly global. For they are currently faced with the temptation to centralise processes using information technology, and it is highly likely that the systematised processes will lean more towards one cultural pole than towards the other. Here are just some of the key issues:

- Collectivists consider the organisation's survival and maintenance to be an end in itself. Since they are likely to identify with it, and since organisational membership is likely to be a salient feature of their selves, this is perfectly understandable. Individualists, on the other hand, perceive the organisation as a means to serve other ends, notably those of stakeholders and especially themselves. Hence the organisation's survival and their identification with it (if any) is contingent on its success in meeting their aspirations.
- Collectivists expect a long-term relational deal with the organisation. Since fitting in with the organisation as a social system is most important, selection is often by recommendation, and there is a long period of intense organisational socialisation at entry. Individualists expect a much more short-term and transactional arrangement, in which the tasks and roles for which they are responsible are spelt out. New employees learn to fit in, and if they fail to do so, tend to exit.[17]
- Because of the importance of membership and socialisation, collectivists blur the boundaries between business relationships and private life. If the company is your metaphorical parent, there may be fewer areas of your life from which you exclude it. Individualists have more varied elements of their selves to express, and seek to draw lines between their work and the rest of their lives (often unsuccessfully).
- Collectivists believe themselves to be accountable to their workgroup or team for such issues as quality of product or service, and to be assessed as a team. Individualists tend to be accountable as individuals to their

line manager. They are usually willing to have their work evaluated on an individual basis by means of performance management processes.

• Collectivists commit their selves to superordinate goals which have been agreed, and they value themselves and others on the basis of their degree of conformity to, and compliance with, these goals. Individualists value themselves for the degree to which they have taken individual initiatives, preferably innovative ones, and succeeded at them.

Table 13 summarises the collectivist and individualist approaches to employment.

Control, compliance, change and trust

To conclude, if the employment relationship involves selves, then culture becomes a central consideration for those managing that relationship. For it is in cultures that selves have their origins, and it is from them that they derive many of their fundamental differences. Successful employment relationships, then, will be those which fulfil organisations' needs and at the same time take account of cultural differences in the workforce.

But there are several clouds on the horizon, which I will mention briefly here but return to at greater length in Chapters 13 and 15. The first is the fundamental issue of *control*. As people become more individualist, they are likely to want greater autonomy and self-determination. As we have seen in our discussions of several of the metaphors, organisations in mainly individualist countries have sought to persuade employees to exercise self-control rather than be controlled overtly by management. In this way targets to be achieved are both externally fixed and internally self-imposed. However, with employees having so many alternative selves to choose from, it will become more and more difficult to persuade such people of the centrality of their work selves.

This is particularly true at the present juncture. Despite all the talk of empowerment in the 1980s, the truth is that IT systems are actually taking discretion away from many individuals (particularly from professionals). In financial lending, insurance, medical diagnosis, house conveyancing, audit accounting and many other decision-making tasks previously the preserve of

Table 13 Collectivists and individualists in employment

Collectivists	Individualists
Organisation an end in itself	Organisation a means to personal ends
Preference for a relational contract	Preference for a transactional contract
Work vs life distinction blurred	Work vs life distinction drawn
Team accountability	Individual accountability
Conformity to corporate goals	Success at individual initiatives

professionals, technical knowledge has been programmed and is put at the service of call centre or other operatives. In one major bank, 95 per cent of lending decisions are taken on the basis of expert systems automatically, the remaining 5 per cent being referred up to head office. Yet the workforce will consist of an ever higher proportion of graduates, who will expect to exercise their own judgement rather than being told by a system what to do. Complete and precise *compliance* with processes is becoming the key requirement for employees in industries such as financial services.

However, calling up the collectivists to meet these compliance requirements may not always work either. One of the major difficulties with collectivists is ensuring that they identify with the 'right' (from the organisation's perspective) group. As large corporations merge and become larger still, they lose their original profile. Collectivist employees feel less inclined to identify with a corporation which transforms itself periodically into something different from what it was. All forms of transformational and structural change threaten any identity which is bound up with the corporation. Hence loyalties and identities may be transferred to smaller groups: the business, the unit, the department, the occupational group, the workgroup. Other organisational units then become outsiders, out-groups, to the likely detriment of collaboration across the corporation. As competitive advantage comes more and more from the speed with which knowledge is shared across the organisation, such limited loyalties become a liability. Individualists are always less likely to share knowledge because it is their stock in trade, their own personal competitive advantage. Now collectivists too may frustrate the organisation's learning because they are too loyal to their group.

Perhaps the most fundamental cross-cultural issues with regard to the employment relationship, however, are those of *change* and *trust*.[18] Individualists are far more likely than collectivists to welcome change for its novelty and for the opportunities to develop new selves which it provides. On the other hand, collectivists are far more likely to trust in management's competence in deciding that the change is the right one, and to stay with the organisation whatever the outcome. Indeed, there is a case for arguing that in many organisations it is more appropriate to have a variety of employment relationships, some of which suit collectivists and others individualists. In the segmented corporations of today, the core employees need to have a fair degree of collectivist loyalty, the contracted experts are likely to be individualists, whilst the peripheral operatives usually have their often surprising degree of loyalty taken for granted.

Trust, however, is about more than competence. Individualists are unlikely to give top management the benefit of any doubt as to their motives when they see them awarding themselves rises in salary much higher in percentage terms both than the rate of inflation and than the rest of the workforce. They assume that top management is in it for themselves. Whilst collectivists may tolerate the difference between rhetoric and reality on the grounds of saving face, it merely makes individualists more cynical. And while collectivists may realise that a promise is to be understood in terms of the context in which it was made, as far as an individualist is concerned, a promise is a promise. Hence organisations in individualist cultures run according to individualist values and staffed mainly by individualist employees are likely to suffer an endemic lack of trust in the employment relationship.

In conclusion, it is worth noting the scope of the implications of only one cultural dimension, individualism vs collectivism, for the employment relationship. If we were to bring all the relevant cultural distinctions into consideration, the implications would be immense. In the era of globalisation, the employer who fails to appreciate the importance of culture as a determinant of the success of the employment relationship is doomed. Whilst a degree of cultural awareness is becoming more common, its fundamental importance for the employment relationship has yet to be fully appreciated. For many employees, the flip sides of the metaphors are more representative of their experience because their employers have failed to understand their selves and the effect their actions are likely to have.

Summary

Perhaps the most formative impact on the self derives from culture. One cultural value distinction, chosen by way of example, is that between collectivism and individualism, and this is evidenced by a wide range of behavioural differences associated with each. Both are associated with a preference for certain forms of self, as a result of favouring certain forms of relationship. Individualist selves are likely to have prominent elements which emphasise the person's uniqueness and personality; collectivist ones elements which emphasise membership, obligations, and character. These different selves have important implications for the success of employment relationships which increasingly require compliance, collaboration and loyalty in times of change.

References

1 Triandis, H. C. (1995) *Individualism and Collectivism*. Boulder CO: Westview Press.
2 Hofstede, G. (1980) *Culture's Consequences*. Beverley Hills CA: Sage.
3 Trompenaars, F. (1993) *Riding the Waves of Culture*. London: Nicholas Brealey.
4 Earley, P. C. and Gibson, C. B. (1998) Taking stock in our progress on individualism–collectivism: 100 years of solidarity and community. *Journal of Management*, 24, 3, 265–304.
5 Triandis, op. cit., p. 2.
6 Erchak, G. M. (1992) *The Anthropology of Self and Behaviour*. New Brunswick NJ: Rutgers University Press.

7 Lukes, S. (1973) *Individualism*. Oxford: Basil Blackwell.
8 Triandis, H. C. (1994) *Culture and Social Behaviour*. New York: McGraw Hill.
9 Giddens, A. (1991) *Modernity and Self-Identity*. Cambridge: Polity Press.
10 Huntington, S. P. (1996) *The Clash of Civilisations and the Remaking of World Order*. New York: Simon and Schuster.
11 United Nations Human Development Report (1999) New York: UN Press.
12 Markus, H. R. and Kitayama, S. (1991) Culture and self: implications for cognition, emotion, and motivation. *Psychological Review*, 98, 224–253.
13 Hirsh, W. and Jackson, C. (1996) *Strategies for Career Development: Promise, Practice, and Pretence*. Brighton: Institute for Employment Studies.
14 Sonnenfeld, J. A. and Peiperl, M. A. (1988) Staffing policy as a strategic response: a typology of career systems. *Academy of Management Review*, 13, 588–600.
15 Schneider, B., Kristof-Brown, A. L., Goldstein, H. W. and Brent Smith, D. (1997) What is this thing called fit? In N. Anderson and P. Herriot (eds) *International Handbook of Selection and Assessment*. Chichester: Wiley.
16 Trompenaars (op. cit.).
17 Schneider, B. (1987) The people make the place. *Personnel Psychology* 40, 437–453.
18 Herriot, P., Hirsh, W. and Reilly, P. (1998) *Change and Transition: Managing Today's Employment Relationship*. Chichester: Wiley.

Chapter 11

Individual differences and employment

The social process revisited

Cultures are the social context from which selves are constructed. Different cultures are likely to lead to different elements of selves being salient in individual members of that culture. This chapter will be concerned with a few of these salient elements in individual selves, and the major way in which they are likely to impact upon employment relationships. As soon as we identify these elements of the self, it becomes immediately apparent that most employers pay relatively little attention to them in their conduct of the employment relationship. Hence, since they are of high impact but ignored, unsatisfactory employment relationships may reasonably be attributed to this ignorance.

However, even to state such an intention is problematic. For example, a reader from a collectivist culture may immediately respond that the very notion of an individual is the product of the individualist culture from which the author comes. The idea of an individual as an autonomous independent person is the cornerstone of individualist cultures; but it certainly does not make much sense to a collectivist, who perceives interdependence rather than independence as the natural social order. Rather, collectivists would suggest, the emphasis on the self which has characterised the previous two chapters is a typical individualist value. It is social relationships rather than subjective selves which best explain their experience, and the statement at the end of Chapter 9 to the effect that we all have selves is yet another example of cultural imperialism. What is more, the reason that was given in that chapter for our continuous search for meaning from our experience – to gain a degree of control over what happens to us – is individualist arrogance run wild. People should learn to accept what life has in store for them.

One response to such objections runs as follows. Human experience is essentially social and reciprocal. A continuous exchange occurs between our social relationships and the sense we make out of them. We choose to call this sense our selves, and refer to the self as a relatively stable way of organising our experience and our actions. It may very well be the case that collectivists pay far more attention to the external social relationships than to the personal experience, and vice versa for individualists. But the fundamental assumptions which we are making are first, that both their personal experience and their social relationships are essential to understanding people of every culture; and second, that the self is a useful construct for organising that experience. We may be more or less conscious of that self, and it may consist more or less of our relationships, but the self is an essential element of our psychology.

Which takes us on to a second potential criticism. Not only is the writer from an individualistic culture. He is also from that peculiar subculture psychology, the members of which appear to believe that individuals consist of, or can be defined by, a set of characteristics or attributes. When you have described and assessed an individual's personality and abilities, what more is there to say?

It is true that many psychologists have appeared to subscribe to this 'essentialist' view of people, and have indeed made their living out of assessing attributes of persons for purposes of organisational selection and placement. However, there are other ways of construing the attributes of people than as permanent dispositions which constitute the structure of their personality or their abilities. Without denying that their inherited physiological structures affect individuals' subsequent development, we may nevertheless treat the personality descriptions beloved of psychologists as our attributions about our own and others' behaviour. Why did John do this or why does Jill behave like that? we may ask. And our answer is often likely to be in terms of various personality traits, hopefully moderated by some mention of the context and situation for the behaviour in question.[1, 2] How have they succeeded in tackling this or that difficult problem? we may query, and respond that they are very bright people, or that they have great ability with numbers. People are in general pretty good at answering questions and questionnaires about themselves, and external assessors can add to the quality of the assessment. However this indicates merely that our language has given us some shared ways of making attributions about the causes of behaviour, and that we are good at using those ways.

Instead of treating psychological assessment as if it were a scientific activity, with the scientist measuring the object of his or her investigation, we should see it as a specific instance of the *reciprocal social process* which underpins all of our experience. To repeat, this process runs as follows:

- Our behaviour in social situations leads both us and others to attend to that behaviour and respond to it. Attributions about why or how we behaved in that way in that situation are one of many possible responses we and others may make.

- We then respond in turn to these responses, be they others' behaviour or utterances, or our own evaluations.
- These second-order responses of ours[3] sometimes result in our changing our self-concept. For example, if others have verbalised their responses in terms of our personality characteristics or abilities, we may internalise those comments and incorporate them into our selves.
- As a consequence, we may interpret the situation somewhat differently on the next similar occasion, and moderate our behaviour accordingly. This changed behaviour will provoke somewhat different responses from others. Such different responses might serve to reinforce our revised selves, or result in further revision.

This process enables us both to be influenced by, and to influence, the social situations which we encounter or create.[4] It brings longer-term social relationships to centre stage in the development of the self, since it is seldom that we change our selves on the basis of a single isolated social interaction (if we do, it is so rare that we characterise it as a conversion experience, or a life-changing event). And finally, the process enables us to maintain a certain degree of stability and continuity in our self-concepts. For if we respond in certain regular ways in particular situations, people will tend to respond to us regularly in the same way. This will confirm our self-concept which will in turn maintain our response to the same situation next time it occurs . . . [5]

Change in our selves is thus likely to depend upon our being faced with (or actively searching out) new situations, or upon our being responded to by new people. Since new situations and new people are an increasing feature of most people's lives, selves are changing faster, and the maintenance of a degree of stability is not always easy. On the other hand, we should never underestimate the huge range of experiences which have formed us and given us the central core of our selves. For many, this springs not so much from current membership of a social group, but from a long-established value base. How else could whistleblowers act against the collective?

The fundamental argument of this part of the book is that the eight metaphors so often turn over on to their flip sides because organisations fail to take account of employees' selves. I have therefore selected four frequently salient elements of selves, not because they are an exhaustive list, but to demonstrate the ways in which the self affects, and is affected by, the employment relationship. They are *gender*, *occupation*, *family*, and *religion*. In the light of the previous paragraph, however, it is important to guard against the idea that these elements of the self are structured components which are static and fixed. On the contrary, both their meaning and their prominence may change for individuals as their selves change.

Now as soon as these four elements of the self are mentioned, it becomes evident that they are rooted in culture, even when we look at only one cultural distinction. For example, it is likely that gender and occupation are more salient elements of the self in individualist cultures, family and religion in collectivist ones. Moreover, the content of the elements will differ across cultures. The gender element will be markedly different, for example, for Dutch and for Iranian women. Recognising, then, that culture and individuals are inextricably linked, we will seek to discover what might be the implications for the employment relationship of these elements of the self.

Finally, by selecting a few elements of the self and treating them separately, I have risked giving the impression that the self is composed of atomised elements rather than existing as a unified and developing narrative. Gender and occupation, for example, or gender and ethnicity interact with each other. They do not simply act as additive factors. Rather, the aggregate and developing self operates within the employment relationship, resulting in a variety of different orientations towards it.[6]

Gender

Gender is the way in which people interpret the biological differences between men and women. Since the biological distinction is a binary one, we tend to see one gender in terms of the other. We see it, not as an 'other', something different, but rather, as the opposite.[7] Individuals from particular cultures bring to the employment relationship the gender element of their identity which is derived from their culture. Sometimes, especially in collectivist cultures, this gender element may not be particularly *salient* in people's identities. Prominent elements of their identity may depend upon gender, for example, wife, sister and mother, but gender itself may not be salient. In individualist cultures, on the other hand, it is likely to be much more so. This is because consciousness has been raised about the fact that men usually hold power, especially in organisations. Cultural stereotypes about men and women are seen both as causes and as post hoc rationalisations for this imbalance of power.

Thus gender as an element in the employment relationship follows the same pattern of development of the self as in other relationships. The individual's 'national' culture suggests a particular view of their own gender, and probably has a considerable effect on the organisation's response to gender (if the organisation is a national one). Hence the employee's gendered self will enable them to fit into the gendered relationships in the organisation. They will tend to behave in line with their gendered self, and since the organisational culture has a similar view of gender, it will reinforce that self.

In many organisations where power is exercised by men, the gender stereotypes describe men as decisive, independent, action-oriented, capable, ambitious, rational, etc., and women as emotional, dependent, indecisive, etc. (the opposite and pejorative terms). Where these stereotypes are culturally supported and part of employees' own gendered selves, the subordinate position and behaviour of women in the organisation and the organisation's own masculine values are continually reinforced, and so are the employees' selves.[8]

However, the raising of women's consciousness regarding gender is itself a cultural phenomenon. By drawing attention to gender stereotypes and the unequal distribution of power and resources which they justify, the women's movement has undoubtedly enhanced the salience of gender in employees' selves. By encouraging groups of women to meet inside and outside the workplace, their gender identity has been supported by group membership.[9] At the levels of the organisation, the occupation, and specific situations and tasks at work (for example, committee meetings), the gender issue has been forced on to the agenda.[10]

More important than gender salience, however, has been the change in the *content* of the gender element. Rather than accepting the culturally defined stereotype, many women have given up seeking to prove themselves more decisive, independent, etc. than men in the workplace. Rather, they have maintained that there are gender differences, but that the selves that women bring to the employment relationship are in no way inferior to those that men bring. Women's selves are characterised by a concern for relationships, which is achieved through qualities of sensitivity, emotional expressiveness and nurturance. They value equality, community and participation.[11] They are not so likely as men to attribute successes to their own individual abilities, particularly since those successes will more likely have been achieved by influencing and empowering others. This whole female gender constellation has been labelled *communion*.[12]

Just as traditional stereotypes define by opposites, it appears at first sight that the new female gendered self is to be contrasted with a male opposite, labelled *agency*. Masculine agency, in this definition, is about self-assertion, independence and competition. It stresses personal responsibility for outcomes, and when these are achieved, takes credit for that achievement. Agency in this sense refers to having an impact and being recognised for it, normally by promotion, added status, and financial reward. As we shall see, some view these male and female selves as mutually incompatible within the organisational setting, others as complementary.

The resemblance of female communion and male agency to collectivist and individualist cultures, respectively, is very clear. However, whereas it is the relationships themselves that are the foremost elements of the self in collectivist cultures, in the new female gender it is the personal qualities which make for successful relationships which are prominent. Women's self-esteem is enhanced as a consequence. Furthermore, theories of adult development which suggest that men only get round to valuing others when they have done with achieving their own goals enhance it still further.[13, 14]

Now many will say that they certainly do not subscribe to such a gendered view of themselves. Men will profess a variety of contents to their notions of their masculinity. Many, in the language of the new gender politics, would claim to be new men who embrace the communion rather than the agency principle. Women, similarly, will avow a wide variety of gendered selves, and there is no reason to disbelieve them (unless their behaviour consistently belies their words). However, there is a considerable and probably growing number for whom their gender is highly salient in their selves. It is these who will pose a major challenge for organisations, since their selves and the employment relationship expected by the organisation may well be incompatible. One or the other party will have to give.

How then will gendered selves and organisations come to a rapprochement so that a satisfactory employment relationship is experienced? Different resolutions have been proposed, as follows:[15]

- *No change*. The competitive business environment means that the trad-itionally male attributes of being decisive, independent, etc. are needed now more than ever. ✗ Mate A
- *Integration*. It is wrong to discriminate against women, so they should be given every opportunity to show themselves as decisive, independent, etc. as men.
- *Complementarity*. Both the masculine and the feminine attributes are necessary for organisations to function well in a business context which requires team working and collaboration as well as competition.
- *Superiority*. Given the radically different nature of the business context in terms of knowledge sharing, diversity of customer, team working, etc., women's attributes are now actually more valuable to organisations than men's.
- *Difference*. Women's values are fundamentally different from men's, and are necessary for the wellbeing of today's and tomorrow's social and business world.

Clearly, many organisations aspire to integration, and have been making considerable progress towards decreasing the degree of sex discrimination that is still present. Nevertheless, even in the least discriminatory of countries, the Scandinavian nations, pay inequality still exists.[16] However, the integration option does not challenge the organisation's values or norms. Complementarity and superiority certainly do, since they require organisations to change their cultural values. In the case of complementarity, they have to add a value set which they may previously have ignored or even denigrated; in the case of superiority, they have to accord such values a prior place. Difference presents an even more profound threat, however, because it challenges the very purpose of organisations. Rather than advocating different values as ways of achieving the same business objectives, difference may require organisations to reassess such fundamental issues as who their stakeholders should be.

Significant positive changes of attitudes towards complementarity, superiority and difference have so far occurred rarely, however. Instead of women with a strong gender identity changing the cultures of organisations, they have struggled to make an impact. If they succeed in retaining their identity, they often find themselves marginalised and their organisational commitment questioned.[17] Hence their employment relationship is a difficult one to maintain, since they are perceived, and perceive themselves, not to fit. Few organisations value the role of constructive internal critic.

The example of the gender element of the self illustrates well the extent to which such elements bring with them a whole array of associated values and assumptions. If the gender element (or any other) is particularly salient in an employee's self, then the reciprocal interplay between the self and the employer is likely to encounter difficulties if the two are inconsistent.

Occupation

We usually think of occupations as sets of work activities. Although they often retain the same labels over time, the activities which those labels subsume may have changed radically. Who remembers the old insurance salesman or bank manager? Yet however much occupations change, they may constitute a salient element of an employee's self. As in the case of gender, the changing social and economic context is profoundly affecting the nature of occupations and hence the salience and content of the occupational element of selves. Once again, employees bring to the employment relationship a salient element of their selves, which both affects and is affected by that relationship.

Indeed, occupation is intimately related both to gender and to status. There is occupational segregation by *gender* in many occupations, with word processors, nurses, call centre workers, shop assistants and teachers being predominantly female, and engineers, scientists, bankers and middle and senior managers in most organisations being predominantly male. Moreover, it is very hard to make a career move between occupations, for example, from word processor to manager.[18]

Occupations are also markers of *social status*. Indeed, the social status of occupations and the skills and qualifications needed for them form the basis of various stratified occupational classifications. Both within societies in general, and inside organisations, occupation, status and gender are inextricably intermixed. In some societies, certain occupations have higher status than in others (for example in Germany and France, teaching has higher status than in the UK and the USA); and in the former communist countries, occupations may not be so segregated by gender. However, in general, this three-way mix operates. It is therefore clear that members of certain occupations are likely to feel lower self-esteem, since these are low status occupations. Furthermore, such lower self-esteem is more likely to be felt by women, since they form the majority of workers in these occupations. Finally, stereotypes of women as less capable are likely to follow.

Occupations are likely to become even more important than they are at present.[19] This is because of the gradual decline of internal labour markets in many organisations, particularly in the USA and the UK. Instead of employees being recruited and developed within organisations for lengthy periods of time to enable jobs to be filled internally, flexibility of employ-ment contract is increasingly occurring. Only the organisational core can have some hope of long-term career progression within the organisation, and many of these favoured few are increasingly finding the grass greener with other organisations. Many other employees have fixed-term contracts, and are held responsible for completing projects according to specification. There is therefore less opportunity for job movement inside the organisa-tion, or any real prospect of an organisational career. Rather, these contract workers move between organisations, and gain their status and value not from their position within an organisation, but rather from their occu-pational skills.

As a consequence of this increased flexibility, and also because of the increasing complexity of much occupational work, occupations are becom-ing more *codified*. That is to say, they increasingly consist of specific skills and knowledge applied to specific tasks and problems. Individuals who have achieved mastery of these skills and knowledge and can keep themselves up to date in them are in a favourable labour market situation if the tasks and problems are important for organisations. They can move between organisa-tions on the basis of their existing skills, creating an occupational labour market. They are thus in marked contrast to those who move between both organisations and also occupations (the secondary labour market). If they can also lay exclusive claim to a fairly broad area of work, emphasise the importance of qualifications, and form associations, they call themselves *professions*.[20]

Thus to call oneself a professional is to lay claim to membership of a high status occupation, and is likely to add considerably to one's self-esteem. Attempts to bolster occupations' status by using the term inappropriately have frequently failed (we balk at calling hairdressers professionals), indicat-ing that the word 'profession' retains a degree of exclusivity. It also implies high standards and competence in maintaining them. Hence a professional element of the self is likely to contain notions of excellence as well as of status. Moreover, the more progress one makes professionally, the greater becomes one's reputation;[21] indeed, professional progress consists of enhancing one's personal reputation. Others refer and defer to this reputa-tion, thereby increasing one's professional self-esteem yet further.

However, there is a flip side to the professional coin. We are all aware of the demise of manual labour in the Western world, and the threat to the identity of miners, steelworkers, fishermen and dockers as 'real men' and family breadwinners. There are also some threats to professionals. And if professions are occupations which have successfully colonised areas of work for themselves, then other less powerful occupations are also likely to face these threats and to be less capable than professions of fighting back.

The first of these threats is that of *dependency*. Many professions simply cannot practice on their own or in small groups of colleagues. Research chemists, engineers, and increasingly even lawyers and doctors can only engage in their professional work if they have extensive technical, administrative and business support. But it is not merely the tools of their trade which professionals need from organisations. They also need the opportunity to operate them; they need professional assignments. Moreover, any role in any project will not do; they need to get assigned to roles which will develop their skills further in projects which will add to their reputation. Finally, many of them are dependent on their organisation for permission to develop their external reputation in the normal ways. Top research chemists in pharmaceutical companies enhance their reputation by publishing in scientific journals and attending international conferences; but the risk of revealing commercially sensitive information might encourage their employer to limit their opportunities for these activities.

The second threat to professionals is to their *autonomy*. They have traditionally sought to establish their own professional standards in terms of the quality of the service they provide. And they have reserved the right to use their own methods to provide it. Engineers have sought for 100 per cent engineering perfection, and doctors have insisted on the primacy of their clinical judgement. Yet commercial imperatives have forced engineers to accept 80/20 solutions, whilst limited medical resources have meant difficult allocation decisions over and above clinical needs. Many professionals are now expected to work in multi-disciplinary teams under the managerial control of a business-oriented project manager, rather than in professional or functional groupings under the leadership of a senior professional. Their work today is invariably determined by the business needs of the organisation; any enhancement of their own skills and reputation is always a happy by-product.

The somewhat schizophrenic attempts of organisations to allow for professional autonomy and trust whilst retaining control are exemplified at Glaxo Wellcome, the pharmaceutical giant. Here the research chemists have 'trust days', when they can be creative in 'their own' time; but individual performance-related pay is retained so that their performance can be effectively managed.[22]

A final and even more powerful threat to professionals is their loss of *exclusiveness*. Governments have deregulated various areas of activity, for example, financial services, so that provision of such services is not limited to bankers, etc. At the same time as opening up opportunities for other occupations (or newly invented ones), however, governments have introduced regulation of standards which were previously policed by professional institutions. This reallocation of regulatory responsibilities removes another element of professional power. However, as I will argue later, it may also provide support for professionals inside organisations.

An even more important threat to exclusiveness than deregulation, however, is that of *systematisation*. The knowledge to which professionals laid sole claim has been captured in expert systems for use by anyone. Call centre employees quote insurance premiums to customers on the basis of a system which has been derived from a combination of professionals' know how and actuarial statistics, but which only needs total and accurate compliance to outperform professional judgement. Audits are now performed by accountancy technicians using audit systems. Hence few professionals can continue to practice simply by performing professional processes which no one else is permitted to perform. Rather, as their stock-in-trade knowledge is being taken away from them, they have to innovate and add value to products and services, and they have to do so faster than these innovations can themselves be systematised. Alternatively, they have to rely on a process of mystification, whereby they give legitimacy to their clients in their struggles to survive in essentially ambiguous situations by mutual confirmation and a shared private language.[23]

Hence the confident levels of self-esteem and the clear value priorities that we would expect to characterise professional selves are under threat. Professionals have had to compromise their standards and hence their integrity, and often cannot fight back because they depend upon their employer for the opportunity to practice. Their identities as professionals and as organisational members may be incompatible. The only recent addition to their armoury has been the increase in the power of regulators. The staff of regulatory agencies are from the same professions as professionals within organisations, and may support them in their efforts to maintain professional standards and autonomy.

However, like other employees, professionals will experience job insecurity. Since their employment now depends upon the value which they can add, they will take good care to retain some of that value for themselves. They may pay lip-service to sharing their knowledge for the good of all their colleagues, but actually retain it for themselves as their own passport to future employment. Thus the popular theory of 'the learning organisation' is noteworthy for the rarity of its practice.

Professionals' commitments to their profession and to their organisation may actually be at odds with each other, and there is strong evidence of professional sub-cultures in many organisations[24] and even of sabotage of the organisation by professionals.[25] On the other hand, provided that good professional practice is rewarded, there need be no such conflict,[26] and many professional organisations are staffed with professionals who appreciate commercial imperatives and are highly committed both to clients and to their employer. Since they are often partners in the enterprise themselves, this is not too onerous a task. Whether professionals who are hired in temporarily to do relatively routine work are similarly committed is another question.

Just as gender as a social issue and therefore as an identity element is in a state of constant change, so too is occupation. And just as gender has to be carefully negotiated in the employment relationship, so too does occupation, particularly if it incorporates a strong value component. In many organisations, particularly those in the UK and the USA, occupations and professions have, on the contrary, been devalued. Professionals who insist on standards at the expense of short-term commercial success have been marginalised or worse. And those who seek to retain their professional identity rather than change it for a managerial one are assumed to lack drive and ambition.

We turn now to two elements of the self which are far less frequently researched and discussed in individualist countries such as the USA and the UK. This is because they are more prominent in collectivist than in individualist selves. They are religion and family.

Religion

Readers will probably be astonished at the inclusion of religion in a book about the employment relationship. This is because they are likely to be members of two sorts of society: European societies where nationally established religion has largely given way to secularism; or American middle-class and educated society, which, if it does attend worship, goes to the established Christian churches or to the synagogue. Even if readers are practising believers, their religion is likely to be a personal and private matter, clearly separated off from their business and their political lives. For some in Western society, their religion may be the most salient and defining element in their identity. But if it is, they are quite likely to have made fundamental career decisions (e.g. to become a nun or a charity worker) which enhance the religious element of their selves whilst maintaining the partition of the sacred from the secular.

Such a Western middle-class perspective totally fails to appreciate the significance of religion in today's and tomorrow's world. Religion is 'the principal defining characteristic of civilisations'.[27] Whilst the proportion of the world's population who are at least nominally Christian has stayed approximately static for the last century at just above 30 per cent, as have Hindus (around 13 per cent), Muslims have increased from 12.4 to 19.2 per cent. The only major religion to have lost adherents is Buddhism, down from 7.8 to 5.7 per cent. The picture of the modern age of science and enlightenment putting paid to the myths of religion is therefore far from the truth. Rather, a revival of religion is occurring in some parts of the world. The big four religions now account for around 70 per cent of the world's population, despite its multiplicative growth this century.

Indeed, rather than modernity destroying the myths of religion, it is in reaction to modernity that the late twentieth-century religious revival occurred. The same global forces that are pushing collectivist societies towards individualism are also causing people to look for alternative sources of meaning, identity and community to those of family and locality.[28] Religion provides such a source, together with clear moral precepts about how one should live in an age of doubt and uncertainty. Or at least, reformist or fundamentalist religion does. The growth in the number of religious adherents is occurring in those religions where there is a strong reform movement within an established religion (e.g. in Islam); or where a proselytising form of religion takes over adherents from an established one (e.g. fundamentalist Protestants winning over Catholics in Mexico); or where new dissenting sects break away from established faiths (continuously in the USA, where some individualists cannot tolerate orthodox church order and discipline).[29] Religion is thus appealing to more people than postmodern irony. Indeed, religious reformation originally provided the moral and intellectual engine for the rise of capitalism.[30] It just might be now in the process of creating a new world order.

These radical forms of religion do not permit the comfortable partition of lives into religious and other elements. They demand a religious perspective on social morality and on political adherence. They colonise the person who embraces them and the culture in which they exist. Thus, for example, in the USA fundamentalist religious groups formed the Moral Majority movement to seek to get politicians elected who were mandated to legislate in accordance with their moral code. In Muslim countries, Islam has become a unifying emergent empire of co-religionists, united by their hostility to the West.[31] Modern Islam is characterised not just by increased religious observance, but also by a renewed emphasis on dress and moral values (in contrast to perceived decadent Western godlessness), and by the provision of services such as education and healthcare

What is more, whilst many of the fundamentalist sects in the USA appeal primarily to poorer and less educated people, the same is not true of Islam. Young intellectuals and the urban middle classes, as well as uprooted rural peasants, embrace a faith which enables them to give form and meaning to their sense of injustice. The high birth rate in Muslim countries further ensures that there will continue to be many young recruits to the cause. For these people, their religion is their life; their religious identity is all encompassing. Moreover, it is yet more sharply defined by those not included within its sphere; when you can identify your enemy as the Great Satan, your own identity as a soldier of the Almighty is secure.

Modernity has spawned this religious revival by breaking down the social structures which gave meaning to people's lives. New meanings had to be sought, but they were found by many in old forms. The purpose of these old forms was to reaffirm separate, and sometimes national, cultural identities. The revival of the Orthodox church in Russia signifies the reaffirmation of one thousand years of Russian nationhood. The moral and dress codes of Islam and its concentration on the teachings of the Koran as the basis for all of life are harking back to a long religious tradition utterly different from the 'irreligious' West. Even the American sects are reaffirming the American Dream, which is why the obviously grasping tele-evangelists' riches are treated by the faithful as evidence of God's blessing upon them.

To liberal readers of established faiths or of no faith at all, these developments often appear ludicrous. We marvel at the credulity of people who seem prepared to trust obvious charlatans, or who treat an ancient text as a literal guide to living their lives in the modern world. Yet to ignore their huge impact upon the employment relationship world-wide is to take a hopelessly insular view. What we have to realise in the globalised world is that for an increasing number of employees, the identity which they bring to the employment relationship will be dominated by their religion. We are used to coping with religious affiliation in terms of expecting religious people to be unwilling to do various things which offend their religious code. For example, many Christians have been unwilling to work on Sunday, or Jews on Saturday. Many will not be willing to cut ethical corners, and some are awkward enough to blow the whistle when they cannot stand by in good conscience.[32]

But the religious identities to which we have been referring obviously have far bigger implications for the global employment relationship than merely the need for organisations to make such allowances. For example, the assumption by multinational organisations that the university-educated Muslim young people whom they employ in their Middle Eastern offices are 'modern' in their outlook is likely to be unfounded. They will certainly be 'modern' in their use of technology, but they are likely to be deeply hostile to any aspect of organisational culture which smacks of the godless West. Yet the entire culture of many international organisations has close links with the culture of their nation of origin, which is most often American or European. We have barely begun to recognise the importance of religion in the late modern world, let alone its likely impact upon the employment relationship. The attribution of the religious response to modernism to a few unhinged fundamentalists is profoundly mistaken and profoundly insular.

Family

In many collectivist countries the *extended* family is the most central relationship of all. Duties to kin have a religious priority in Confucianism; even the awesome project of Mao's Cultural Revolution failed to dent the family's supremacy in China. Family identity is likely to be highly salient in the selves of many collectivists, together with the values of loyalty, support, respect and obligation which are associated with it. In particular, the social virtue of trust (of others in the family) is dominant in the individual's view of the family and their own position within it.[33]

For many in more individualist cultures, the *nuclear* family has recently held a similarly important position, with personal role within that family as a salient element of identity. With the breakdown of an ever higher proportion of nuclear families, it is relationships with partner and/or with children which now dominate for many. Such relationships are likely to be especially salient for women.

The range of relationships between the self as family member and the organisation spans the spectrum. In China, parts of Italy, and several Muslim countries, most organisations *are* the family. With little trust in larger social or government institutions, families who found a business seek to keep it in the family for generations. They compensate for being unable as a consequence to expand to become large corporations in two main ways: first, by engaging in flexible specialisation of goods or services;[34] and second, by forming networks with other local family firms with whom they forge working relationships.[35, 36] Thus in some cultures, the elements of self which relate to family and those which relate to organisation and work are largely synonymous, or at the least are highly compatible.

In the case of other cultures, however, the small family firm, if it grows, rapidly becomes a professionally managed organisation. For rather than handing over the business to their children to manage, the founding owners hire professional managers to run it. With the use of joint-stock investment to finance the business to expand, all the short-term demands of shareholders soon become paramount. The need for short-term profits leads to an emphasis on productivity and performance, and to the bureaucratic controls necessary to ensure them. In countries such as Japan, which have both a strong family tradition but also many wider forms of association, the large corporations act as surrogate family.[37]

Once the transition to bureaucratic organisation has been made, work becomes distinct and separate from family. Indeed, one of the many reasons for the masculine culture of many organisations is their definition as being not family, as having nothing to do with the rest of employees' lives. 'Family' comes to mean the rest of one's life which is not engaged in work, one's 'personal' or 'private' life (although that private life may contain much public activity). And one of the cardinal sins in Western organisations is to let one's private life intrude into one's work life. Furthermore, the less personal life one appears to have, the more committed one is assumed to be; the 'long-hours culture' is the natural result. Such a work/family contest is the inevitable result of attempting to create an impermeable boundary between the two in the first place.[38]

If one comes from a culture where work is very central and salient to identity, such as Japan or Israel,[39] then the contest may not be so painful as, for example, in the Netherlands or the UK, where work is less central. What is certain is that the contest inevitably results in considerable spillover, with family affecting work deleteriously and vice versa. Some may solve the dilemma by compensating for failure in one of the two areas by putting all their effort into the other. Others will devise all sorts of arrangements with their spouse or partner so that their careers advance at different times.[40]

Elements of the self and the employment relationship

However, this problem is entirely consequent upon a particular definition of the employment relationship: one which fails to take account of the employee's self. In this case the element of self which is ignored has been labelled 'family', but gender, occupation, and religion could be cited just as easily. In all these elements, and many more (e.g. ethnicity, sexuality and social class), the individual's self-concept is developing and changing. Yet most organisations fail to take account of the selves which employees bring to the employment relationship. It is due to this failure that the flip side of our metaphors is so often uppermost in the experience of most employees.

Disregard of all four elements of the self which I have explored in this chapter leads directly to the flip side of the metaphors. Organisations which fail to appreciate gender create Outsiders instead of Clubs, little understanding the underlying masculine nature of the rules of acceptability. Those which denigrate the craftsmanship or professionalism inherent in occupations give the lie to their profession of the value of human Resources. The widespread failure to recognise religion as core to the selves of many employees world-wide runs the risk of turning Partners into antagonists. And ignoring the family and treating it as a sphere of life outside the concern of the organisation ironically splits up the organisational Family.

So the economists' attempt to treat the employment relationship as a simple business transaction is doomed to failure. However rational, specific and detailed the transaction, at least one of the four elements of the self which I have described, if not others, will be implicated. For what seems reasonable and rational to top managers is very likely to threaten the selves of individual employees, or at the least to rub up against them uncomfortably. The emotional reactions which result do not assist the development of the relationship.

Summary

Individual differences are taken to refer not to essentialist elements of individuals, but to the result of social relationships. Hence it is differences between selves which are crucial to the nature of employment relationships.

Four elements of selves are discussed: gender, occupation, religion and family. These differ in their prominence, partly as a function of the individualist or collectivist values of individuals. They are each likely to have a profound influence upon the employment relationship from the employee's perspective, yet are seldom taken much into account by organisations. As a consequence of this neglect, the employment relationship is likely to suffer.

References

1　Hogan, R. T. (1992) Personality and personality measurement. In M. D. Dunnette and L. M. Hough (eds) *Handbook of Industrial and Organisational Psychology*, (2nd edn, vol. 2). Palo Alto CA: Consulting Psychologists Press.
2　Matthews, G. (1997) The big five as a framework for personality assessment. In N. Anderson and P. Herriot (eds) *International Handbook of Selection and Assessment*. Chichester: Wiley.
3　Weick, K. E. (1995) *Sensemaking in Organisations*. Thousand Oaks CA: Sage.
4　Hinde, R. A. (1997) *Relationships: A Dialectical Perspective*. Hove: Psychology Press.
5　Mischel, W. and Shoda, Y. (1995) A cognitive-affective system theory of personality: reconceptualising situations, dispositions, dynamics, and invariance in personality structure. *Psychological Review*, 102, 246–268.
6　Bailyn, L. (1989) Understanding individual experience at work: comments on the theory and practice of careers. In M. B. Arthur, D. T. Hall and B. S. Lawrence (eds) *Handbook of Career Theory*. Cambridge: Cambridge University Press.
7　Marecek, J. (1995) Gender, politics, and psychology's ways of knowing. *American Psychologist*, 50, 3, 162–163.
8　Ridgeway, C. (1991) The social construction of status value: gender and other nominal characteristics. *Social Forces*, 70, 2, 367–386.
9　Nkomo, S. M. and Cox, T. (1996) Diverse identities in organisations. In S. Clegg, C. Hardy and W. R. Nord (eds) *Handbook of Organisation Studies*. London: Sage.
10　Wharton, A. S. (1992) The social construction of gender and race in organisations: a social identity and group mobilisation perspective. *Research in the Sociology of Organisations*, 10, 55–84.
11　Calas, M. B. and Smircich, L. (1996) From 'the woman's' point of view: feminist approaches to organisation studies. In S. Clegg, C. Hardy and W. R. Nord (eds) *Handbook of Organisation Studies*. London: Sage.
12　Marshall, J. (1989) Revisioning career concepts: a feminist invitation. In M. B. Arthur, D. T. Hall and B. S. Lawrence (eds) *Handbook of Career Theory*. Cambridge: Cambridge University Press.
13　Gallos, J. V. (1989) Exploring women's development: implications for career theory, practice, and research. In M. B. Arthur, D. T. Hall and B. S. Lawrence (eds) *Handbook of Career Theory*. Cambridge: Cambridge University Press.
14　Gilligan, C. (1982) *In a Different Voice: Psychological Theory and Women's Development*. Cambridge MA: Harvard University Press.
15　Marshall (op. cit.).
16　United Nations Human Development Report (1994) New York: United Nations.
17　Marshall, J. (1984) *Women Managers: Travellers in a Male World*. Chichester: Wiley.
18　Baron, J. N., Davis-Blake, A. and Bielby, W. T. (1986) The structure of opportunity: how promotion ladders vary within and among organisations. *Administrative Science Quarterly*, 31, 248–273.

19 Tolbert, P. S. (1996) Occupations, organisations, and boundaryless careers. In M. B. Arthur and D. M. Rousseau (eds) *The Boundaryless Career*. New York: Oxford University Press.

20 Abbott, A. (1988) *The System of Professions: An Essay on the Division of Expert Labour*. Chicago: University of Chicago Press.

21 Kanter, R. M. (1989) Careers and the wealth of nations: a macro-perspective on the structure and implications of career forms. In M. B. Arthur, D. T. Hall, and B. S. Lawrence (eds) *Handbook of Career Theory*. Cambridge: Cambridge University Press.

22 Randle, K. and Rainnie, A. (1997) Managing creativity, maintaining control: a study in pharmaceutical research. *Human Resource Management Journal*, 7, 2, 32–46.

23 Alvesson, M. (1993) Organisations as rhetoric: knowledge-intensive firms and the struggle with ambiguity. *Journal of Management Studies*, 30, 6, 997–1015.

24 Gerpott, T. J., Domsch, M. and Keller, R. T. (1988) Career orientations in different countries and companies: an empirical investigation of West German, British, and US industrial R&D professionals. *Journal of Management Studies*, 25, 5, 439–462.

25 LaNuez, D. and Jermier, J. M. (1994) Sabotage by managers and technocrats: neglected patterns of resistance at work. In J. M. Jermier, D. Knights and W. R. Nord (eds) *Resistance and Power in Organisations: Critical Perspectives on Work and Organisation*. London: Routledge.

26 Bartol, K. M. (1979) Professionalism as a predictor of organisational commitment, role stress, and turnover: a multi-dimensional approach. *Academy of Management Journal*, 22, 815–821.

27 Huntington, S. P. (1996) *The Clash of Civilisations and the Remaking of World Order*. New York: Simon and Schuster.

28 Marty, M. E. and Appleby, R. S. (1993) *Fundamentalisms and Society*. Chicago: University of Chicago Press.

29 Fukuyama, F. (1995) *Trust: The Social Virtues and the Creation of Prosperity*. New York: Free Press.

30 Tawney, R. H. (1962) *Religion and the Rise of Capitalism*. New York: Harcourt, Brace and World.

31 Esposito, J. L. (1992) *The Islamic Threat: Myth or Reality?* New York: Oxford University Press.

32 Rothschild, J. and Miethe, T. D. (1994) Whistleblowing as resistance in modern work organisations: the politics of revealing organisational deception and abuse. In J. M. Jermier, D. Knights and W. R. Nord (eds) *Resistance and Power in Organisations*. London: Routledge.

33 Fukuyama (op. cit.).

34 Sabel, C. and Piore, M. J. (1984) *The Second Industrial Divide*. New York: Basic Books.

35 Ohmae, K. (1995) *The End of the Nation State*. New York: Free Press.

36 Granrose, C. S. and Chua, B. L. (1996) Global boundaryless careers: lessons from Chinese family businesses. In M. B. Arthur and D. M. Rousseau (eds) *The Boundaryless Career*. New York: Oxford University Press.

37 Abegglen, J. C. and Stalk, G. (1985) *Kaisha: the Japanese Corporation*. New York: Basic Books.

38 Fletcher, J. K. and Bailyn, L. (1996) Challenging the last boundary: reconnecting work and family. In M. B. Arthur and D. M. Rousseau (eds) *The Boundaryless Career*. New York: Oxford University Press.

39 Meaning of Working International Research Team (1987) *The Meaning of Working: An Eight Country Comparative Study*. London: Academic Press.
40 Sekaran, U. and Hall, D. T. (1989) Asynchronism in dual-career and family linkages. In M. B. Arthur, D. T. Hall and B. S. Lawrence (eds) *Handbook of Career Theory*. Cambridge: Cambridge University Press.

Chapter 12

Organisations and employment

Some fashionable definitions

But who is the employee's relationship with? Until now I have used the phrase 'the organisation' without attempting to define what is meant. I have discussed the individual's employment relationship as being with the organisation, but we only normally speak of relationships with people. I needed to spend Chapter 9 defining 'the individual' in terms of social psychology. 'The organisation' is even harder to come to terms with as a concept.

Commentators have come up with innumerable metaphors to describe organisations.[1] They range from the organisation as machine and as organism through to the organisation as brain or as a series of conversations. The preferred metaphor for each group of commentators is a function of the theoretical framework within which they work. So more traditional scholars who view organisations as serving functions and consisting of systems favour the machine and organism metaphors, whilst postmodernists talk in terms of organisations as conversations.[2] But wherever the metaphors come from, a wide variety is likely to be necessary if we are to adequately express the extraordinary range of difference in organisational forms.

This immense variety is a consequence of the litany of changes which every management text recites. Deregulation, enhanced competition, the globalisation of business, the impact of IT and the power of the stock and money markets are the interconnected drivers which have forced a proliferation of changes of organisational shape.

- Alliances have helped firms to manage the supply chain better and achieve economies of scale.
- Decentralisation into business units has enabled customer needs to be met more appropriately and tighter control to be exercised on targets and budgets.
- Reductions in the number of levels in the organisational hierarchy have also resulted in devolution of responsibility to those dealing with the customer or making the product.
- Flexibility has been encouraged by outsourcing functions, by novel

employment contracts, and by increased movement into and out of organisations.

These changes are the ones most frequently noted, and, one suspects, favoured by commentators. However, another set of organisational changes could be specified which are arguably just as common responses to the multiple drivers of change. The overwhelming need to cut costs and enhance productivity in the face of global competition has resulted in a spate of *mergers* and *acquisitions*, especially in such sectors as oil, pharmaceuticals, and banking. Mergers and acquisitions rather than alliances are the archetypal restructurings of our times. The opportunities for economies of scale are too great to pass over, and strength makes one less easy prey for predators. Hence the law of the Jungle seems just as appropriate a metaphor as the collegiality of allies. *Recentralisation* is proceeding apace, as the economies of scale made possible by information technology render central processing units the new first choice. The option of economy and control has often proved more attractive than that of decentralisation, devolution and empowerment. The levelling down of the hierarchy has seldom been carried out with the prime intention of delegating authority further down the line. Rather, middle management offered tempting targets for *downsizing* in the interests of cutting costs, with the outcomes of a greater workload for the survivors, and control by budget accountability rather than by manager. Finally, labour flexibility from the organisation's perspective may be *job insecurity* from the employee's.

The organisational forms favoured by commentators – alliances, decentralisation, delayering, and flexibility – have indeed increased in some sectors as a consequence of the drivers of change. Yet so have these others listed in the previous paragraph – mergers and acquisitions, recentralisation and downsizing. The result is a multiplicity of organisational forms.

In order to understand employment relationships, we cannot adopt a particular theory on the nature of organisations now and in the future. We need instead to take a psychological perspective. We need to define 'the organisation' in terms of the perceptions of the employee rather than in terms of commentators' analyses. Just as the employees' self is affected by the treatment they receive from 'the organisation', so 'the organisation' has to be defined in terms of the self's perceptions. Then the psychological nature of the employment relationship may be elucidated. So how *do* employees perceive the organisations for which they work?

Us and them

A motto in common use during the development of Nissan UK[3] was 'from us and them to just us'. The implication, of course, was that employees began to identify with the organisation to the extent that control was exercised entirely by themselves. This assumes that the success of the business was as salient a value within their own self-concept as it was in the interests of top management. Or, at the least, it assumes that even if this was not true of everyone, then those for whom business success was highly salient would ensure that the rest of their colleagues acted as though it was for them too.[4]

Whilst one does hear people in large organisations use 'we', this is much more likely to refer to their work team or to their business unit than to the organisation itself. Rather, they tend to use the word 'the organisation' as though they are speaking of a person. 'The organisation did this or said that', they say. They are normally referring to the organisation's top management, or less probably, to its representative in the form of their local manager. But the situation is complex. Local management may be willing and committed agents of top management. They may be complying through fear of punishment. They may pay mere lip service to top management's policies whilst pursuing their own agenda. Or they may actively subvert them. Thus 'the organisation' may be giving out contradictory messages, and 'them' may mean different things at different times.

Of course, in some organisations there is only 'me' or 'us'. If people are self-employed, or work in a mutually owned co-operative, or in a 'fourth wave' organisation of self-managing professionals, then there is no 'them', no 'other', with whom to have an employment relationship. Even in these cases, however, demanding clients may play the psychological role of demanding employers. The client contract manager, having screwed down the contract to a tight specification, may look over one's self-employed shoulder in just as controlling a manner as one's line manager of yore.

Again, in small family-based organisations, there may be only 'us'. Even when the family organisation becomes medium-sized, it may work within a network of similar organisations which are so tied to each other by mutual obligation and trust that the collective 'us' does not imply an 'other'.[5] On the other hand, if you are an employee of a family firm but not a family member, then 'them' immediately becomes a likely category of use. One can be as much at the mercy of an immediate head of the family as dependent upon a distant group of executives. In these cases it is likely to be a matter of 'me and them', or 'me and him (or her)'.

In larger organisations, 'us' and 'them' become the usual categories.[6] The attempt to depict large organisations as only consisting of 'us' ignores both the realities of power and also the recognition of those realities by employees.[7] It is the size of large organisations which allows 'me' to become 'us'; there are many potential allies against 'them'. What is more, there are many possible different definitions of who 'us' represents. These definitions may embody those elements of the self which employees feel that 'they' have ignored.

So, for example, 'we' may be my *work group* upon whom 'they' up there regularly dump from a great height. Or it may be my *project team*, who have been given impossible deadlines and inadequate resources. Or my *local branch*, whom 'they' never even visit, let alone value. Or my *union*, which represents people like me against people like 'them'. Or my women's or ethnic *minority group*, whom 'they' discriminate against. Or my *occupational group*, which supports 'our' professional standards against the erosion caused by 'their' constant pressures for cost cutting. All of these categories can comprise 'us'. They are likely to do so if the elements of employees' selves which the categories represent are ignored in the conduct of the employment relationship.

Socialisation and fit

So we have at last defined the final element in the employment relationship, 'the organisation'. It is the employee's perception of the organisation, and usually consists of senior management. Now we can finally start looking at the employment relationship as a psychological whole, an ongoing social process. Hitherto in this part of the book we have considered at length the psychological nature of relationships in general, giving us the process model for the employment relationship too (Chapter 9). We then concentrated heavily upon selves as the most important constituent element of the relationship, considering the cultural context (Chapter 10), and some specific elements of the self (Chapter 11). Having defined the other element, 'the organisation', in this chapter, we can finally look at the theory and research about the employment relationship itself. Unfortunately, little attention has been paid to the relationship as a whole process. Rather, researchers and commentators have concentrated either upon the organisation's actions and their impact upon the employee, or, less frequently, upon the reverse.

The vast preponderance of attention has been paid to one direction of the process of the employment relationship rather than to the other. What has primarily concerned us is how organisations can socialise employees so that they fit well into the organisation and the job. In other words, commentators and researchers have been concerned with helping 'them' to create an organisation in which there is no 'them' and 'us', but rather a generalised 'us', defined in the way 'they' see fit. What has concerned employees just as much, however, is how they can have some impact upon the organisation so that it takes more account of their own needs and identities as they perceive them.

Socialisation occurs both at the organisational and at the job levels of analysis. At the organisational level, socialisation is a usually conscious effort to enhance new employees' adoption of the officially sponsored values, goals and culture of the organisation. At the job level, more and more attention is being paid to assisting the learning of the tasks and duties of the job and to fitting the employee to it.[8]

The primary features of the socialisation process are as follows:

- It occurs over a period of time until new employees eventually become accepted by colleagues and management as fully fledged organisational members.
- It requires the employee to get a wide range of information about the task, the role, the work group and the organisation.
- It also involves social learning, as the employee becomes integrated into the organisation's culture.
- Since culture includes values, attitudes and norms of behaviour, the employee is also likely to undergo personal change where these cultural features do not coincide with their own.
- To the extent that the employee has little influence over the socialisation process, the changes in their selves which it brings about are not necessarily those which they would have otherwise chosen.
- The outcomes may be positive for the organisation and the individual; the organisation gaining a committed employee, the individual gaining self-esteem, a sense of belonging and job satisfaction. Alternatively, the employee may not welcome the changes in their selves which they have had to make in order to adapt to the organisation's culture.

A variety of models of the development of organisational socialisation have been proposed. Most of them suggest three stages: an information-gaining and sense-making stage; a stage of accommodating one's prior expectations to the experience of the realities; and the development of longer-term acceptance and commitment. It is quite clear that the process of socialisation cannot consist merely of the compliant acceptance of what one is told. Evidence demonstrates that employees have to have an attitudinal and affective response to the organisation if they are to be committed enough to go the extra mile. They have either to identify with it or else internalise its values.[9] Organisations can foster such commitment if they invest in employees[10] and support them.[11, 12]

Thus positive results of socialisation are contingent upon organisational support and employee personal change. Yet such personal change as is necessary for the individual to fit into the organisational culture may be incompatible with their existing selves. In particular, new value priorities may clash with strongly held values or ideologies; or a very salient element of the self may be devalued; or self-esteem may be threatened. Some socialisation procedures, coyly labelled 'divestiture',[13] actively seek to change radically the employee's self. They use such methods as initiation rituals, endurance of physical hardship, group bonding and removal from all contact with one's previous existence, to impose new elements of the self.

However, in most organisations other than the military, a far more subtle process occurs, so subtle that it certainly cannot be termed conscious socialisation. It has been characterised as the Attraction Selection Attrition process,[14] and results in the snuggest of fits between employees and organisations. Individuals are naturally *attracted* to occupations and organisations which they believe demonstrate a congruence with their selves. The representatives of that organisation then *select* from amongst these already self-selected applicants those who are most like themselves. As these newly appointed employees are socialised into the organisation, there is a degree of *attrition* amongst those who realise that their selves and their new colleagues are incompatible. The outcome is a very good socialisation and fit indeed! One may even mistake certain organisations for sets of clones. The evidence clearly shows that even within accountancy, a profession noted for its stereotypical membership, different firms are distinguished from each other by the sets of value priorities held by their members. They stay longer in the firm as a consequence.[15]

Of our eight metaphors for the employment relationship, Crusade best expresses the divestiture face of socialisation, Club the snug fit. But whatever the metaphor, the fact remains that the relationship is usually dominated by the organisational partner. It is the organisation which makes the running in the relationship and seeks to socialise other selves into its own culture. As the Attraction Selection Attrition model suggests, individuals can at least decide whether they wish to enter (although many have to go after any job which they think they have a chance of getting). But thereafter the pressure to conform is powerfully exerted. It is important to note the multiple and interlocking sources of this organisational power:

- Top management ('them') take those decisions that most affect employees in big ways; regarding, for example, mergers, downsizing, restructuring, change programmes and the employment contract.
- Top management control most of the resources which support employees in carrying out their work.
- The structures, norms and values of the organisation are likely to support the exercise of top management's authority, so that it is accepted without question.
- In particular, extensive systems of discipline and control are available to top management.
- The modes of exercising power (the game and its rules) are only learnable by those who have the opportunity to play the game.
- Management divides and rules by dealing with employees individually rather than collectively.
- Surveillance methods have increased in their effectiveness and use.
- Employees who have a weak sense of self and low self-esteem can regain them by the effective and efficient exercise of their work roles; they may identify with the organisation.
- Top management can employ communication strategies which give meaning and legitimacy to management decisions.

The futility of resistance can be made clear: to quote the situation of the majority of the world's employees:

> The necessity of dull compulsion in order to earn one's living, the nature of busy work, arduous exertion and ceaseless activity as routinely deadening, compulsory, and invariable: such techniques of power may easily discipline the blithest of theoretically free spirits when the conditions of that freedom become evident.[16]

Employee influence

But the situation is not entirely one-sided. Many would argue that the current restructuring, fluidity and ambiguity within many organisations offers far more opportunity for individual employees, and groups of them, to exercise power in the employment relationship. If there are fewer middle managers; if roles are constantly changing and are ill-defined; if people are selected for the roles that they might play rather than for job vacancies; if structural change is constantly occurring: then there is a vacuum which the individual can fill.

Furthermore, if messages from top management as to what is expected are mutually contradictory, then employees can choose to hear the message which suits them better, or otherwise exploit the contradiction. The same applies if there is a single message but it is an ambiguous one. Individuals can create roles to better suit their selves. They can use the situation to enhance their curriculum vitae and gain training and development. They can organise in their own way in their local situation without being found out. They can, in fact, enact organisation themselves, thereby becoming 'the organisation' as far as they are concerned.[17, 18]

Of course, some are more individually suited to taking these bold unilateral initiatives than others. Those who think in ways independent of the contextual constraints and who attribute outcomes to themselves rather than to their situation are strong candidates. So are those with a high need for power and autonomy, those for whom work is a central element of their selves, and those who especially value creativity, challenge, and entrepreneurship as their 'career anchors'.[19] However, *individual* resilience and determination is not the only thing that can bring a degree of power and influence to individuals. In the corporate chaos it becomes easier to create *groups* of people tied together by shared elements of the self that they wish to enhance: occupational, gender, ethnic or special interest groups, for example. The networks of influence that such groups can exercise across the organisation by sharing and using information can be powerful indeed.

Control may be gained by employees over their *outcomes*: their pay, for example, or their contracts, but usually only if they have strong labour market power or union representation. It may also be gained over their *actions*:

how they behave at work, how they carry out their tasks. And their power may derive from *information* about what is likely to happen, which enables them to prepare for organisational events. Even when these forms of control are unattainable, employees can still assert their power by 'misbehaving', demonstrating that they can still choose not to conform completely to what 'they' have decided is right and proper.[20] A sense of self-esteem and autonomy is maintained somehow.

Control may also be exercised by defining for oneself a *subjective* career in which one can make progress despite the fact that one's 'objective' career (i.e. that defined as desirable by 'them') may languish. To the extent that individuals have met their own needs, such a career can in a sense be independent of the fact that they have been compelled to meet the organisation's needs. For example, people have succeeded in adding skills to their c.v. which were not immediately vital to the organisation: IT professionals learn another system despite its lack of applicability to their current work.

These examples of individual influence and control, however, are interestingly selected. They focus upon employee needs which are mostly consistent with, or at the least, not actively hostile to, organisational needs. It is as though commentators limit the elements of the employee's self to those which result in 'win–win outcomes'. For example, the story of the individual's learning coincides with the story of the organisation's innovation. There are many other elements of the self, however, which are likely to be incompatible with organisational needs. It is worth pursuing the topic of 'organisational misbehaviour' at greater length in order to make this point more clearly.

There has always been a wide range of 'misbehaviour' in organisations, from timewasting, absenteeism, slowing down the rate of working, pilfering and sabotage through to subversive humour and overt sexuality. The earlier examples in this list may be attributed to a rational attempt to diminish or compensate for the intensification of work pressure. The later ones are only explicable in other ways, however. In particular, they may be seen as techniques for affirming elements of employees' selves which are not taken into account by management. Clowning is a way of actively subverting management's seriousness, thereby demonstrating that there are other things in life that are more important than work. Satire indicates that the satirist is not such a fool as to be taken in by the latest management rhetoric or fad. Displays of bawdy humour indicate that people are really male or really female, not desiccated units of production; or else they draw attention to the fact that someone is going to get married.[21] And note that all of this 'misbehaviour' is social in its nature: the audience has to laugh at the clown or the satirist. It is definitely 'us' getting one over 'them'.

Relationships between us and them

The previous two sections of this chapter, dealing with the influence of the organisation upon the individual and the influence of the individual upon the organisation, have a curiously static feel about them. However, we have already rejected such linear models of the employment relationship in favour of a far more dynamic two-way model in which the actions of each party affect the other, and the other's actions, reciprocally. Hence to talk, for example, about employees impacting upon 'organisations' without reference to what 'the organisation' has recently done to employees is to tell much less than half of the story. Rather, we need to return to our psychological model and ask again what it tells us about the process of relating: the process of constructing and conducting an employment relationship in which each party acts upon and reacts to the other.

We first need to return to our insistence that relationships are essentially between people; the employment relationship is between individual employees and those with most power and influence over what happens to them at work – normally top management. The employment relationship is between 'us' and 'them', or between 'me' and 'them'. This means that we can allocate the same psychological processes to either end of the relationship. Just as employees have selves which are expressed in their actions and reactions, so too do top managers. And just as employees' selves may be affected and changed by top management's actions and by their own, so top management's selves are also in principle malleable. The employment relationship is not between abstractions: 'the individual' and 'the organisation'. It is rather between people and groups of people.

Of course, the extent to which the selves of employees and top management change as a consequence of their relationship will vary. Some employees may suffer severe damage to their self-esteem or a huge enhancement of it as a consequence of the way in which their annual appraisal was conducted; others will merely laugh cynically. Some top managers will moderate their view of themselves as socially concerned when they have made a large part of a local workforce redundant; others will treat it all as a business success and reserve their notions of social morality for their 'private' lives.

Thus each party will have a different story to tell. Their narratives will be based on the retrospective sense they have made of the history of their employment relationship. Big events and small; their own actions and the other's; their own responses to the other's actions and vice versa; the whole sequence of escalating actions and reactions; the changes they saw happening in their selves and in the other's; all of these are likely to feature in the parties' *accounts*.

Accounts

Sensemaking is the fundamental way in which people develop these accounts of the employment relationship, and their sensemaking tends towards coherence and reason. They need to be able to explain why things happened, and are each apt to find their own explanation.[22] The particular events which they are keen to explain are normally those which stand out as unusual and which have most impact upon them. These are particularly likely to be events which resulted in people having to undertake major transitions.

Why, employees ask, did 'they' agree to the merger? Why did 'they' employ those consultants to 're-engineer' us? Or from top management's perspective: Why wasn't she willing to take an overseas posting? Why didn't they accept our generous wage offer? And the answers which people supply to such questions as these tend to be attributional: they agreed to the merger because they were greedy for the shares; they introduced re-engineering because they didn't know what else to do; she refused to go because she lacks ambition; they refused our offer because they don't understand the pressures we are under to cut costs. All the above causal attributions are to the person rather than to the situation, a direction of attribution more likely when the parties are particularly salient in each other's mind. And the less the parties talk to each other, the easier it is for them to make motivational attributions which are based on ignorance.

Of course, attributions are not the only component of accounts. People may also seek to capture the essence of their employment relationship by using metaphor, as we have seen. They may seek to compare their own employment relationship with those of others, to see if theirs is typical or if there is something unusual about it. They may downgrade (or upgrade) its importance relative to other relationships, so as to defend or enhance their self-esteem. The fundamental point is that they will seek to create an account which:

- is coherent in itself, thereby providing meaning
- both expresses and maintains their selves
- and guides their conduct of the relationship.

This is true of employees and also of top management. Both parties develop their own accounts of the employment relationship hitherto. But these accounts are likely to be highly divergent. This is because the selves which the accounts were created to support and display were probably markedly different. Work and identification with the business and its success are likely to be far more salient elements in top management's selves than in those of their employees. And their conduct of the relationship and the sense they make of it is derived from their own selves. They frequently appear to take little notice of the selves of their employees. All those elements which are not about performance and productivity may in their view be of little relevance, unfortunate occasional intrusions into their relationship with their human resources. As far as they are concerned, skills, effort and compliance are the key elements of employees' selves.

All this talk of sense-making and causal attribution should not, however, detract our attention from the fundamentally *emotional* nature of accounts. Making sense and attributing causes sound as though they are searches for reason; they are *post hoc* efforts at rationalisation. However, accounts are accounts of people's experience, and a great deal of experience is emotional. It is how we felt at the time about the news of our promotion, or of our colleagues' redundancy, or of the next management change initiative, which is central to our experience and therefore to our accounts of it. Any account of an episode in the employment relationship will be an account of how we felt about it as well as of why we think it happened. Unfortunately, whilst we are very good at rationalising long after an episode has occurred, we are not so good at recalling how we felt at the time, nor at putting these feelings into words.

Accounts, then, are our ways of summarising our past experiences of a particular employment relationship. They deal with the historic episodes upon which the relationship is based, and they inform our present and future actions within it. Accounts, however, belong to individual parties to the relationship, and are the results of talking and thinking about it. How are we to manage better the actual conduct of the relationship?

Dialogues

I will argue in the last part of this book that unless top managers take greater account of employees' selves, they will be unable to achieve their companies' survival and prosperity in the global environment. The establishment of *dialogue* is therefore necessary, since it enables the parties to understand each other's selves. I will therefore propose dialogue as the fundamental process through which the employment relationship should be negotiated.

One way of defining dialogue is to state what it is not. Dialogue is the opposite of rhetoric. Rhetoric seeks to persuade the other to take the perspective that one wishes them to. This perspective is not necessarily the other's own perspective; it is more likely to be the perspective which will result in the other doing what we want them to do. Dialogue seeks, on the contrary, to discover what the other's perspective is, and to discover and reveal one's own.

An initial step towards dialogue is to exchange *accounts* of past episodes in the relationship. The reasons which are given for actions may be *post hoc* rationalisations, and people's story of how they felt at the time may be hazy and full of self-defence. But the accounts which parties give certainly allow the other to see the background they are assuming, their overall perspective. They may also allow the identification of the salient elements of their selves.

However, accounts are about the past. Dialogues are about the present and the future as well as about the past. The present is far more emotionally charged than the past, since the past is perceived through a rationalising memory which makes experience more reasonable, whilst feelings have faded. A process as cool as the exchange of accounts is therefore unlikely to continue to succeed when parties are talking about the here and now of the employment relationship; about episodes in which both are heavily involved and about which they both feel strongly. Rather, dialogue needs to permit the expression of emotion.

Given the destructive potential of some forms of emotional expression, however, it has been argued[23] that dialogues about the present need to be managed in particular ways. Specifically, a situation needs to be created in which people can disclose their experience and feelings to others for them to interpret and provide feedback. In other words, we first need to discover our own true feelings and reflect upon them. Where the 'us and them' gulf is deep and wide, third parties are needed to perform this function, so that each of the two parties to the employment relationship can subsequently engage in gradual disclosure to each other of what they have learned in this way.

The idea that it is only front-line employees in service industries who have to perform emotional labour is mistaken. Most junior and middle managers are under great pressure to appear optimistic and upbeat whatever they are actually feeling. Most employees are expected to appear enthusiastic and highly motivated. The elicitation of authentic feelings is therefore counter-cultural and difficult, particularly if they are feelings of shame or fear or inadequacy. Although facilitation by a third party is one solution, another is for top managers to initiate authentic emotional dialogue by volunteering their own current feelings and setting up situations for safe dialogue (as practised, for example, by Ricardo Semler in Brazil). However, unless they have already earned the trust of employees, they are more likely to interpret their emotional expression as an attempt at impression management.

Dialogue about the present is fundamental to the success of the employment relationship because it is the only situation in which the full influence of feelings upon the relationship can be revealed. As I have argued, feelings about past episodes fade and are rationalised. Feelings about the future are likely to be limited to a certain set of emotions only, such as optimism, anxiety, resignation, etc. It is only in the midst of an episode that feelings are present in all their variety and power.

Yet it is at this point that feelings are most crucial, since the successful management of an episode depends upon the understanding by both parties of what the other feels about the situation and why. The usual good management practice of releasing as much information about, for example, redundancies or mergers as possible is therefore inadequate. This is because the information which top managers release may neither address employees' emotional needs nor reveal their own. They may, for example, assume that employees who survive are feeling relieved and grateful, whereas they may actually be feeling angry or guilty. Only if the two parties understand the other's feelings, and thence salient elements of their selves, will they act in ways which sustain and enhance the employment relationship.

So feelings about and perceptions of the present, and fears and aspirations for the future need to be exchanged as well as accounts of the past. In human relationships, dialogue at best enables parties to create together a story with which both can agree. This may be an extremely minimalist story: 'our relationship always has been, and continues to be, a strictly transactional one of high performance in exchange for good financial rewards', for example. But the point is that if true dialogue, in which feelings have been disclosed, has occurred, the parties will understand each other's selves. They will realise what the other thinks and feels. They will adapt accordingly, for they will better appreciate the likely effects of their own actions. Instead of an escalating cycle of action and reaction, real negotiation and compromise can occur, and the relationship develop and prosper.

It is extraordinarily hard for top management to engage in dialogue, however. Normally, they hold the *balance of power*, and see little reason to divulge their accounts, let alone to engage in dialogue. Yet unless they do so, they stand little chance of acting in ways which take account of employees' selves. Moreover, unless employees understand better the perspective of top managers, their own actions and reactions are similarly unlikely to form the foundation for a fruitful relationship.

The *use of rhetoric* by top managers is another major obstacle to the occurrence of true dialogue. In order to demonstrate the depth of this problem, I will describe in the final part of the book three fundamental areas of organisational practice which illustrate it. They are the issues of control and compliance; of the segmentation of the employment relationship within organisations; and of organisational change. All of these issues are obfuscated by rhetoric from top managers and by prevailing managerialist discourse, which misrepresent the experience of the majority of employees. Such rhetoric is by definition likely to prevent both parties understanding the feelings and selves of the other, since it is not aimed at understanding but at persuasion. The need, therefore, is to enable top managers to substitute dialogue for rhetoric. In the final chapter I will seek to explore ways of setting up the conditions for dialogue.

Summary

The final element of the employment relationship is 'the organisation'. From the employee's perspective, this term normally refers to the senior management of the organisation. The employment relationship has typically been considered from the organisation's perspective, or, more rarely, from the employees'. As far as the organisation (top management) is concerned, the socialisation and compliance of employees are crucial. Many succeed in creating organisations that are so well socialised as to consist of conformist clones. When the relationship is viewed from the employee's perspective, we discover that employees find ways of influencing the relationship so as to affirm their selves. When it is examined as a dynamic ongoing process of events in real time, it becomes clear that it will only be facilitated by dialogue. Dialogue is contrasted with rhetoric, in that dialogue entails the discovery of the other's feelings and the revealing of one's own, thereby enabling the selves of the parties to become clearer to each other. Rhetoric seeks to influence the other's perceptions and feelings. Whilst accounts of the past and talk about the future are important elements of dialogue, its most powerful use relates to present experience, where emotions are most prominent.

References

1 Morgan, G. (1997) *Images of Organisation* (2nd edn). Thousand Oaks CA: Sage.
2 Clegg, S. R. and Hardy, C. (1996) Organisations, organisation, and organising. In S. R. Clegg, C. Hardy and W. R. Nord, (eds) *Handbook of Organisation Studies.* London: Sage.
3 Wickens, P. D. (1987) *The Road to Nissan.* London: Macmillan.
4 Garraghan, P. and Stewart, P. (1992) *The Nissan Enigma: Flexibility at Work in a Local Economy.* London: Mansell.
5 Granrose, C. S. and Chua, B. L. (1996) Global boundaryless careers: lessons from Chinese family businesses. In M. B. Arthur and D. M. Rousseau (eds) *The Boundaryless Career.* New York: Oxford University Press.
6 Kelly, J. and Kelly, C. (1991) Them and us: social psychology and the new industrial relations. *British Journal of Industrial Relations*, 29, 1, 25–48.
7 Hardy, C. and Clegg, S. R. (1996) Some dare call it power. In S. R. Clegg, C. Hardy and W. R. Nord (eds) *Handbook of Organisation Studies.* London: Sage.
8 Anderson, N. R. and Ostroff, C. (1998) Selection as socialisation. In N. Anderson and P. Herriot (eds) *International Handbook of Selection and Assessment.* Chichester: Wiley.
9 O'Reilly, C. and Chatman, J. (1986) Organisational commitment and psychological attachment: the effects of compliance, identification, and internalisation on pro-social behaviour. *Journal of Applied Psychology*, 71, 3, 492–499.
10 Tsui, A. S., Pearce, J. L., Porter, L. W. and Tripoli, A. M. (1997) Alternative approaches to the employee–organisation relationship: does investment in employees pay off? *Academy of Management Journal*, 40, 5, 1089–1121.
11 Eisenberger, R., Fasolo, P. and Davis-Lamastro, V. (1990) Perceived organisational support and employee diligence, commitment, and innovation. *Journal of Applied Psychology*, 75, 1, 51–59.
12 Wayne, S. J., Shore, L. M. and Liden, R. C. (1997) Perceived organisational support and leader–member exchange: a social exchange perspective. *Academy of Management Journal*, 40, 1, 82–111.
13 Van Maanen, J. and Schein, E. W. (1979) Towards a theory of organisational socialisation. *Research in Organisational Behaviour*, 1, 209–264.
14 Schneider, B. (1987) The people make the place. *Personnel Psychology*, 40, 437–453.
15 O'Reilly, C. A., Chatman, J. A. and Caldwell, D. (1991) People and organisational

culture: a profile comparison approach to assessing person–organisation fit. *Academy of Management Journal*, 3, 2, 487–516.

16 Hardy and Clegg, op. cit., p. 628.

17 Bell, N. E. and Staw, B. M. (1988) People as sculptors versus sculpture: the roles of personality and personal control in organisations. In M. B. Arthur, D. T. Hall and B. S. Lawrence (eds) *Handbook of Career Theory*. Cambridge: Cambridge University Press.

18 Weick, K. E. (1996) Enactment and the boundaryless career: organising as we work. In M. B. Arthur and D. M. Rousseau (eds) *The Boundaryless Career*. New York: Oxford University Press.

19 Schein, E. (1993) *Career Anchors: Discovering Your Real Values* (rev. edn). London: Pfeiffer.

20 Ackroyd, S. and Thompson, P. (1999) *Organisational Misbehaviour*. London: Sage.

21 Westwood, S. (1984) *All Day Every Day: Factory and Family in the Making of Women's Lives*. London: Pluto Press.

22 Isabella, L. A. (1990) Evolving interpretations as a change unfolds: how managers construe key organisational events. *Academy of Management Journal*, 33, 1, 7–41.

23 Fulop, L. and Rifkin, W. (1997) Representing fear in learning in organisations. *Management Learning*, 28, 1, 45–63.

Part 3

Employment dialogues

Chapter 13

The compliance dialogue

The second part of this book was theoretical in nature, as I sought to establish a psychological framework for the employment relationship. The framework chosen was that of a social process, in which the parties' actions and reactions were affected by, and also affected, their selves. I argued that the reason why many employees experienced their employment relationship in terms of the flip sides rather than the top sides of the eight metaphors was because organisations have failed in general to take account of the elements of self which employees bring to the relationship. The relationship process, in other words, was failing because fundamental elements within it were being ignored. I concluded that the process needed facilitation, and that the basic tool for facilitation was likely to be dialogue.

Whereas dialogue discovered the other's feelings and selves and revealed one's own, rhetoric, currently a more common activity, sought to change them. In the next three chapters I seek to anchor these theoretical notions in current and likely future organisational issues. These chapters will thus provide a reality check for the theoretical framework and its associated tool of dialogue. Given the current prevalence of rhetoric, I will start each chapter with an analysis of how the real issue has been concealed by managerialist rhetoric. I will then seek to demonstrate how a process of dialogue might address the issue so as to improve the employment relationship. This chapter addresses the rhetoric of commitment and the likely reality of compliance.

The rhetoric: commitment

Both the Crusade and the Customer metaphors are favourite elements of top management rhetoric. Crusade has been used to suggest that all the troops share the aspirations, values and assumptions of their charismatic leader. They, too, treat the Holy Grail as the most important thing in the world, worth dying for in a foreign field. They, too, are totally committed to the cause.

Used by top management, the Crusade metaphor seeks to persuade employees that there exists just such a commonality of basic assumptions and values across the organisation: a common culture. The use of culture change programmes by top management is thus essentially an admission that a common culture has not yet been 'bought into' by everyone. However, such a change initiative sends a message that a common culture is perfectly possible, and certainly highly desirable in terms of the beneficial outcomes to the business (and therefore to all). It usually fails to conceal the fact that the values and assumptions to be shared are those proposed by top management.[1]

From a shared set of values and assumptions arises a shared commitment, the rhetoric continues. This commitment is towards the organisation, and contains a strong affective component: the employee feels favourably towards the organisation, identifies with its failures and successes, and is willing to go the extra mile on its behalf. The committed employee is constructive and productive, and furthermore, feels tied to the organisation so that he or she wishes to stay.

Now the Customer metaphor clicks into the rhetoric. The employees share the values and assumptions of the business, and so are in business for themselves. They have bought into, and taken part ownership of, the business. Therefore they can be expected to accept responsibility and accountability. Indeed, they should expect and demand these things for themselves as business partners, and therefore customers, of top management.[2] They should be empowered to act as business people in their own right, so that they can be free to exercise their entrepreneurial talents. Then they can take initiatives for themselves, create innovation, and do deals.

Finally, just to ensure that the message is clear, the rhetoric contrasts the centrepiece of the story, organisational commitment, with another concept: 'mere' compliance.[3] Commitment comes from within, from shared values; compliance is surface behaviour. Compliance is based upon a transactional relationship, motivated by reward, or by fear of punishment if you break the transactional terms. It used to be policed by old-fashioned bureaucratic managers, assisted by their handmaiden the personnel manager (now replaced by shiny new Human Resources). Of course, all these vestiges of the bad old past are only to be found in failing organisations. We are successful, so by definition all of you, our employees, are deeply committed; and we value that commitment.

Culture, not structure

The reality is a far cry from the rhetoric. But the perceived size of this gap depends upon what we observe. When we look at organisational *structures*, there is considerable support for the rhetoric. The extraordinary rate of change in organisations' environment has forced them to adapt themselves in a variety of ways to the markets in which they operate. Changes in the structure and form of organisations have been described as 'protean': constantly changing, and hard to get a grip on. Research into 450 European firms[4] indicated that between 1992 and 1996, operational decision-making was decentralised, project working increased, and so did the incidence of outsourcing and strategic alliances. The trend towards decentralisation in particular suggests a degree of local empowerment and the possibility of delegation, autonomy and entrepreneurship in the interests of the business.

However, changes in structure do not necessarily relate directly to the experience of employees and the nature of the employment relationship. For example, decision-making may be devolved to local business units, but the centre may maintain control by setting frequent and demanding targets and requiring a constant flow of operational information back to base. Employees may feel just as much under management control as before they were devolved.

The best source of evidence about the reality is not structure, but rather, organisational *culture*. After all, the analysis of culture centres upon the discovery of the assumptions and values commonly found in an organisation, and these are the very same terms in which the rhetoric is couched. There are numerous definitions of organisational culture, and many different models which seek to describe and understand it. However, the one most useful to our present discussion is the Competing Values model.[5] This specifies four different cultural orientations, which should, of course, be treated as ideal types rather than mutually exclusive categories. They are as follows:

- *Support* values highly affiliation, participation, co-operation, mutual trust, team spirit, and individual growth. Informal communication and decision-making is the order of the day, feelings and ideas are expressed freely, and individual commitment is emphasised.
- *Innovation* involves searching for environmental information, anticipating change, creative thinking and activity, openness to change and willingness to experiment and take risks. Involvement and commitment from employees is assumed and expected.
- *Goals* is about rationality, competitiveness, performance indicators, performance management, accountability, contingent rewards, and the efficacy of processes such as appraisal. Its artefacts include mission statements, objective-setting and budget targets.
- *Rules* emphasises hierarchy, authority, order and stability, compliance, responsibilities, procedures, job descriptions, rules and discipline.

Clearly, support and innovation imply less control than do goals and rules. if the commitment and empowerment rhetorics represent reality, then we would expect that the support and innovation cultural orientations would be winning out at the expense of rules and goals. I will argue that the opposite is the case in the experience of most employees.

Innovation and support or rules and goals?

This broad-brush interpretation of current trends is certainly at odds with that of most commentators and management thinkers. They argue that organisations are moving even more strongly away from control. Rules are giving way to innovation, they suggest, and support too is increasing as organisations recognise they have to learn by helping employees to share knowledge and skills. Rules, characterised as insupportable old-fashioned bureaucracy, are the *bête-noir* of most commentators, and viewed as down-graded in all successful companies. These views are another example of mis-taking prescription for description; what is desired for what is happening, and, in particular, for what most employees are experiencing.

Certainly, global competition has been the primary driver in forcing organ-isations to concentrate upon an external focus in preference to an internal one. Top managements have had to focus more carefully upon competitor performance, global business trends, market segmentation, customer requirements and shareholder expectations. Their strategic responses have been varied. Young organisations in young industries have indeed developed innovative and supportive cultures. Young communications, media, software and consulting companies, for example, thrive on adhocracy, teamworking and creative thinking.

Yet even within these relatively new and expanding sectors, more mature companies move inexorably towards the other cultural dimensions. Ask any member of a large consulting, accountancy, or law firm about the tyranny of timesheets and the pervasive demands of revenue targets. The up or out career structures of the professional sector are alive and well.[6] This is why the creative top managers of rapidly growing firms in new industries soon give way to more management-oriented CEOs and directors. Business sector certainly does influence organisational culture, since the competitive environment of the sector, the requirements of customers, and indeed the expectations of society are unique to the sector.[7] But the increasing age and size of the organisation and its developing business strategy soon rebalance the cultural focus. In particular, goals is likely to supplant support, and maybe innovation too, as the primary orientation.

It is when we consider the less young and glamorous sectors, however, that the commentators' scenario becomes obviously unsupportable. The fastest growing occupations in the West are certainly in the service sector, but they are not those of the innovative knowledge worker, as repeatedly claimed. Rather, they are in such jobs as fast food (in the UK, there are more employees working in Indian curry houses than in the coal, steel and shipbuilding industries combined!). In the USA, the five fastest growing occupations, nearly all in the service sector, are predicted to be janitorial, custodial, medical, sales and restaurant jobs requiring low-technology skills only. The single occupation of security guard for buildings accounted for more jobs than the five fastest growing high technology occupations combined.

Only 6 per cent of jobs in the USA are sufficiently technically oriented to require two or more years of higher education.[8] In the UK, there is a similar increase in the proportion of the workforce in the service sector, with employment in the manufacturing sector dropping from 34.5 per cent in 1954 to less than 20 per cent in 2000. Today some 3 per cent of the UK working population is employed in call centres, and call centre work is the fastest growing occupation. Those employed in these growing occupations by and large experience an organisational culture which is oriented towards rules and goals much more than towards innovation and support.

There are two main reasons for the move towards these cultural orientations for the majority of service workers. The first is the strategic direction which most such service providers have taken: to compete primarily on the basis of cost competitiveness and productivity. The requirements to control costs and to enhance productivity per worker have inevitably resulted in rules and goals cultures, aimed at maximising management control over the workforce. The second reason is the increased systematisation of knowledge, whereby expert systems automate and make available the knowledge previously located with professional employees. Here again, strong control is exercised to ensure complete and accurate compliance with the rules for using the system.

Call centres: a case of rules and goals

The growing *call centre* phenomenon puts flesh on to this generalisation, and perfectly illustrates both the push towards enhanced productivity and the impact of the systematisation of knowledge.[9] Call centres have been characterised as the new sweatshops, and as the return of Taylorism. Some call centres in the UK suffer an 80 per cent turnover rate per annum, and the cost of recruiting and training replacements is more than £100 million. The first strike in UK call centres occurred in November 1999.

Call centres beautifully illustrate the push towards *productivity goals*. Essentially, each employee has targets in terms of the number of calls they have to make, or respond to. In order to enable progress towards these targets to be assessed, time spent on each call, time between calls, and time to respond to the call are all recorded automatically and monitored by a supervisor. Usually, an upper limit to the length of a call is set, and employees are called to account if it is exceeded. All calls are recorded, and the supervisor may listen in to a call at any time without the employee being aware.

The enhancement of the productivity of each employee is the key objective, as in many cases the call centre is outsourced, and the client organisation can switch to another supplier if a cheaper service is offered. Hence the managers of the call centres are themselves driven by budget and productivity targets and the targets of individual operatives are derived from these. The call centre may be given a great deal of autonomy in structural terms: 'a business in its own right'. But control is exercised by the central imposition of goals and targets.

It is hardly surprising that the better call centre staff are not vocal extroverts, but rather rule-conscious, dutiful, conscientious, perfectionist and introverted. They are still people-centred, however, whereas, again unsurprisingly, their supervisors and managers are far more driving and task-centred.

The *systematisation of knowledge* is also a key element of call centre operations. Consider, for example, a call centre for the purpose of offering insurance quotations to potential customers. The accumulated knowledge of insurance professionals, together with actuarial calculations, has been reduced to a software programme. All the call centre operator has to do is to ask the caller a number of pre-set questions, the answers to which will determine the policy offer made. The operators have to stick rigidly to the procedure. As a result of their experience, they may feel that they can give a superior offer to the one given by the system, but they must not do so. They have to obey the *rules*. If possible, they have to understand the difficult idea that even if their particular solution to a specific case might have been a better one, nevertheless sticking rigidly to the formula is more profitable for the company overall. Even the firsthand contact which the operator has with the potential customer is seldom utilised. Rather, consumer trends are analysed by the central processing and analysis of data from the call centres.

Now of course, the financial services company ultimately employing the call centre staff also has to come up with new and competitive insurance products. There has to be an element of innovation culture around to maintain the company's competitive advantage. But this element is likely to be limited to a relatively few individuals located together in a small part of the organisation: innovation as sub-culture. The main operation and its management, however, are driven by goals and rules, and their main concern is control. The only sort of flexibility which they are interested in is flexibility of labour so that a 24-hour-per-day, seven-day-per-week service can be provided.

This discussion demonstrates the dangers of characterising an organisation's culture on the basis of the strategic orientation of its top management. The financial services company concerned may be recognised by the business press as producing innovative products and as meeting the expectations of shareholders well. But these virtues are the consequence of a highly segmented structure and a highly specific subculture, such that the call centre operators would consider the new product developers to be creatures from another planet, and vice versa. So, in most larger and more mature organisations in most business sectors, the dominant cultural orientations are goals and rules, in the sense that these are the orientations experienced by the majority of employees. And the drivers of these orientations are the perceived imperatives to cut costs, enhance productivity and automate processes.

Rhetoric, dialogue, and trust

The gap between the rhetoric and the reality is immense. In fact, most employees' experience consists of the direct opposite of the rhetoric. They are not so committed to the organisation that they act as entrepreneurs on its behalf. They are not Crusaders or business Customers. On the contrary, they feel that they are unlikely to share top managers' values, and hence to commit their selves to 'the organisation'. What is more, even if they wanted to, they would not be able to. For in truth, top managers do not want them to take initiatives or exercise entrepreneurial autonomy. They are unwilling to develop a culture of support or innovation. In fact, what they want them to do is to comply. Most employees have to comply with the rules, because management need procedures to be carried out precisely as they require. And they have to comply with the goals because management requires the achievement of productivity targets within budget in the interests of cost competitiveness.

The existence of this reality gap is the first threat to the employment relationship. Regardless of the content of the rhetoric, what matters is its extreme distance from employees' experienced reality. The natural emotional responses to such rhetoric are mistrust of, and cynicism towards, its authors.[10]

The mistrust may take several forms. Some employees may take the rhetoric at face value, that is, as top managers' expression of what they actually believe and expect to happen. The fundamental and most obvious form of mistrust in this case will be mistrust of top management's *reliability*. There was an implied promise in the rhetoric, and it was not kept. The implied promise of empowerment, for example, is experienced as more responsibility for the same pay with less resources. The other form of mistrust when rhetoric is taken at face value is of *competence*. 'How can they possibly believe that we work like they say we do', they ask. 'They must be completely out of touch with what's really going on.'

Others may perceive the rhetoric to be an attempt at persuasion, and make attributions as to why top managers should be seeking to persuade them of a different version of events to their own. These attributions may well be to top management's *motives*. 'They are trying to pull the wool over our eyes', they may feel, or 'They are trying to get more out of us for less once again.' Or employees may infer what top managers' *perception* of them must be if they engage in such unreal rhetoric: 'They must think I'm a complete idiot to believe in that sort of rubbish.' Frequent feelings of mistrust of this nature, arising out of several rhetorical episodes, are likely to lead to cynicism and breakdown of the employment relationship.

The only way to re-establish a relationship in which the parties begin to trust each other is for top managers to stop using rhetoric and to substitute for it the practice of dialogue. The use of *rhetoric* both demonstrates and breeds mistrust. It demonstrates the mistrust of top managers in employees' competence and motives, since by definition it seeks to change their perceptions of their experience. It breeds mistrust in employees because it ignores their concept of themselves as capable of evaluating what they see and hear and making their own sense out of it. It can even be construed in its extreme forms as the thought police seeking to enforce ideological conformity.

Dialogue, on the other hand, both demands and engenders trust. The parties are explicit to each other about how they feel or felt about an episode in the employment relationship (for example, a downsizing exercise). Indeed, in true dialogue they both elicit the other's feelings and help them to make sense of them. The expression of emotions about the past, the present, and the future reveals the nature of each of the parties' selves to the other.[11] Such self-disclosure is known to engender trust. Moreover, dialogue about intentions enables commitment to be generated for the agreed actions.

The compliance dialogue

The gap between commitment rhetoric and compliance reality is not the only problem, however. Top management's need for compliance is in itself a major issue. The fundamental question is whether the compliance required is sufficiently compatible with employees' selves to make the employment relationship sustainable.

The requirement to comply is hard to reconcile with employees' selves, especially with the selves of those who are more individualist in their values. They see themselves as having agency in their lives: the ability to affect what happens to them. They react adversely to attempts to coerce them. They believe that they are unique individuals who are autonomous and strive towards authenticity, being true to their selves. At the very least, they like to think, they will only comply on the basis of their informed consent.

Yet their experience is only too often one of being offered no choice. The option of informed consent is not on offer. The only option open is that of leaving if you don't like it. Some of the recent attempts to segment markets in the financial services sector offer a good example of new compliance requirements which are contrary to many employees' values. Customer service has long been a key rhetoric in the industry, and many customer-facing employees certainly feel strongly in favour of providing a good service to the individual and corporate customers with whom they deal. Now, however, customers are being segmented into 'plums' and 'lemons', i.e. those individuals 'of high net worth' from whom the banks will make a good profit, and those from whom little can be expected. Instead of seeking to meet all clients' needs as best they can, employees will be expected to deliver different qualities of service depending on the customer's potential profitability.

Employees' *emotional reactions* to being forced to respond in ways contrary to their inclinations are likely to include frustration at not being able to do what they think right, and, consequently, aggression towards those perceived to be responsible: top management. Confrontation is one possible behavioural response, but a more frequent one is subversion. Here is a case of an employee making sure the customer always wins at the expense of the company:

> To counter-balance the callous pursuit of efficiency, I concede all guarantee claims to customers without question. If a customer complains, I repair or replace at our cost. If I questioned more closely, or examined receipts of purchase, I am sure many would be out of date.[12]

The first task of any dialogue about compliance, then, is to understand the other party's perspective upon it. And the most powerful way of so doing is to discover their feelings when expecting compliance and when having it expected of them. Given their position of power, it is top managers' responsibility to initiate the dialogue. This they should do by explaining their reasons for requiring compliance and expressing their feelings about having to do so. Then they should elicit employees' feelings about being expected to comply.

To return to the call centre example, the *frustration* of employees at being unable to take any initiatives of their own on the customer's behalf is likely to be considerable. Management may justify the expert systems in use as necessary, since they can demonstrate that they are more profitable, although many employees will need convincing that they could not have done better through their own personal knowledge of the customer. Since 50 per cent of all employees are soon likely to be graduates in the Western world, such self-confidence and initiative is going to be typical of many call centre employees.

However, employee frustration and aggression is more likely to be felt regarding the systems for control and surveillance. Instead of using the technology to enable employees to monitor their own performance and improve upon it, most call centre managers use it to monitor performance themselves. The systems are used to control rather than to 'informate'.[13] Instead of the perception of employees that they are being continuously controlled, both by the expert system and by the surveillance systems, dialogue could lead to a mixture of system control and self-control. Whilst the expert system required total compliance, the surveillance system could be used by operatives rather than by their supervisors. The overwhelming rules and goals culture could then be tempered by a perception of support. Paradoxically, it is only when a culture of support and, to a lesser extent, one of goals is present that organisational commitment is likely to occur.[14, 15]

Table 14 The compliance dialogue

Rhetoric	Reality	Results	Dialogue outcome
Shared culture	Rules	Mistrust	Admission, justification of
Commitment	Goals	Frustration	compliance
Empowerment	Compliance	Subversion	Surrender some control

A major requirement, then, is for top managers to stop engaging in rhetoric about empowerment and commitment and to start engaging in dialogue. Such dialogue will reveal that what they need and will continue to need from most employees is compliance. An appreciation of the difficulty of reconciling compliance with the selves of many employees will result in the granting of as much autonomy as possible in areas where compliance is not essential. But before they can engage in dialogue effectively, top managements will have to regain the trust which they have lost through their use of rhetoric which is at odds with employees' experience. Table 14 summarises the compliance dialogue.

Summary

Recent managerialist rhetoric has promoted the idea that employees are being, and should be, empowered to take initiatives and decisions on the organisation's behalf. It assumes that employees share the same values and culture with top managers, and that therefore they will feel committed to the organisation. In most organisations and for most employees, this rhetoric contradicts their experience. For their experience is of a requirement to be continuously compliant, both in terms of following the rules and of achieving the goals. Call centres are a good current example. The mistrust caused by this gap between rhetoric and reality as experienced creates a problem, even before the issue of compliance can be addressed. When compliance is required, elements of employees' selves and value systems may be incompatible with compliance, and they may react strongly and emotionally. Dialogue will need to explore these reactions and come up with ways in which the agreed and recognised need for compliance can be tempered with a degree of autonomy.

References

1 Beer, M., Eisenstat, R. A. and Spector, B. (1990) Why change programmes don't produce change. *Harvard Business Review*, 68, 6, 158–166.
2 du Gay, P. (1996) *Consumption and Identity at Work*. London: Sage.
3 Legge, K. (1995) *Human Resource Management: Rhetorics and Realities*. London: Macmillan.
4 Ruigrok, W., Pettigrew, A., Peck, S. and Whittington, R. (1999) Corporate

restructuring and new forms of organising: evidence from Europe. *Management International Review*, 39, 2, 41–64.

5 Quinn, R. E. (1988) *Beyond Rational Management*. San Francisco: Jossey Bass.

6 Morris, T. (2000) Promotion practices and knowledge bases in the professional service firm. In M. Peiperl, M. Arthur, R. Goffee and T. Morris (eds) *Career Frontiers: New Conceptions of Working Lives*. Oxford: Oxford University Press.

7 Gordon, G. G. (1991) Industry determinants of organisational culture. *Academy of Management Review*, 16, 2, 396–415.

8 Perrow, C. (1996) The bounded career and the demise of civil society. In M. B. Arthur and D. M. Rousseau (eds) *The Boundaryless Career*. New York: Oxford University Press.

9 Whitehead, M. (1999) Churning questions. *People Management*, 5, 19, 46–48.

10 Kramer, R. M. (1996) Divergent realities and convergent disappointments in the hierarchic relation: trust and the intuitive auditor at work. In R. M. Kramer and T. R. Tyler (eds) *Trust in Organisations: Frontiers of Theory and Research*. Thousand Oaks CA: Sage.

11 Fineman, S. (1996) Emotion and organising. In S. R. Clegg, C. Hardy and W. R. Nord (eds) *Handbook of Organisation Studies*. London: Sage.

12 Manning, W. E. G. (1992) PhD thesis (unpublished), University of London.

13 Zuboff, S. (1988) *In the Age of the Smart Machine*. London: Heinemann.

14 Sheridan, J. E. (1992) Organisational culture and employee retention. *Academy of Management Journal*, 35, 4, 1036–1056.

15 Vandenberghe, C. and Peiro, J. M. (2000) Organisational and individual values: their main and combined effects on work attitudes and perceptions. *European Journal of Work and Organisational Psychology* (in press).

Chapter 14

The difference dialogue

The rhetoric: inclusiveness

The rhetoric about commitment, which I reviewed in the previous chapter, implies that everyone in the organisation holds the same values, and is therefore committed to its success. Rhetoric about *inclusiveness* implies that everyone belongs and is treated in a way which recognises their membership.

Several of our eight metaphors are frequently enlisted to assist the inclusiveness rhetoric:

- Family implies that all belong, and there is a connotation of care and equal treatment.
- All belong to the Club, too, although some members are more senior than others, and there has to be a committee to get things done.
- The Contract metaphor has been cleverly converted from notions of individual deals to a single contract: '*the* psychological contract has now become flexibility in exchange for employability'. A single contract implies that all are on the same footing.
- 'We value everyone', says the Resource metaphor. The recent emphasis on best practice in Human Resource processes implies that all will benefit from its application.
- On the rare occasions when the Citizen metaphor is used, equal rights for all are usually implied, with justice most prominent amongst them.
- And finally, Partnership implies everyone sharing in the benefits which result from shared risks and shared effort.

The Resource metaphor, in particular, has recently come to be used to imply a general inclusiveness, over and above that derived from belonging in an organisation. The message is that Human Resource processes have now been refined to such a degree that they have been clearly demonstrated to benefit the organisation's bottom line. Thus best practice in HR is rapidly becoming *universal*, since of course organisations seize upon every method of enhancing their bottom line and hence their competitive advantage. Thus all employees are likely to benefit, since those organisations which fail to engage in good HR practice will go to the wall.

More pervasive, however, is the rhetoric *within* organisations about inclusion. The rhetorical devices are several. The language of metaphor is often supported by the creation of cultural artefacts designed to point to underlying shared values. Single status employment contracts, staff magazines, and the removal of certain visible status differentials, such as different canteens or parking spaces, are such artefacts. All have the purpose of persuading employees that they are all included, recognised, and valued. And the inclusion is into the organisation as a whole, not so much into the business centre, occupational group, local office, work group, or any other 'approved' category. It is certainly not into less approved groups, such as pressure groups for a better life–work balance.

Reality: exclusiveness across organisations

The free use of metaphors to persuade employees that their experience is one of inclusion is likely to backfire catastrophically. For it gives them the chance to seize upon the flip side of the metaphors as more accurately expressing their experience. From their perspective:

- One big happy Family is more accurately portrayed as favourite sons and ignored siblings.
- The congenial Club is actually run by a cabal, who only admit to their number those, like themselves, of whom they approve.
- The so-called mutually agreed Contract is unilaterally imposed by top managers.
- The 'valued' Resources are either over-valued and over-paid or, mostly, used up rather than invested in.
- Citizenship is supposed to imply equity and justice, but it's one law for them and another for us.
- And speaking of equity, we put in comparable effort to them, but they take far far more back than us: hardly the basis for an equal Partnership.

These common hostile reactions to inclusiveness rhetoric are supported by a variety of arguments. First, I will critique the rhetoric that suggests that *across organisations* in general, Human Resource policies, processes and practices are rapidly improving the employment relationship. Recently, a lot of attention has focused upon the findings[1] (see Chapter 4) that the use of a set of mutually integrated and consistent HR processes enhances firms' bottom line performance. The implication has mistakenly been drawn that there exists a model of best employment practice for organisations in general. Hence the employment relationship will run smoothly and uniformly, and all employees, as well as the organisations themselves, will benefit.

A frequently added qualification to this optimistic inference suggests that there also has to be a degree of fit between the set of HR processes and the organisation's strategic direction if bottom line benefits are to accrue. Hence an organisation with a strategy of cost competitiveness will need a somewhat different bundle of HR processes, and indeed a different set of practices, policies, and philosophy[2] from one seeking to succeed by means of innovating new products and services or entering new markets. An organisation which concentrated heavily upon attracting, developing and retaining highly qualified employees would be making a mistake in so doing if its strategy is one of cost competitiveness.

These assumptions of *best practice* and *best fit* are both mistaken, the first profoundly so.[3] Recent advances in theory and research in the area of organisational strategy indicate that HR processes do not act in a direct and uniform way upon corporate performance.[4] Rather, they have indirect and organisation-specific effects. They are more the outcome of underlying philosophies than the cause of advantage. Instead, long-term competitive advantage comes from the rare and inimitable ways in which HR and business philosophies, policies, practices and processes are interwoven with each other and embedded deep within particular organisations.

The key issue is therefore about how human and non-human resources are integrated, and the history and depth of this inter-penetration. Expressing this issue in relational terms, true integration is unlikely to have occurred if, for example, the HR function has failed to develop close working relationships with finance, marketing, sales, etc. (or, if the organisation is project based, with project leaders and managers and with central office). Such integration is hard to imitate and takes time. However, its benefits become clear when change is navigated successfully. For it is the relationships resulting from integration which enable companies to adapt to change by, for example, enhancing their rate of innovation.[5]

Thus instead of a simplistic and static contingency view of certain HR strategies fitting certain business strategies, a much more dynamic view of strategic fit is required. Only such a dynamic view is capable of dealing with the increasingly *ad hoc* and emergent nature of strategy in rapidly changing business environments. Moreover, only a dynamic and historically embedded account of integration can explain why some firms are markedly more successful than others. For if success is dependent upon best practice and simple fit, which are easy to imitate, why are all firms not embracing them and becoming equally successful?[6] The answer to this rhetorical question is, of course, that success depends upon the existence of mutually supportive relationships across the organisation which enable rapid and yet sound management of change to occur. And such relationships exist only as a result of successful long-term integration of business and people factors, which is very hard to imitate.[7]

So, rather than an increasingly homogeneous universe of organisations all improving their chances of success by embracing best practice and best fit, we see an increasingly heterogeneous and differentially successful universe, the successful organisations being those which have become uniquely well integrated. The picture of a homogeneously well-treated labour force is usually a rhetorical fiction.

Reality: exclusiveness within organisations

Not only are there considerable differences in the nature of the employment relationship *between* organisations within the same country and the same sector, however. There are, more importantly, acute differences *within* organisations. For many, often for most, the relationship is best characterised as one of compliance in respect of goals and of behaviour, as I argued in the previous chapter. But organisations are sharply segmented. There is a wide variety of other forms of relationship for different categories of employee.[8] These range from temporary agency employees who are sent away if they fail to get up to speed in their first couple of hours in the organisation, through to the pool of talented individuals just below the Board whose immediate development is considered of paramount importance.

Consider, for example, another group of employees. Despite the recent rhetoric regarding 'the end of the career' for all, many organisations continue to spend major resources in recruiting, training, and retaining graduates whom they regard as of high potential and as longer-term seedcorn for the business. Whilst not necessarily envisaging career paths which lead to the Board, they certainly expect to offer development opportunities which will result in such employees becoming highly marketable both inside and outside the company.[9]

The expectations held *by* this group of employees are even higher than those held *of* them. They want challenging international work, good pay, a commitment to develop them, and team support. One such from amongst a sample of international high flyers said:

> I want a change in the frame of mind from a traditional style investment banking attitude to a dynamic organisation that is quick to adapt and innovate. If these aspects don't surface, then I'll leave.[10]

When asked what type of company they would most like to work for if they left their current employer, they mentioned start-ups and small entrepreneurial niche players, and criticised their organisation's bureaucracy, hierarchy and politics. Yet the biggest single complaint was about lack of investment by the organisation in their personal development, despite the fact that, paradoxically, the more marketable they become the more likely they are to stay. And, incidentally, they want to 'have it all', work–life balance being a central career value for around half of the sample. Their loyalties are towards their colleagues, their manager, their clients, their employer and the senior managers, in that order of priority.

With the boundaries of the organisation becoming so indistinct, and the drive towards 'flexibility' so seemingly inexorable (see Chapter 5), a wide variety of employment relationships are on offer.[11, 12, 13] Individual agency workers such as temps have already been mentioned. What is their relationship with the organisation where they are currently placed? Some of them become almost permanent fixtures and stay longer than some so-called permanent staff. Are they asked to the Christmas party?

What of teams of consultants, formally employed by a management consultancy, but again often long-term fixtures in a client organisation? What of temporary employees of the organisation itself, or part-timers, or those on fixed term contracts? What of those who work at home, or are constantly mobile away from the office, or work in the back office rather than in front of house?

Perceptions of these employees by top managers may include such stereotypical features as casual, low skill, poor quality, short-term, disposable, uncommitted, female, and poorly paid. As a consequence the employment relationship may become exploitative in a variety of ways.[14] For example:

- The employer may want an agency employee or a contractor to integrate successfully within the internal team, but be unwilling to invest in any training to ease this integration.
- An employer of temporary labour operating in a buyer's market for such labour may push that workforce beyond acceptable limits in the sure knowledge that they can find others to take these workers' places should they object or leave.
- An employer may offer merely a sequence of short-term contracts, thereby depriving employees of employment rights and retaining the possibility of dismissing them.

Likewise, flexible workers themselves may take advantage of their situation:

- Consultants may 'steal' solutions, which they find or have developed in a client organisation, and use them with their next client who happens to be a competitor of the first.
- Those permitted to work flexible hours to enable them to fulfil domestic responsibilities may arrive later and finish earlier than is compatible with their overall working time.

Both parties in these cases are failing to appreciate the employment relationship from the other's perspective:

- The employer enforcing a variable hours or a zero hours contract may ignore the disruptive effect these contracts have upon employees' arrangements for child care, etc.

- The employer offering casual employment to a large proportion of the workforce may be unaware or unconcerned that the consequence for the employee is an inability to obtain financial credit.
- Employees with scarce skills on fixed term contracts may hold employers to ransom, failing to understand or care about the difficulties they are causing in the employment relationship with jealous permanent employees.
- Employees abusing overtime or stealing time have clearly failed to appreciate the employer's need to compete on cost and productivity.

In sum, from those just below the Board and the young high flyers with their high expectations, through the full-timers whose employment relationship is dominated by compliance, via external contractors who nevertheless have to be managed, down to the lowliest temp or casual worker at continuous risk of exploitation, a wide variety of relationships exists in every large organisation and in most medium-sized ones. This variety gives the lie to rhetoric of inclusivity. So does the ever-increasing gap (certainly in the USA and the UK) between the rewards gained by top managers and the average rewards in the organisation. In truth, today's organisations are deeply segmented.

Feelings of inequity and injustice

As I argued in the previous chapter, the first reaction to the gap between inclusion rhetoric and exclusion reality is one of mistrust, simply because of the gap. However, here I will concentrate upon the likely reactions of the majority of employees to the increasing segmentation and diversity of employment relationships.

Feelings of *inequity*, and the anger and resentment which often accompany them, are likely reactions to segmentation. I have already discussed (Chapter 6) the importance of feelings of distributive and procedural justice for the employment relationship.[15] The central element of equity is comparison; one compares the ratio of one's own inputs to one's outcomes with the ratios of others. It therefore depends considerably upon who is chosen as a comparison group as to whether there is a perception of equitable treatment or not.

One common comparison is with others doing a similar job in *other* organisations in the same sector, and indeed such comparisons are often made explicitly in the setting of reward levels. If employees perceive that others doing a similar job to a similar level of performance have altogether more favourable employment outcomes, they will feel inequitably treated. The same applies to perceptions of procedural justice, provided that employees can get information about the processes and the degree of respect enjoyed in other companies. Yet, as I discussed above, organisations within the same sector may differ markedly in the nature of their employment relationships with their employees, and for very good business reasons. Any constructive difference dialogue requires top management to explain these reasons.

A second common comparison when employees are assessing equity is with others in *their own* organisation. Given the ever-increasing variety of employment relationships within organisations, the opportunities for unfavourable comparisons are also increasing all the time:

- Long-serving full-time employees may compare their input/outcome ratios unfavourably with fixed-term or contract staff, for example, especially if they spend a lot of their own time showing them the organisational ropes.
- Hard-pressed middle managers, who perceive themselves to be holding the organisation together under continuous pressure to perform or leave, may contrast their own lot with that of top management, who receive huge bonuses despite the mediocre financial performance of the company.
- Ambitious young employees who have worked themselves up the ranks compare their own occasional training experiences with the long-term career development lavished upon the high flyer cohort.

Feelings of inequity are primarily about *distributive* injustice. However, equally strong feelings are aroused by the experience of *interactional* injustice. The rhetoric of equal value is denied by the payment of differential respect to different categories of staff. Making support staff redundant and making accountants redundant are conducted very differently in some of the big accountancy firms. Accountants, after all, may be subsequent future clients. Feelings of interactional injustice relate clearly to fundamental elements of self-esteem and identity. 'I am a human being and a person', thinks the employee, 'yet they treat me inhumanly and impersonally. I'm just another number as far as they are concerned.' The fundamental ways in which respect is shown to others as fellow human beings, let alone as those in a relationship with us, are not always recognised as appropriate actions within the employment context.

Yet the deep emotions which arise in reaction to the differential treatment which employees receive are of fundamental importance to the future of the employment relationship. For they are indicative of the elements of the self which are brought into play in the conduct of that relationship. Indeed, their expression is the fundamental condition for dialogue to commence. These aspects of the dialogue are summarised in Table 15.

The second rhetorical wave: flexibility

It is absolutely clear that top managers feel the need to segment the employment relationship within their organisation. Yet the commitment and the

Table 15 The inclusiveness dialogue

Rhetoric	Reality	Results	Dialogue outcomes
Inclusiveness	Segmentation	Exploitation	Justification of
Commitment	Varied practices	Inequity	segmentation
Common practices		Injustice	Different dialogues

inclusivity rhetorics are hopelessly at odds with increasing segmentation. Like a second wave, the *flexibility* rhetoric has been developed to rationalise such segmentation.[16]

Now the flexibility rhetoric is an attempt by top managers to make sense, both for themselves and for others, of their recent and ongoing segmentation of the organisation. It is indeed a very logical and rational account, using as it does the theory of 'the flexible firm' provided by commentators some 15 years ago.[17] It runs as follows. The needs for functional and numerical flexibility, obtained from core and peripheral workers respectively, derive from the perceived need for companies to be versatile to compete successfully. Such versatility is required both in terms of supply of labour (numerical flexibility) and its use (functional flexibility).

The flexibility rhetoric therefore suggests that top managers have taken a conscious strategic decision to segment the workforce yet further, and then carried it out. Such rational decision-making is what both top managers themselves and their employees believe that they should be doing. Moreover, not only have they been virtuously strategic; flexibility is also by definition a virtuous objective to pursue.[18] Its opposite, after all, is rigidity, and who can afford the handicap of rigidity in a free and rapidly changing marketplace?[19] To anticipate the Darwinist rhetoric of change which will be described in Chapter 15, flexibility enables adaptation to the environment rather than corporate extinction.

The evidence, however, suggests that increased segmentation has occurred for a variety of reasons. It has been much more opportunistic than strategic, with probably the most frequent opportunities seized being those to cut costs.[20] Moreover, much of the added flexibility has been the result of local management decisions rather than corporate policy. Furthermore, the availability of expert systems has enabled much work to be deskilled and undertaken by part-time or contract employees. And the customer expectation of 24-hour-per-day, seven-day-per-week, service makes numerical flexibility a necessity.

Functional flexibility, too, has often been a by-product of other management actions rather than a strategic policy. When the numbers of employees are reduced in the interests of cost competitiveness, those that are left often have an increased range of tasks to perform. Hence they are forced to become functionally flexible through the intensification of their work.

Rather than experiencing the benefits of flexibility, however, employees may feel uncomfortably stretched.

In general, employees' reactions are likely to be less emotionally charged to the flexibility than to the inclusiveness rhetoric. The discourse of the free market and the survival of the fittest within it has become pervasive, and 'flexibility' is a common-sense response which fits into these stories nicely. On the other hand, a very fundamental social principle is at issue here, the perceived violation of which is likely to lead to profound, if less hot, emotional reactions on the part of employees. That principle is *social reciprocity*. As with the commitment rhetoric, so with flexibility: the expectation of flexibility held by top management needs to take into account our own needs for flexibility, feel employees. If they want us to be committed to the organisation, we need some commitment from them in return. If they are asking for more than just competence and effort from us, we need to get from them something more than just our wages. And since job security and a balance between life and work are important to us, there is every reason for us to expect the same from them as they want from us: commitment and flexibility.

Thus the rhetorics of inclusiveness and flexibility are likely to lead to different emotional reactions from employees. Employees will feel mistrust of top management because the inclusiveness rhetoric is at such odds with their experience. They will feel angry about the inequities and injustice which that rhetoric seeks to conceal. In the case of the flexibility and the commitment rhetorics, however, the feelings may be deeper. Employees may perceive the employment relationship to be so hopelessly out of balance that they may become alienated from it altogether.

Different dialogues and the difference dialogue

The implications for dialogue are clear. There will have to be different forms of dialogue with different segments of the organisation. These dialogues will be around commitment, co-operation, and compliance. For core employees, the dialogue will involve top management asking for *commitment* to the organisation and offering commitment back. Mutual commitment implies a high level of trust and a longer-term relationship. Top managers will have to reveal why they themselves are committed to the organisation, and they will have to elicit and listen carefully to the limits to commitment that such employees are likely to express. Fundamental issues regarding the values implied in identification with the organisation in question will have to be raised and answered. And, in the longer term, commitment will have to be expressed by both parties by actions which are not immediately reciprocated.

For others, the dialogue will be more about *co-operation* than commitment. Top management will expect many employees to co-operate with, and implement effectively, the changes which they wish to make. Their use of the 'flexibility' rhetoric is top managers' attempt to justify their requirement of employees to make the personal and work transitions that are necessary for such changes to occur. Co-operation implies goodwill, however, and a fundamental condition for goodwill is a degree of reciprocity in the relationship. Thus flexibility on the part of employees requires flexibility on the part of management; employees' co-operation with top management's expectations implies managers' co-operation with those of employees. And employees' most fundamental expectation when they are asked to make transitions is a degree of management support and understanding of the elements of their selves which are implicated in these transitions.

Another condition of co-operation is a perceived willingness on the part of top management to explain and justify changes, and an effort to provide a degree of structure and continuity which enables employees to make meaning out of their working lives. Both the commitment and the co-operation forms of difference dialogue imply a certain length of time in the employment relationship. Both require a sequence of reciprocal actions before commitment or co-operative goodwill can be established. Both depend to a greater or lesser degree on mutual trust. Hence, both depend upon the expression of feelings and the appreciation of the other's self. A third form of dialogue, however, requires *compliance*. Co-operation implies goodwill, whereas compliance merely implies a transaction. Compliance does involve feelings, since parties can feel satisfied or dissatisfied with the terms of the transaction and angry, frustrated or cynical if they are perceived to have been broken. However, there is no implication of any other element to the relationship than the terms of the transaction, and therefore compliance with those terms is its central concern.

These are three different forms of dialogue, each appropriate to different segments of the segmented organisation (and subject, of course, to individual variation, since dialogues are in the end with individuals at the local if not at the organisational level). In addition to these different dialogues, however, there also needs to be a *dialogue of difference*. That is, employees and top managers need to engage in an exchange which justifies and explains why different forms of dialogue are undertaken with different segments of the workforce. Specifically, top managers may need to address the questions:

- Why are there different employment relationships in our organisation from those pertaining in other comparable organisations?
- Why are the relationships in our organisation so different from each other?
- Why is each of these relationships necessary and appropriate?

The flexibility rhetoric is an attempt by top management to justify segmentation itself. Dialogue, however, by definition is not rhetoric, but rather an exchange between parties in an effort to understand the other. Its purpose is to enable the parties to act reciprocally in a mutually satisfactory relationship.

Of particular importance in the difference dialogue are the attempts by top managers to understand the selves of employees in different segments. The danger of projection of one's own self on to others' is very obvious, even when the attraction, selection and attrition process[21] has already resulted in a degree of cloning. In the *commitment* dialogue, for example, top managers who were formed in a different social climate may expect a similar level of organisational commitment to that which they themselves have demonstrated. In the *co-operation* dialogue, they may assume a level of loyalty and goodwill which was typical of more deferential times and less conditional on reciprocity. With regard to the *compliance* dialogue, they may have difficulty in understanding why large numbers of employees work to live rather than live to work; or alternatively, why compliance alone is not very satisfying to a large proportion of a modern workforce.

On the other hand, top managers should be able to admit unequivocally that there are different dialogues going on with different segments of employees. Such an admission will by definition contradict much of the inclusiveness rhetoric which they may have been putting out previously. They will have considerable difficulty in explaining the increasing gap between the rewards of those who are at or near the top and those of the rest. However, they should at the least be able to point out that there is reciprocity in each of the three forms of dialogue. Those who are highly committed to the organisation and who live to work get tangible and intangible commitment back. Those who demonstrate goodwill and co-operation have their own personal needs considered. And those who comply reliably receive their return according to the terms of the transaction.

What the difference dialogue might achieve then, is recognition that there is a degree of reciprocity apparent in all the forms of the employment relationship. The situation will then be avoided whereby top managers engage in the rhetorical expression of expectations which are not appropriate to the form of dialogue in which they are engaged. It is foolish and counter-productive to expect organisational commitment from employees engaged in a compliance dialogue. Hence employees may be less likely to become alienated by inappropriate expectations. Top managers will also have to make it clear in the difference dialogue that the opportunity for employees to engage in a different form of dialogue to the one they are currently in is in principle open.

To conclude with the concrete: if different dialogues occur, we might expect to see such outcomes as the following:

• Developmental roles for specialists which allow them to contribute primarily from their expertise, but which provide the minimum commercial and managerial development necessary to ensure that they add value.
• Duty rosters which mesh in with employees' family and community obligations.

- Managers who have been trained specifically in the management of flexible staff, and training programmes designed to ensure that flexible staff can get quickly up to speed, achieve their targets, and understand the organisation.
- Integration strategies to ensure that home and teleworkers feel part of the organisation.

In all of these cases, a degree of reciprocity[22] has been achieved, since each party has satisfied some of their own needs in satisfying those of the other. The outcomes of such mutuality are normally increased motivation and intention to stay. For example, Littlewoods, a UK retailing and mail order company, report that 98 per cent of women return after maternity leave and 30 per cent of senior management positions are filled by women as a result of their job-sharing and term-time contract provisions. Littlewoods appraise their managers on their family-friendly approach as well as on their achievement of conventional business targets. As family structures change, more women go to work, the elderly live longer and need caring for, and livelihoods become less secure, efforts to take account of these concerns in a variety of employment relationships demonstrate the value of dialogue.

The strategic benefits of mutuality for top management are clear. Dialogues which result in mutually beneficial agreements, which are subsequently kept, generate trusting relationships. Such relationships form the deeply embedded social capital which combines business and people philosophies, policies, and practices and secures unique competitive advantage.[23] These aspects of the four dialogues are summarised in Table 16.

Summary

There are two forms of managerialist rhetoric which address the issue of differences between employment relationships. The first form, the inclusiveness rhetoric, seeks to persuade employees that such differences are minimal. Employees' own experience of differences between and within organisations gives the lie to such rhetoric, resulting in feelings of mistrust because of the rhetoric. The differences themselves may result in feelings of inequity and injustice. A second form of rhetoric explains the differences in terms of the need for organisational flexibility. Although this is more convincing, the

Table 16 The flexibility dialogue

Rhetoric	Reality	Results	Dialogues
Flexibility Strategic intent	Little reciprocity Opportunism	Anxiety Alienation	Commitment, co-operation, compliance, and difference dialogues

absence of a reciprocal flexibility to fit employees' own needs may lead to feelings of alienation from the employment relationship itself. Different dialogues along the themes of mutual commitment, mutual co-operation, and mutual compliance were recommended, together with a difference dialogue which sought to understand the need for these three forms of dialogue.

References

1 Huselid, M. (1995) The impact of human resource management practices on turnover, productivity, and corporate financial performance. *Academy of Management Journal*, 38, 3, 635–672.
2 Schuler, M. (1998) Human resource management. In M. Poole and M. Warner (eds) *The Handbook of Human Resource Management*. London: Thomson.
3 Purcell, J. (1999) Best practice and best fit: chimera or cul-de-sac? *Human Resource Management Journal*, 9, 3, 26–41.
4 Lepak, D. P. and Snell, S. A. (1999) The human resource architecture: toward a theory of human capital allocation and development. *Academy of Management Review*, 24, 1, 31–48.
5 Tsai, W. and Ghoshal, S. (1998) Social capital and value creation: the role of intrafirm networks. *Academy of Management Journal*, 41, 4, 464–476.
6 Purcell (op. cit.).
7 Becker, B. E. and Huselid, M. A. (1998) High performance work systems and firm performance: a synthesis of research and managerial implications. *Research in Personnel and Human Resources Management*, 16, 53–101.
8 Hirsh, W. and Jackson, C. (1996) *Strategies for Career Development: Promise, Practice, and Pretence*. Brighton: Institute for Employment Studies, Report 305.
9 Arnold, J. and Mackenzie Davey, K. (1994) Graduate experiences of organisational career management. *International Journal of Career Management*, 6, 1, 14–18.
10 Winter, J. and Jackson, C. (1999) *Riding the Wave: The New Global Career Culture*. Redhill: Career Innovation Research Group.
11 Reilly, P. (1998) Flexibility in Europe. *European Journal of Work and Organisational Psychology*, 7, 1, 1–12
12 Emmott, M. and Hutchinson, S. (1998) Employment flexibility: threat or promise? In P. Sparrow and M. Marchington (eds) *Human Resource Management: the New Agenda*. London: Financial Times and Pitman.
13 Brewster, C. (1998) Flexible working in Europe: extent, growth, and the challenge for HRM. In P. Sparrow and M. Marchington (eds) *Human Resource Management: the New Agenda*. London: Financial Times and Pitman.
14 Noon, M. and Blyton, P. (1997) *The Realities of Work*. London: Macmillan.
15 Folger, R. and Cropanzano, R. (1998) *Organisational Justice and Human Resource Management*. Thousand Oaks CA: Sage.
16 Legge, K. (1995) *Human Resource Management: Rhetorics and Realities*. London: Macmillan.
17 Atkinson, J. and Meager, N. (1984) *New Forms of Work Organisation*. Brighton: Institute of Manpower Studies, Report 121.
18 Hyman, R. (1991) Plus ça change: the theory of production and the production of theory. In A. Pollert (ed.) *Farewell to Flexibility?* Oxford: Basil Blackwell.
19 Pollert, A. (1988) The flexible firm: fixation or fact? *Work, Employment, and Society*, 2, 3, 281–316.
20 Hunter, L., McGregor, A., MacInnes, J. and Sproull, A. (1993) The flexible firm: strategy and segmentation. *British Journal of Industrial Relations*, 31, 3, 383–407.

21 Schneider, B. (1987) The people make the place. *Personnel Psychology*, 40, 437–453.
22 Schein, E. H. (1978) *Career Dynamics: Matching Individual and Organisational Needs*. Reading MA: Addison-Wesley.
23 Nahapiet, J. and Ghoshal, S. (1997) Social capital, intellectual capital, and the creation of value in firms. *Academy of Management Best Paper Proceedings*, 35–39.

Chapter 15

The change dialogue

The survival rhetoric

So far I have taken for granted the fundamental assumption that organisations have to change and adapt if they are to survive in an increasingly competitive environment. Yet this assumption conceals the metaphor which underlies it: the Darwinian evolutionary metaphor. It is only the fittest organisations which adapt and survive in their markets, we say, applying the biological model of evolution to the social sphere: social Darwinism. However, just as the central concepts of the employment relationship, 'the individual' and 'the organisation', are anything but simple, so the relationship between 'the organisation' and 'its environment' also conceals some difficulties of interpretation and meaning. The rhetoric of 'change or perish' certainly fails to do justice to these complexities.

Top management, in particular, has nevertheless found the evolutionary metaphor extremely useful in justifying its actions and interventions.[1] The metaphor puts a premium on adaptation or extinction as the only two alternatives available; hence change can be represented as essential to survival. Thus, if employees fail to change and adapt, they can be represented as not merely obstructing progress but even as dooming the organisation to becoming as extinct as a dinosaur. Any who resist change are stigmatised as dead wood, too old or too set in their ways to adapt. Thus employees who may accept the need to change, but who can see difficulties with top management's specific strategy or tactics, can be dismissed as obstructive.

The evolutionary metaphor is a powerful rhetorical tool because it has permeated our language to such an extent that we often fail to question the assumptions which it conceals. Evolution is a natural process, following natural laws, and hence carries with it a strong connotation of inevitability. Once we have accepted the metaphor of the organisation as an organism and 'the market' as its natural environment, then the inevitability of organisational change is indisputable. If the market is a jungle where the weakest go to the wall, then organisations need to be lean, fit and hungry to survive the competition and to search out new environmental niches. Then they need to adapt rapidly to fill those niches successfully.

Yet even given the power of the evolutionary metaphor, the gap between the managerial rhetoric and the reality of employees' experience is still a yawning chasm. Here is a selection of commonly used rhetorics of change, together with the more frequent experiences which contradict them:

Old is bad and new is good, so change is good
Change has unexpected and often harmful outcomes

People who reject change are dead wood and incapable of changing
They were often right in their predictions

Most employees support the change initiative
They were not asked whether they did or not

Change initiatives are part of an overall organisational strategy
They are usually one-off reactions to external events

Change initiatives support each other
They are often mutually incompatible

Change initiatives have proven and predictable success outcomes
They normally have ambiguous and unexpected outcomes

Change initiatives, once selected, are implemented throughout organisations
Implementation is usually patchy and seldom completed

Change initiatives are exciting and stimulating
They might be if there were fewer of them

Employees are benefited by change because it develops them
Development requires building on prior learning

The entire organisation radically changed its culture
Some managers bought in, everyone else just complied wearily

The two merger partners developed a new common culture
The more powerful partner's culture prevailed

Change is for the whole organisation
Change is what 'they' do to 'us'.

The change experience

The gap between rhetoric and reality, once again, is likely to give rise to feelings of mistrust and cynicism. But employees' experience of change initiatives has given rise to more profoundly felt emotions. The sheer volume of initiatives that have hit employees in the last two decades is phenomenal. They have often faced simultaneously both structural changes and specific change programmes. Structural changes have included downsizing, delayering, mergers and acquisitions, and a seemingly cyclical process of decentralisation and recentralisation. Change programmes have included culture change programmes such as Total Quality Management, process changes such as Business Process Re-engineering, and certification processes such as Baldridge or ISO 9000.

From top management's perspective, these changes are all justifiable in terms of seeking to ensure the organisation's survival and prosperity. Their motives may also be somewhat more personal, and related to the maintenance and enhancement of their selves. Top managers may identify strongly with the organisation. Their reputation and self-esteem may be bound up in its survival and success. Their future career may be contingent upon their taking a change initiative. Whatever their motives, top managers' change initiatives are unlikely to be based primarily upon their consequences for employees. Indeed, top managers will often assume that what is in their view in the interests of the business is by definition also in the interests of employees.

Yet the consequences for employees are potentially immense, and, as in the case of top managers, are intimately bound up with their selves.[2] Some of the change programmes are structural, and any impact upon employees is seen as a by-product. Others are directly aimed at changing employees' values, attitudes, and behaviour. In these latter, top managers typically recognise that it is important to get employees' to 'buy-in', but assume that this will not be a problem except for those few who resist change because they cannot or will not adapt.

As far as employees are concerned, however, change initiatives may affect their selves profoundly in ways which top management typically fails to comprehend or take into account. Change initiatives and their impacts will also affect employees' perceptions of top management, thus changing the nature of the employment relationship.

First, then, I will consider the impact of structural and programmatic change upon employees' selves. Here are some selected examples of the possible effects of various changes:

- Compulsory redundancy: a loss of self-esteem; of the sense of personal agency; of identification with the organisation; of identification with one's work group; of identity as worker and breadwinner; the possibility of creating new elements of the self and of jettisoning old ones.
- Merger: a loss of organisational identity, and perhaps of work group identity; the fear of redundancy, but the possibility of an enlarged job and thence possibly enhanced self-efficacy.
- Functional flexibility: a loss of professional or functional identity, but a possible gain in self-efficacy as one acquires a wider range of skills.

- Temporal flexibility: a change (gain or loss) in one's identity as partner, parent, spouse, etc.
- Resource reduction: loss of self-esteem if one's performance fails to reach target; loss of personal agency if one cannot do anything about it.
- Certification initiative: response of reactance and refusal to participate, or possible increase in cynicism at the amount of bureaucracy involved.
- An accumulation of change initiatives which cannot possibly all be properly implemented: a loss of self-efficacy and of agency, and anger at the lack of awareness of top management.

Such impacts as these upon employees' selves are likely to provoke very profound emotional reactions to the constant introduction of change initiatives. Top managers thrive on change initiatives, enhancing their self-esteem and organisational identification by their efforts at pleasing the shareholders, increasing share price, and making the organisation less vulnerable to merger or acquisition. Employees, on the other hand, may be less than happy because reduced resources and higher targets have decreased their chances of being considered successful. So many elements of their selves are potentially under threat in periods of repeated change initiatives that feelings of anxiety, fear, impotence and resentment may well ensue.

Given these very different outcomes of change initiatives for the selves of top managers and for those of employees, it is hardly surprising that such initiatives are a constant source of friction for the employment relationship. Top managers are perceived as initiating change in response to the demands of stakeholders other than employees (whom they may not consider to be stakeholders at all). Indeed, employees may attribute the introduction of change initiatives to top managers' motives rather than as a rational response to business pressures. Top management may be seen to stand to gain, for example, from the merger they are planning. Or the constant repetition of initiative after initiative may be attributed to their incompetence; they are thrashing around searching for solutions.

Many of the outcomes of change initiatives for the employment relationship could not therefore be much worse. Not only is the rhetoric once again a long way from experienced reality, but the outcomes for the two parties, top management and other employees, are markedly different. Major threats to the selves of employees are often experienced, and consequently strong emotions are aroused within them. Top managers, however, usually gain reputation and self-esteem.

The realities of change

Even research which has used the evolutionary metaphor as the basis for its theory has certainly not come up with a simple 'survival of the fittest' message,[3] however. The evidence clearly shows that it is not so much survival of the *fittest* which occurs, but rather, survival of the *biggest*. This finding holds true when a variety of indices of size are employed. And when the effects of organisation size and organisation age are separated out for analytic purposes, it is size which predicts survival rather than age. So the lean and mean organisations of management rhetoric are in danger of perishing through anorexia; on the contrary, being old is no handicap, and being fat has its advantages. Recent instances of even large organisations being taken over are not sufficient to overturn this generalisation. Research on the outcomes of organisational downsizing programmes reinforces it: the results have certainly not been uniformly positive in financial business terms;[4] and they have been mostly negative in other terms.[5]

Furthermore, if the evolutionary metaphor implies that fleet-footed and opportunistic organisations always stand greater chances of survival than their more staid competitors, it is mistaken again. Whilst glamorous opportunists do well when a niche market is new, the evidence demonstrates that it is the boring and efficient organisations which survive and prosper as those niches mature.[6] The brave new world of Internet commerce will soon mature into a few market leaders. The market environment selects out those organisations which do not have the competencies and activities which fit them in the longer term for their niche.[7]

So even from research predicated upon the evolutionary metaphor, the notion that constant change is of itself virtuous and necessary for organisational survival is at best a gross over-simplification. Instead, theory and evidence point towards the conclusion that efforts to restructure organisations so that they fit better with their markets are fraught with danger.[8] Efforts to intervene radically have several hidden costs:

- They run the risk of destroying the reliability and accountability which clients and customers value
- They usually throw away all the sunk costs of the organisational processes, people, and plant associated with the former structure
- They may lose the organisational memory of how to deal successfully with problems and issues which was embedded in the former structure
- They have to develop rapidly the roles, policies, processes and practices which are implied by the new structure.

Hence it may well be true that organisations which can remain reliable, accountable, and stable over time are more likely to survive than those which run the risks of changing when it may not be necessary to do so. Such stability depends upon being able to adjust without having to make periodic major changes.

If the core features of organisations are their goals, their forms of authority, their core technology, and their marketing strategy, then it is in these arenas that external change may seem to require a radical overhaul. Yet it is such changes that pose the greatest risk. An organisation loses legitimacy if it decides to change its *goals*; it runs huge risks of losing control if it changes its *authority systems*; it puts operational efficiency at risk if it changes its *core technology*; and it risks losing its cash cows if it changes its *marketing strategy*.

Thus the undertaking of radical change is a momentous decision to make; it requires as careful an analysis of the balance of possible costs and benefits as is possible in an uncertain environment. Only in relatively few circumstances is the decision a clear-cut one. One such circumstance is when a *new technology* so revolutionises the nature and cost of the product or service that it is impossible to compete unless one adopts it.[9] Once again, the finance sector provides a good example. The face-to-face 'technology' of banking in branches has been partly superseded by telephone banking. Internet banking, in its turn, now offers a far cheaper service than either of the two previous technologies. Large banks and insurance companies are now scrambling to change their core technologies to adapt to these innovations. Yet one can still imagine a company achieving unique competitive advantage by continuing to provide face-to-face service.

A second environmental circumstance which often forces change is change in the *institutional context* of the organisation. Government regulatory regimes may require fundamental changes in the way goods or services are produced or sold. Professional institutions may require standards of professional practice to be maintained. But perhaps the most fundamental change in recent years has been the increase in the number of individuals indirectly involved in the ownership of companies, and hence in the power of investing institutions such as pension funds (investing on clients' behalf) to demand high and immediate dividends. It could be argued that this is a major reason for the recent rash of mergers and acquisitions, which permit costs to be cut and profitability increased by means of the economies of scale that result. There is no greater structural change than the merger of two like-sized organisations; but close behind in terms of magnitude come the changes undertaken by those seeking to defend themselves against acquisition.

The social determinants of change interventions

However, even when the desperately difficult decision has been taken whether or not to undertake radical change, the nature of any such change has still to be chosen. The objectives of the change may be clear: to cut costs and increase profitability; to defend against an acquisition threat; or to become international, for example. Or maybe objectives are not so clearly specified. Indeed, sometimes the rationale may simply be that 'in the present crisis we have to be seen to be doing something'. But the way to succeed is often anything but clear. The myth of rational action has to be maintained in a situation where there is little or no evidence about what will or will not work for a particular organisation. Hence top managements search around for ways of legitimising their change intervention, since hard evidence that it will have the desired effects is unlikely to be available to them.[10]

One way of selecting and legitimising change is to point to other admired organisations which have undertaken the same intervention, the *modelling solution*. There is unlikely to be any sound evidence that the intervention has actually worked for these so-called 'leading edge', 'best of class' companies, but the fact that they have undertaken them is treated as a guarantee of effectiveness. It could be argued that the recent obsession with benchmarking, characteristic of Western management, has its roots in the same need to legitimate management interventions. Certainly, the bandwagon effect that accompanies such interventions as Business Process Re-engineering is well evidenced. There comes a point at which the critical mass of organisations which have conducted a particular intervention render it an act of managerial courage not to do so.

What is more, the modelling solution enhances the myth of planned and rational management action. The very names of the favoured interventions imply that they are highly targeted and accurate (e.g. 're-engineering', 'architecture'). They are 'projects' which can be planned, scheduled, managed, monitored, concluded and evaluated in terms of their stated objectives. Those who have conducted them become experts, gurus of the intervention in question, who can tell you how it should be done properly. The intervention in question may become legitimised and respectable, with certificating institutions set up to grant awards for successful implementation (e.g. Total Quality). All of these features create confidence that it is the right solution.

Another way to legitimate change is to continue to carry out the same changes that one's own organisation has previously conducted in the past: a *routine* of change becomes established.[11] The implementation of the change in question then becomes more efficient each time it is carried through. Repetition is justified by the reasoning that it worked in the past, so it is likely to do so again. Indeed, a momentum may build up such that the most recent change is the most likely to be repeated, and with a lesser time gap. If the major purpose of radical change is to fit the organisation to meet the demands of environmental change; and if environmental change, by definition, presents new problems and issues to be addressed; then, necessarily, routine change is likely to be counter-productive.

Both the myths of rational practices and routine change sequences may inhibit future appropriate change. Indeed, the changes made may serve a merely symbolic function. Actual organisational practices on the ground and the new structure consequent upon the change may become completely *decoupled* from each other: change at the front of the stage, but not at the back.[12] If the audience to the drama is the employees, then this decoupling can only result immediately in increased cynicism at such window dressing. If it is the outside world, such as the investment community, the penny may take longer to drop, but will do so unforgivingly when financial results fail to improve.

Although the practices and processes of leading edge companies are used as models to imitate, we should not overlook the more *personal networks* of top managers as a potential source of ideas for change interventions. These networks may be surprisingly limited. Top managers tend to talk only to those at their own level or above who have faced or are facing the same issues. They may limit themselves to those in the same or related business sectors, believing that the issues are unique to their sector, or that solutions which appeared to work in other sectors would not work in theirs. There is nevertheless a considerable interlocking of directors across organisations such that any one director may have a seat on several Boards as a non-executive. The result is a charmed inner circle of the business elite who have lines to government, set the business agenda and provide accepted accounts of the business environment.[13] Furthermore, many had early jobs with, and continue to employ, certain elite management consultancies such as McKinsey with change products to sell.

Nor should we ignore the *professional formation* of top managers as a determinant of their choice of change intervention. Directors with finance, marketing, and operational backgrounds are likely to favour different approaches. To the extent that their profession is dominant at Board level, their own favoured approaches are more likely to be adopted (especially if they are the Chief Executive).

In sum, decisions about whether to undertake fundamental organisational change, and about what form it should take, are fraught with risk and difficulty. So ambiguous is the organisational environment, and so difficult is it to predict the outcomes of interventions, that top managers seek social support from amongst their peers. Their purpose is to discover what they should do, and then to legitimate their intervention when they have decided upon it. For top managers need to present to the outside world, and perhaps to themselves too, a picture of themselves as rational actors taking decisions for change which permit them to control the organisation's destiny.

Thus the dangers inherent in radical change initiatives and in the social grounds for undertaking them underlie the findings that downsizings, mergers, culture change programmes, and business process re-engineering have failed to live up to their prospectuses.[14, 15, 16, 17] What they have succeeded in doing instead is to threaten the employment relationship.

Establishing the change dialogue

The auguries are hardly propitious, then, for establishing a fruitful dialogue about change:

- Top management's rhetoric and employees' experience are once again discordant

- The impacts of change initiatives upon the two parties are markedly different
- Their emotional reactions to change initiatives are therefore equally different
- Perceptions of the other party are consequently unfavourable.

Yet both parties' accounts of the most recent change initiatives are likely to be available to memory. In particular, the emotions felt will be fresh enough to be recalled without too much difficulty. What is important is that the dialogue focuses upon these emotions. Top managers will need to discover that many employees felt hostile, fearful, resigned, or helpless, rather than excited and optimistic. They will find this discovery hard to make and hard to accept, since they probably sincerely expected to find the opposite emotions.

Next, they will need to ask *why* employees felt these negative emotions. They will have to avoid well-practised attributions, such as the idea that people in general, and particularly people of a certain age, are fearful of the very idea of change itself. Employees, in turn, will have to ask why top managers were well pleased with the initiative when their own experience was anything but pleasing. And they will have to explore management's impatience with the pace of change and with those they perceive as blocking it.

More fundamentally, the occurrence of change initiatives raises once again the issue of *power*. The imposition of a change initiative by top management, and the use of evolutionary rhetoric to persuade employees that it is inevitable, are both very strong assertions of power. Yet there are few organisational scenarios which have more impact upon employees' selves, and which stir up stronger emotions as a consequence. The absence of dialogue is thus no more than a reflection of the unilateral use of power in a situation where most is at stake for both parties.

Yet such use of power is actively hostile to the development of a sound employment relationship. It ignores the impact of change initiatives upon employees' selves and also upon employees' perceptions of top managers. It provides a series of episodes for an employee narrative which consistently demonstrates the absence of reciprocity, and it renders any subsequent attempt to involve employees unlikely to succeed.

The only hope for change dialogue to succeed is to concentrate upon the process of dialogue as a means of *learning*. The biological language of evolution needs to give way to the social language of learning. The time is currently ripe for a review of change initiatives, as evidence and experience point more and more powerfully to the conclusion that they do not generally work. Such a review should be carried out in dialogue rather than at the Board. For only when it occurs within the process of dialogue will the parties be able to recognise that the very process they are engaging in is the means for establishing and maintaining a good employment relationship.

Table 17 The change dialogue

Rhetoric	Reality	Results	Dialogue
Survival of the fittest Change is good Rational choice of programme	Survival of the biggest Change is overwhelming and risky Social choice of programme Little reciprocity	Weariness Changed selves	Learning review

And it is the resulting deeply embedded networks of relationships across the business which bring long-term competitive advantage. The final chapter will therefore reaffirm the importance of dialogue and explore the ways in which the organisation can provide a context within which it can flourish. The change dialogue is summarised in Table 17.

Summary

The current managerial rhetoric regarding change is unsupported by the evidence. It is bigger organisations which survive rather than 'leaner' ones, and radical organisational change is both highly dangerous and relatively seldom successful. Most change initiatives are chosen for social rather than rational reasons. Whilst they are consistent with top managers' selves, they seldom are for employees'. Rather, change initiatives frequently have results which are inconsistent with, and potentially damaging to, employees' selves. As a consequence, employees tend to make attributions about top management's motives and to distrust the change rhetoric which they continuously use. The way forward is to use dialogue as a means of learning about why change programmes do not work, and to base subsequent efforts to achieve competitive advantage upon the improved employment relationship which will ensue.

References

1 Legge, K. (1995) *Human Resource Management: Rhetorics and Realities*. London: Macmillan.
2 Herriot, P., Hirsh, W. and Reilly, P. (1998) *Trust and Transition: Managing Today's Employment Relationship*. Chichester: Wiley.
3 Baum, J. A. C. (1996) Organisational ecology. In S. R. Clegg, C. Hardy and W. R. Nord (eds) *Handbook of Organisation Studies*. London: Sage.
4 Cameron, K. S., Freeman, S. J. and Mishra, A. K. (1993) Downsizing and redesigning organisations. In G. P. Huber and W. H. Glick (eds) *Organisational Change and Redesign*. New York: Oxford University Press.
5 Kozlowski, S. W., Chao, G. T., Smith, E. M. and Hedlund, J. (1993) Organisational downsizing: strategies, interventions, and research implications. In C. L. Cooper and I. T. Robertson (eds) *International Review of Industrial and Organisational Psychology*. New York: Wiley.

6 Nelson, R. R. (1994) The co-evolution of technology, industrial structure, and supporting institutions. *Industrial and Corporate Change*, 3, 47–64.
7 Hannan, M. T. and Freeman, J. H. (1989). *Organisational Ecology*. Cambridge MA: Harvard University Press.
8 Davis, G. F. and Powell, W. W. (1992) Organisation-environment relations. In M. D. Dunnette and L. M. Hough (eds) *Handbook of Industrial and Organisational Psychology*, vol. III. Palo Alto CA: Consulting Psychologists Press.
9 Nelson (op. cit.).
10 Tolbert, P. S. and Zucker, L. G. (1996) The institutionalisation of institutional theory. In S. R. Clegg, C. Hardy and W. R. Nord (eds) *Handbook of Organisational Studies*. London: Sage.
11 Nelson, R. R. and Winter, S. G. (1982) *An Evolutionary Theory of Economic Change*. Cambridge MA: Harvard University Press.
12 Tolbert and Zucker (op. cit.).
13 Useem, M. (1984) *The Inner Circle: Large Corporations and the Rise of Business Political Activity in the US and UK*. New York: Oxford University Press.
14 Herriot *et al.* (op. cit.).
15 Cameron *et al.* (op. cit.).
16 Mirvis, P. H. and Marks, M. L. (1992) *Managing the Merger*. Englewood Cliffs NJ: Prentice Hall.
17 Beer, M., Eisenstat, R. and Spector, B. (1990) Why change programmes don't produce change. *Harvard Business Review*, 68, 6, 158–166.

Chapter 16

The dialogue dialogue

Facts and feelings

We return once again, and finally, to the metaphors with which we started: Family, Crusade, Contract, Club, Resource, Citizen, Partner, and Customer. Each of them draws attention to particular features of the employment relationship, since each is distinguished from the others by such features. So, Family is about care and security; Crusade about vision and values; Contract about obligations and transactions; Club about belonging and fitting in; Resource about assets and their utilisation; Citizen about rights and responsibilities; Partnership about shared interests; and Customer about service to consumers.

Some of these metaphors express elements of standard managerial discourse, of the language in which managerial communications and managerialist books are normally written. So, for example, Resource proclaims that the business and its needs are paramount, and employees are assets to be used to that end. Crusade emphasises the unitarist perspective, which argues that all should share the same values and vision for the business. Contract puts the relationship on a business footing, with outcomes specified and accountabilities established. Customer reinforces the notion that business principles permeate every feature of the relationship.

The remaining metaphors, however, do not fall within a rational business perspective, driven by 'the bottom line'.[1] Care and security, belonging and fitting in, rights and responsibilities, shared but different interests – all of these represent concerns of different constituencies of employees. These concerns are expressed by the Family, Club, Citizen, and Partner metaphors respectively.

It is important to note that these latter metaphors are not used only by employees. They are also sometimes used by top managers. It may be that the latter use them mostly rhetorically. Their purpose may be to persuade employees that the particular needs implied by these metaphors are being met by the organisation. But even this rhetorical use signifies the realisation by top management that these needs exist. There are other perspectives besides the bottom line, and they are legitimate subjects for dialogue.

Unless this realisation occurs, dialogue is doomed. For the alternative is the privileging of the business language and the business metaphors to the exclusion of all others. Business language implies *rationality*, with measurement as the ultimate proof that something exists and is worth considering, and indices of the bottom line as the only relevant outcomes. Feelings are usually excluded from the business dialogue. If they are permitted, they only appear in the guise of shared values, where those values are selected by top management as appropriate motivators whereby to exercise control.

Moreover, the business dialogue runs according to certain unspoken *rules*. For example, there are two main criteria for the right to claim the floor and for having added weight given to one's contributions. These are, first, position in the management hierarchy and second, professional expertise on the topic under discussion. The notion, therefore, that employees may be more expert about their work than their managers is hard to incorporate. The undoubted fact that individuals of whatever level in the organisation are the only experts on how they really feel is right out of court. Their feelings are not a business issue.

Yet care and security, belonging, rights and interests are outcomes of the employment relationship which are likely to arouse profound feelings. The long-term and regular presence or absence of these outcomes, the top or the flip sides of the metaphorical coin, will lead to more stable and lasting emotional states, such as satisfaction or cynicism. It is when outcomes change for the better or worse, when the coin turns over on to its top or its flip side, that the hotter and more extreme emotions, such as joy and delight or anger and despair, are likely to occur.[2]

Such feelings are very important. Subsequent reflection upon them and the episode in which they occurred often forces the parties to reflect in turn upon their selves, their perception of the other party, and the nature of the relationship. Reflection is likely to lead to change in all three. Whilst the expression of emotions during the course of an episode can itself affect the relationship there and then, it is subsequent discussion and reflection which are perhaps more likely to result in long-term change in the relationship and in selves.

The previous three chapters have presented us with examples of how these changes can occur. Rhetoric may have raised expectations of increased autonomy and empowerment, but the experience for most is of increased control and compliance (Chapter 13). The disappointment of expectations may lead to anger and mistrust, the experience of compliance over the longer term to resentment or resignation. The relationship will suffer immediately, whereas change in the self may take longer, as employees change their view of themselves at work to one of victim or automaton or resister. Marked differences in the nature of the relationship enjoyed by oneself and others (Chapter 14) may likewise lead to strong feelings, in this case of distributive or interactional injustice. The relationship will be perceived to be unfair, and the employees will see themselves as victims or plaintiffs. And finally, the experience of constant and unsupported change (Chapter 15) leads to feelings of anxiety, bewilderment, disorientation, and ultimately resignation and helplessness. Self-esteem and self-efficacy are likely to plummet and trust in top management to disappear.

Dialogue to the rescue

How can the process of dialogue help avoid such outcomes as these? Essentially, dialogue is to be seen as accompanying the episodes from which the employment relationship is derived, and in which it is expressed in actions. Dialogue is not often about the relationship in general, but more frequently concerns the episode that is occurring at present. It will concern, first, the events within the episode that have already happened, and of which the parties will have accounts available; second, the immediately current events, in which they will be deeply involved and about which they will be experiencing strong emotions; and third, the likely future course of the episode and its outcomes, probably accompanied by emotions such as hope, anxiety and anticipation.

Here, by way of example, is an episode without benefit of accompanying dialogue which relates, as do so many, to organisational change:

- Important shareholders express dissatisfaction with the company's profits, which have failed to increase despite a recent round of redundancies.
- Top management hires a firm of consultants to engage in a business process re-engineering (BPR) project in order to enhance productivity.
- Employees learn of this project informally and interpret the action as an intention to cut costs through further redundancies.
- They support their union's suggestion to refuse co-operation with the consultants.
- Top management assures the union that they will not make further redundancies during or as a result of the BPR project.
- Top management instructs the consultants (and copies to the union representative) to concentrate solely upon recommending improvements to business processes.
- Employees welcome this assurance, but warn that their co-operation with the consultants is contingent upon it being kept.
- Top management receive the consultants' report, make process changes, and redeploy those staff elsewhere whom the process improvement has made superfluous.

- Employees subsequently quietly readapt the re-engineered processes to suit their existing ways of working.

Top management may feel pleased to have headed off trouble and to have been seen to listen, but regret that a threat could be construed to have succeeded. Employees may feel angry that they have not been consulted or informed, anxious about potential redundancy, relieved that they have avoided it, and encouraged that they may have changed the course of events in their favour. Reflecting upon the employment relationship, top management may decide that they need to enhance the security of their communications systems and set about decreasing the influence of the union. Employees may be reinforced in their perception of the relationship as one in which top management try to do things to placate shareholders without concern for what happens to employees. Solidarity in opposition appears to be the appropriate stance to take.

In this episode, the actions of each party were essentially unilateral in nature and in response to the actions of the other. Each party was seeking to interpret the other's actions in terms of their intention and motive, in the absence of clear communication. For example, it seems likely that employees assumed, rightly or wrongly, that at least part of the objective of BPR was to make further redundancies. If the top managers had not assured the union representatives that they would not make redundancies, the episode could have escalated, with each party responding more extremely to the other so that strike action followed. The important shareholders and the business analysts and commentators would then have been even less impressed.

If, however, a process of dialogue had accompanied the episode, it might have turned out quite differently, as follows:

- Important shareholders express dissatisfaction with the company's profits, which have failed to increase despite a recent round of redundancies.
- Top management inform key constituencies of employees of this expression. They express their own surprise and disappointment, given the recent redundancy programme. They also indicate their anxiety that shareholders will take hostile action unless they are seen to address the profitability issue.
- The union facilitates dialogues with representatives of key constituencies, who are asked for their reactions. The dominant emotion expressed is fear that top management will make further redundancies to cut costs and thereby enhance profits in the short term.
- Some representatives seek to reframe the issue in terms of productivity. They tell stories of considerable increases in productivity at local level. They argue that if these practices were shared across the company, productivity overall would increase.
- Top management ask to see these practices at work *in situ*, since they

were previously unaware of their existence. Having seen them in operation, and had them explained to them by local operatives, they are convinced that there is potential for spreading some of the practices across the company.

- They bring local managers together and promise them that they will not lose out by sharing with each other the tricks which have brought them added performance bonuses.
- They consult with local managers to discover how long it will take to implement the changes and how much more profit will ensue. They persuade them to collaborate with each other in the implementation process. They then give the shareholders a plan for increasing profitability over a given period which exceeds the savings which could have been achieved by more redundancies.

The key elements of dialogue (see Chapter 12 pp. 171–173) are now present in this episode:

- Each party expressed its feelings to the other, as well as its perception of the situation.
- A degree of understanding of the other's position and self ensued.
- Stories of recent experiences were told, rather than longstanding myths or models which are best used to maintain existing relationships.
- These stories helped to reframe the problem into a form which both parties agreed.
- Ways of addressing the problem were shared by establishing new relationships.

Particularly if the episode is subsequently reviewed, the parties' perception of the employment relationship itself may change; for example, in terms of the perceived willingness to collaborate in the face of external threat. Thus it is the use of dialogue during episodes which results in enhanced collaboration. The reframing of problems and issues enables change to proceed incrementally rather than by major transformational projects, and the employment relationship develops in tandem.[3]

There is, therefore, every reason for top managers to engage in dialogue with employees. Dialogue enables collaboration in addressing real problems whilst also developing relationships with employees which will result in better collaboration in future. Since organisations are essentially ways of enabling people to collaborate in achieving their purposes, any way of aiding collaboration is worthwhile. Employees also have every incentive to engage, since it is only by means of expressing their feelings and having them listened to that their selves are taken into account.

Obstacles to dialogue

Unfortunately, there is also a long list of reasons why both parties find it hard to engage in dialogue.[4] The first is that most dialogue between top management and employees is inevitably *mediated* through third parties.[5] Employees use their representatives to talk with top management, whilst top managers usually seek to cascade their communications down the line so that the employee's line manager is the person from whom the message comes. However, both of these mediating parties may have their own agendas. What employees or top management wish to communicate may be converted, simplified, reduced, summarised, or made purposely ambiguous on its way through to the intended recipient. What's more, the message may have been intended in the first place to mislead through its plausibility; or at the very least, to persuade rhetorically.

Moreover, the 'official' channels are not of course the only ones; often they are not even the dominant ones. The parties may learn of each other's supposed feelings, attitudes or intentions on the grapevine; and there are some key individuals at strategic points on that grapevine who act as gate-keepers or have privileged access or deal more with the external world.[6]

Alternatively, top management may come to treat *actions within episodes* as its preferred way of communicating; for example, establishing a performance-related pay system is often referred to as 'sending a clear message'. Yet it can be just as hard to understand actions as words. Parties may not know in detail what the actions were and in what context they occurred. Even if they do know, it may still be extremely difficult to attribute causes and intentions to them. The consequence may be that the organisation is awash with conflicting interpretations of events and actions. Sometimes, indeed, the only way to succeed in putting a meaning on to another's action is to act oneself.[7] Then one can perhaps tell from the other's reaction what they intended to convey in the first place.

Another obstacle to dialogue is the increasingly *temporary* nature of top management, and indeed, of other positions. If several episodes, each accompanied by dialogue, have to be experienced before a relationship can be properly established and a degree of trust built up, then today there is decreasing opportunity for good employment relationships to be forged between the parties. For top managers come and go, and it becomes far easier to think of oneself as dealing with a faceless 'them' rather than with individual persons. Some middle managers have seen their companies change ownership half a dozen times whilst remaining in the 'same' job.

Moreover, communication is increasingly likely to be *virtual*, for a variety of reasons. The geographical spread of organisations makes it much more convenient, whilst the wide variety of different employment relationships within the organisation (Chapter 14) demand different forms and contents of communication. In principle, electronic forms of communication permit free interaction, but in practice they make it easier for parties to ignore reply and deny voice.[8] However thoroughly stage-managed a face-to-face meeting, the opportunity for voice is usually available somewhere.

Thus the search after meaning to explain the other party's actions in an uncertain world is constant, and the temptation to provide ready-made meaning rather than permitting the other to come to their own imperfect understanding is therefore great. For example, an almost universal managerial framework for meaning is the *rational action* model.[9] This assumes that dialogue is about the communication of business-related information in order for parties to make rational decisions and take action.

Yet, as I have argued already, the use of this rational framework is actively hostile towards dialogue. First, it excludes as irrelevant all elements of self other than the work role. If dialogue is to occur and to contribute to the development of the employment relationship, selves are central. Second, it implies one-way communication rather than two-way dialogue: management releases information and takes strategic decisions, which it passes on down for implementation.

Another framework for meaning are the *myths* (or stories with meanings) put about and elaborated as they pass around the organisation. Top managements who favour the Crusade metaphor are particularly fond of myths which emphasise the company's vision and the heroics which people perform in its pursuit. Myths can be powerful carriers of meaning, since they can enthuse and motivate. They are a specific example of rhetorical symbols whose purpose is to persuade. Company logos, rites and rituals, and the rhetorical use of metaphor are other such symbols, all aimed at persuading employees to adopt the perspective which top management desires.[10] Such symbols serve to socialise new employees, increase their organisational identification, legitimate management's power, and justify their past actions. They are hostile to dialogue, since their purpose is to persuade the other rather than to understand them.

Of course, myths and stories can start with employees. They can be laced with a wicked and subversive humour, and they can drip with irony.[11] The creator of the Dilbert cartoons does not need to be creative; employees constantly inform him of the scenarios his cartoon depicts. Employees can express only too clearly the flip side rather than the top side of the metaphors. All such responses are unlikely to be heard, since there is no dialogue. Rather, those few accounts of authentic experience which emerge are couched in language totally incompatible with the official rhetoric.

Indeed, when real dialogue is not sought by top management, employees use language to express their voice which managers would never understand. The early expressions of feminism in the workplace were couched in terms which afforded the women who used them great comfort and solidarity, but which were incomprehensible to the men at the top.[12] The use of a common language implies a willingness to engage in dialogue itself.

But even when employees and top management seek dialogue rather than to persuade or to protest, there are still major obstacles to overcome. The first is that parties are so confused and disturbed by the ambiguity and rate of change that they are unable to construct a *coherent account* which they can communicate. Given that such accounts are normally *post hoc* rationalisations anyway, we need to broaden our understanding of accounts to include the expression of our feelings. Employees' feelings of, for example, insecurity, uncertainty or ambition, and top managers' of anxiety, impatience or optimism are important elements of dialogue, since, if listened to, they assist the parties to understand each other better. Unfortunately, feelings are more difficult than rational accounts both to express and to receive in organisational settings.[13]

Alternatively, the parties may have an account to give but be *unwilling* to *engage in dialogue*. This unwillingness may arise because they do not wish to take the risk of revealing their selves when the other party has hitherto engaged only in rhetoric, protest or apathy. It is the task of top management to take the first risk and break this cycle of non-dialogue. Yet if top managers retain the labour-market power and exercise tight internal control, they may consider there to be no good reason why they should. Only if they understand that *the social capital of a successful employment relationship is the key to unique competitive advantage through more effective collaboration* are they likely to initiate dialogue.

Obstacles to dialogue about dialogue

There are, then, major difficulties to be overcome before dialogue can occur, but they are not insurmountable. Moreover, part of conducting dialogue is normally reflexive, so *dialogue about dialogue* should also be possible. However, dialogue about dialogue has problems of its own to overcome before it can become commonplace in organisations. Reflection requires the appreciation of the underlying assumptions about people which form a major part of the culture of any organisation.[14] Such assumptions may have their roots in the national culture of the organisation's country of origin as well as in its specific history.

The major such assumption in the West is that of the *employee as consumer*. If top managers hold that employees are customers (Chapter 8), then they will seek to market to them. Whilst marketers themselves would argue that their practice is indeed one of dialogue rather than message, they are now commonly perceived as seeking to persuade. Devices such as opinion questionnaires are thus seen as efforts to discover how better to target their persuasive communications, rather than as genuine attempts to understand employees' perspectives. To uncover this assumption and question it would force a dialogue about the employment relationship. Yet to do so would be to question the very fundamental premise upon which many organisations now believe they should base themselves.

It is the marketing approach which has spawned the rhetorical use of many of the metaphors for the employment relationship. Top managers have sought to persuade employees that the relationship is like a Family or a Crusade, that they are valued Resources or Partners in the business. Of course, such attempts to persuade are tested by employees against their own experience of the reality of the relationship. If they are found wanting, then the rhetoric is not welcomed as providing a powerful framework of meaning for their experience (one of the elements of charismatic leadership).[15] Rather it is seen for what it is: an attempt to persuade them of the truth of a perspective on their experience different from their own. We have, however, become more and more sophisticated in our capacities to spot all such marketing attempts, and we treat them with an ironic cynicism. The proliferation of television advertisements which are wittily ironic about the product or service which they promote bears witness to this increased sophistication.

Hence the assumption that employees are customers and can be marketed to is actively hostile to a dialogue about the employment relationship. For it prevents top managers from trying to understand employees' views of the relationship except for the purpose of changing those views. Moreover, the use of rhetorical persuasion to this end will lead to an active deterioration in the relationship. For employees will come to mistrust top managers' communications. They will mistrust their truthfulness, since these communications are incompatible with their own experiences. And they will mistrust their motives, since they will suspect that the purpose of the persuasion is to obtain their acquiescence to a course of action which they do not at present support.[16]

Establishing dialogues through politics

A dangerous ambiguity has bedevilled my argument throughout this book. A psychological perspective which emphasises the importance of the self surely has to argue that the employment relationship is experienced uniquely by each employee. Each employee, after all, enters the relationship bringing a self which has been created largely through their own past social experience. And that experience is unique to themselves. Different selves therefore lead to different reactions to top management's actions, different perceptions of top management, and different accounts of episodes and of the employment relationship itself. Yet the very notion of top managers entering into a different relationship with each individual employee is enough to send them gibbering justifiably to the corporate hospitality cabinet. Most of the discussion in this book has implied that, at the very least, different relationships are maintained with different groups or segments of employees.

Of course, top managers have more recently sought to address employees individually, by-passing their representatives. Their purpose, however, has been to weaken the power of the unions, not to create different relationships with each employee. Further, it can be argued that top managers have frequently empowered local managers to do more individualised deals with their subordinates. However, this has usually only occurred in a piecemeal way, and the increased centralisation and outsourcing of Human Resource processes and systems renders such flexibilities less likely in the future. Moreover, neither of the above attempts to individualise the relationship necessarily implies the use of dialogue as the means for doing so.

The solution, however is not an individual but a *political* one, as it always is when we are dealing with different interests.[17] That is, it involves dialogues between top managers and a variety of constituencies amongst employees. Different constituencies represent different sets of interests. One such constituency, for example, could consist of those for whom childcare or elder-care is currently a pressing concern; another of those whose occupational membership or professional reputation is of paramount importance to them. These constituencies are defined by the constituents themselves; they do not consist of the categories into which top management has segmented employees for business purposes. This definition of constituencies according to interests implies the recognition by top management of the pluralistic nature of organisational life. It requires them to abandon the assumption, or perhaps merely the rhetoric, of unity of purpose and interest.

Each individual employee may, of course, be a member of several different constituencies of interest. To continue with the examples above, an individual employee could be represented in both the childcare and the occupational constituencies. Hence it is possible for different elements of the employee's self to be taken into account through their multiple membership of constituencies. In this case, the elements of family and occupational identification would both be considered in their employment relationship.

Why should top managers engage in potentially conflictual political relations with several different constituencies of interests? There are three reasons for them to do so: they might soon have *little choice*; it will be *to their advantage*; and it is something which they *ought to do*. Ignoring employees' diverse interests is becoming less and less of an option. Governmental regulation of course plays a part here, but its degree varies considerably across nations. Various exemptions often make a mockery of the spirit of the regulations, and their enforcement is patchy. On the other hand, the deterrent effect of punitive damages awarded in civil actions can be powerful, especially in such areas as discrimination, harassment and stress. Moreover, whilst the formal power of trade unions has been diminishing in most countries, their role in supporting employees' rights in accord with regulations is growing.

However, another potent source of support for employees lies in other non-governmental organisations (NGOs). For example, ecological pressure groups have supported employees who have concerns about their organisation's environmental policies and practices. Organisations supporting ethnic or other minorities, such as the disabled, have lobbied on behalf of their constituencies or helped individual employees to bring legal actions against their employer. Internal constituencies of employees do not therefore have to rely solely upon their own resources to promote their interests.

In a more general way, the boundaries between employing organisations are becoming more and more blurred. A whole range of communities impinge upon organisations; no organisation can now remain an island unto itself. Industry, occupational, regional, and ideological communities, among others, all impact upon today's companies.[18] The consequence is that individual employees need no longer feel so isolated and powerless as hitherto.

To ignore employee constituencies of interest is therefore less of an option for top managers to take today. Moreover, it is unlikely to be in their interest to do so. To concentrate upon their political dealings with shareholders to the exclusion of other constituencies is the avowed strategic stance of some companies and the unspoken one of many others. Yet it has to be continuously reaffirmed that most companies' profits depend upon the organised collaboration of employees in carrying out certain activities. To achieve employees' compliance, co-operation or commitment in these activities, top managers have to take their interests into account. And they can only do so by discovering through dialogue what those interests are and how they can best be served within the context of the interests of the other stakeholders in the business.

When this happens, conflict is extremely likely. Many of the interests of the different stakeholders will be incompatible. However, the political process of dialogue between conflicted and interested parties is often generative. It can result in new frames of reference for activity, supported by new institutions, or by new coalitions of existing ones. Certain companies have, for example, acquired a whole new legitimacy and a wider range of institutional support by accepting their impact upon the environment as a fundamental responsibility.

It is no accident that much of the creative achievement of the human race has emerged from societies in which democratic dialogue flowered at a particular juncture in their history. The commodification of politics and the growth of democratically unaccountable global corporations currently threaten the processes of democratic dialogue and conflict resolution. So does 'the culture of contentment'.[19] However, when the voice of such constituencies as are represented amongst employees is heard and responded to, the potential of dialogue may be realised. Then their capacities for creative collaboration will be released.

Which is why it ought to happen.

Summary

Some of the eight metaphors are consistent with managerial discourse, which is predominantly rational in nature. Others, however, indicate the existence of employee needs in the employment relationship. These needs are closely associated with emotions. The process of dialogue allows the expression of such emotions, and, when conducted in the context of an organisational episode, can result in enhanced collaboration. Later reflection upon the episode and dialogue about dialogue can change perceptions of self, the other and the relationship. However, there are a number of potential obstacles to dialogue and to dialogue about dialogue. They include the mediated, temporary and virtual nature of much contemporary organisational communication; the difficulty of initiating dialogue in the absence of a felt need for it; and the dominance of the marketing ethos and practice within organisations. However, the different needs of employees and of top management may be addressed through the political process of resolving conflict over incompatible interests.

References

1 Addleson, M. (2000) What is good organisation? Learning organisations, community, and the rhetoric of the bottom line. *European Journal of Work and Organisational Psychology* (in press).
2 Herriot, P. (2000) Future work and its emotional implications. In R. Payne and C. Cooper (eds) *Emotions in Organisations*. Chichester: Wiley (in press).
3 Hosking, D. M., Dachler, H. P. and Gergen, K. J. (eds) (1995) *Management and Organisation: Relational Alternatives to Individualism*. Aldershot: Avebury.
4 Putnam, L. L., Phillips, N. and Chapman, P. (1996) *Metaphors of communication and organisation*. In S. R. Clegg, C. Hardy and W. R. Nord (eds) *Handbook of Organisation Studies*. London: Sage.
5 Eisenberg, E. N. and Goodall, H. L. (1993) *Organisational Communication: Balancing Creativity and Constraint*. New York: St. Martin's Press.
6 Stohl, C. (1995) *Organisational Communication: Connectedness in Action*. Thousand Oaks CA: Sage.
7 Weick, K. (1995) *Sensemaking in Organisations*. Thousand Oaks CA: Sage.
8 Fulk, J., Steinfield, C. and Schmitz, J. (1990) The social influence model of technology use. In J. Fulk and C. Steinfield (eds) *Organisations and Communication Technology*. Newbury Park CA: Sage.
9 Putnam, L. and Mumby, D. K. (1993) Organisations, emotion, and the myth of rationality. In S. Fineman (ed.) *Emotion in Organisations*. London: Sage.
10 Alvesson, M. and Berg, P. O. (1993) *Corporate Culture and Organisational Symbolism*. Berlin: de Gruyter.
11 Ackroyd, S. and Thompson, P. (1999) *Organisational Misbehaviour*. London: Sage.
12 Marshall, J. (1989) Revisioning career concepts: a feminist invitation. In M. B. Arthur, D. T. Hall and B. S. Lawrence (eds) *Handbook of Career Theory*. Cambridge: Cambridge University Press.
13 Fineman, S. (1996) Emotion and organising. In S. R. Clegg, C. Hardy and W. R. Nord (eds) *Handbook of Organisation Studies*. London: Sage.
14 Schein, E. H. (1985) *Organisational Culture and Leadership*. New York: Jossey Bass.

15 Conger, J. A. and Kanungo, R. (1987) Toward a behavioural theory of charismatic leadership in organisational settings. *Academy of Management Review*, 12, 637–647.
16 Lewicki, R. J. and Bunker, B. B. (1996) Developing and maintaining trust in work relationships. In R. M. Kramer and T. R. Tyler (eds) *Trust in Organisations: Frontiers of Theory and Research*. Thousand Oaks CA: Sage.
17 Coopey, J. and Burgoyne, J. (2000) Politics and organisational learning. *Journal of Management Studies* (in press).
18 Parker, P. and Arthur, M. B. (2000) Careers, organising, and community. In M. Peiperl, M. Arthur, R. Goffee and T. Morris (eds) *Career Frontiers: New Conceptions of Working Lives*. Oxford: Oxford University Press.
19 Galbraith, J. K. (1992) *The Culture of Contentment*. New York: Houghton-Mifflin.

Index